Studying the Gospels

an introduction

Studying the Gospels

an introduction

**Gideon Goosen &
Margaret Tomlinson**

E.J.DWYER

First published in 1994 by
E.J. Dwyer (Australia) Pty Ltd
3/32–72 Alice Street
Newtown NSW 2042
Australia
Phone: (02) 550 2355
Fax: (02) 519 3218

National Library of Australia
Cataloguing-in-Publication data

Goosen, Gideon C.
Studying the Gospels: an introduction.

Bibliography.
Includes index.
ISBN 0 85574 389 1.

1. Jesus Christ—Biography. 2. Bible. N.T.
Gospels—Introduction. 3. Bible. N.T.
Gospels—Criticism, interpretation, etc. 4.
Jews—History—To 70 A.D. I. Tomlinson,
Margaret, 1941– . II. Goosen, Gideon C. Jesus,
mystery and surprise. III. Title. IV. Title: Jesus,
mystery and surprise.

232.901

Cover design by Simon Leong
Text design by Katrina Rendell
Typeset in 11/13 pt Bembo by DOCUPRO,
Sydney
Printed in Australia by Australian Print Group

10 9 8 7 6 5 4 3 2 1
98 97 96 95 94

Distributed in Canada by:
Meakin and Associates
Unit 17
81 Auriga Drive
NEPEAN, ONT K2E 7Y5
Ph: (613) 226 4381
Fax: (613) 226 1687

Distributed in the United States by:
Morehouse Publishing
871 Ethan Allen Highway
RIDGEFIELD CT 06877
Ph: (203) 431 3927
Fax: (203) 431 3964

Distributed in Ireland and the U.K. by:
Columba Book Service
93 The Rise
Mount Merrion
BLACKROCK CO. DUBLIN
Ph: (01) 283 2954
Fax: (01) 288 3770

Acknowledgments

We wish to thank those who in various ways, and at different times, have contributed to the writing of this book by their constructive ideas and suggestions.

Our thanks too go to June Pereira who, over many months, patiently did the keying in and editing of this manuscript. We are also grateful to those tertiary students who, for a number of years, have given us valuable feedback on both the running text and the exercises contained in these pages. Finally our sincere gratitude to our editor, Catherine Hammond of E. J. Dwyer, whose fine eye for detail has helped to improve the manuscript in so many ways.

The Scripture quotations in this publication are taken from the Jerusalem Bible, copyright 1966, 1967, 1968 by Darton, Longman and Todd Ltd., and Doubleday and Company Inc., and used with kind permission.

Other acknowledgments are: photos on pp. 4, 13, 31, 36, 39, 175 by G. Goosen; photos on pp. 16 & 37 from *The Holy Land*, by M. Avi-Yonah, 1969, with permission from Steimatzky Ltd., Israel; Harvard University Library for the *Dead Sea Scrolls* on p. 21; the diagrams on pp. 50 and 52 with permission of MacMillan Publishing Company from *Anatomy of the New Testament*, Third Edition by Robert A. Spivey and D. Moody Smith, copyright 1982 by MacMillan Company Inc.; photos on pp. 65 and 86, from *Daughters of the Church*, by R. Tucker and W. Liefeld, with permission from Academie Books, Michigan; photos of manuscripts of Mark, Matthew and John, on pp. 73, 80 and 96, with permission from Chester Beatty Library, Dublin; art from the *Vatican Collection*, Rome, on pp. 108, 117, 164; Blind Man by Di Buoninsegna, p.137, London National Gallery; *Persecution* by Weaver Hawkins on p.150, from *Images of Religion in*

Australian Art, by R. Crumlin, 1982, with permission from Bay Books, Sydney; *The Holy Women at the Sepulchre*, (Gospels of 1038, Erevan, Armenia, p.154) in *Art of the Byzantine Era* by D. Rice, Thames and Hudson, 1963; quotation on p.169 from J. N. Kelly, *Early Christian Creeds*, 3rd Edition, with permission from Longman Group Ltd., Harlow, Essex, U.K.

CONTENTS

HOW TO USE THIS BOOK

This book, which is designed for those commencing a study of the Gospels, can be used as a text in

1. a formal class situation;

or

2. adult study/discussion groups

In either case the book is suitable for adults, tertiary and senior high school students. It can also be used for *private* study.

Central to the fruitful use of this book are the *EXERCISES*, irrespective of who uses the book. They are many and varied. Some require a written response, others are more suited for discussion. Some are for individual work, others for small groups. There are those that primarily challenge the brain, while others engage the heart and personal faith. Choose the ones that suit your needs!

The exercises for discussion are designated by this symbol:

Some hints regarding the use of this book:

Formal Class Situation

It is strongly recommended that students should familiarize themselves with at least one Gospel by reading it in its entirety prior to any study of the text. Appendix A provides guidelines for this task.

While working through the text it is important to do the exercises which are designed to reinforce, illustrate and expand on the material presented.

A glossary at the end of the book will assist readers in quickly recalling the meaning of any technical terms in the text.

A lengthy bibliography is included to indicate both the sources consulted and further reading suggestions.

Adult Study/Discussion Groups

If you intend to use this book as a stimulus for small study/discussion groups, a few handy hints may prove useful:

Size of Group. Five or six interested adults are enough to form a group. It is not advisable to go beyond nine or ten as the group then becomes too difficult to hold together in discussions. If you have a large number of interested adults, form two or three groups.

Place to Meet. Private homes prove a great success. You can take it in turns to hold meetings in the homes of the group members. School staff rooms or parish halls can be used, but in general large rooms are too impersonal and cold for small group meetings.

Frequency of Meetings. This is for the group to decide. Groups meet anything from once a month to once a week. School holidays are best avoided. A short commitment by group members of a term, of two or three months, is likely to be more popular than longer commitments.

Seating. Arrange the seats so that every person can be seen and heard by everyone else. Check that the room is ventilated and neither too hot nor too cold.

Facilitator. This person is the group leader, and can be male or female, priest or layperson. His/her duties are to:

— plan and organize the session;
— make people feel at ease and comfortable;
— initiate discussion;
— invite others to discuss;
— ensure that all those who want to talk get a chance;
— encourage the timid and prevent the garrulous from dominating the discussion;
— be sensitive to each individual in the group.

The facilitator should definitely NOT:

• present himself/herself as a know-all;
• talk too much or attempt to respond to, or comment on, all things said;
• demand a response from everyone (some people, for a variety of reasons, including lack of knowledge, may prefer to listen rather than speak).

HOW TO PLAN EACH SESSION

Each session should run for not more than ninety minutes. Longer sessions may put people off, especially after a hard day's work.

Choose the session you wish to discuss from the suggested sessions below. (Other parts of the book may be used for background reading.)

Prepare for the meeting by reading the relevant pages and become familiar with the appropriate scriptural passages.

Ideally, each session should have:

(i) a brief period for commenting on the material prepared, e.g. was it easy to follow? difficult? interesting? (15–20 minutes);
(ii) a discussion session using the discussion workshop questions provided in the text or ones that arise from the reading (30–45 minutes);

(iii) a concluding prayer and reflection section which could mean using formal prayers (Our Father, prayers from a missal, psalms etc.) or spontaneous prayers, especially ones that arise out of the scriptural passages being studied. The singing of a hymn can be added (use a tape if necessary!). In general it helps to create a prayerful atmosphere. This can be further promoted if a candle is lit and placed on a table. The lights can be lowered and soft music provided. Spontaneous prayers work best when group members know each other fairly well. It might take a few sessions for a new group to be ready for this kind of sharing (10–15 minutes).

After each session refreshments can be provided to assist the social nature of coming together. Those who need to leave then have the opportunity to do so.

LIST OF SUGGESTED SESSIONS FOR STUDY/DISCUSSION GROUPS

These are only suggested sessions. Some will expand into two or three sessions, others may contract into one. Be flexible as regards the needs and interests of the group.

LIST OF ABBREVIATIONS

The books of the Bible in alphabetical order

Ac	Acts	Jude	Jude
Am	Amos	1 K	1 Kings
Ba	Baruch	2 K	2 Kings
1 Ch	1 Chronicles	Lk	Luke
2 Ch	2 Chronicles	Lm	Lamentations
1 Co	1 Corinthians	Lv	Leviticus
2 Co	2 Corinthians	1 M	1 Maccabees
Col	Colossians	2 M	2 Maccabees
Dn	Daniel	Mi	Micah
Dt	Deuteronomy	Mk	Mark
Ep	Ephesians	Ml	Malachi
Est	Esther	Mt	Matthew
Ex	Exodus	Na	Nahum
Ezk	Ezekiel	Nb	Numbers
Ezr	Ezr	Ne	Nehemiah
Ga	Galatians	Ob	Obadiah
Gn	Genesis	1 P	1 Peter
Hab	Habakkuk	2 P	2 Peter
Heb	Hebrews	Ph	Philippians
Hg	Haggai	Phm	Philemon
Ho	Hosea	Pr	Proverbs
Is	Isaiah	Ps	Psalms
Jb	Job	Qo	Ecclesiastes
Jdt	Judith	Rm	Romans
Jg	Judges	Rt	Ruth
Jl	Joel	Rv	Revelation
Jm	James	1 S	1 Samuel
Jn	John	2 S	2 Samuel
1 Jn	1 John	Sg	Song of Songs
2 Jn	2 John	Si	Ecclesiasticus
3 Jn	3 John	Tb	Tobit
Jon	Jonah	1 Th	1 Thessalonians
Jos	Joshua	2 Th	2 Thessalonians
Jr	Jeremiah	1 Tm	1 Timothy

2 Tm	2 Timothy	Zp	Zephaniah
Tt	Titus	NJBC	New Jerome Biblical
Ws	Wisdom		Commentary
Zc	Zechariah		

References are made in the text to the author, year of publication and page number, e.g. (McBrien, 1980: 403–4). Complete references are given, chapter by chapter, in the Bibliography at the end of the book. The lists are alphabetically arranged according to author.

CHAPTER 1

▼

THE SETTING
FOR THE STORY

In taking on the huge task of telling the story of Jesus, a good place to start is with the background or setting for the story. Indeed this is essential if one is to enter into the time and place, the events and people that formed the world into which Jesus was born 2000 years ago. Stories that make an impact on us are often those which successfully re-create the times in which the characters lived and against which we can better understand the actions and decisions of individuals. The success of television productions such as *War and Remembrance* and *A Town Like Alice* can no doubt be attributed to a greater or lesser degree of care in re-creating the appropriate epoch, down to details like uniforms and language usage.

The story of Jesus is of course already found in book form in the New Testament, and more specifically in the Gospels. However, as we shall see, these documents are not simple. There are many customs, words, idioms, ways of speaking, places etc. that need explaining. Much effort has already been put into studying the individual books of the Bible and in trying to piece together the background to biblical events.

The need to do this background work was stressed by the Second Vatican Council (1962–65). In the document on Revelation (referred to by its Latin name, *Dei Verbum*, meaning "Word of God") specific attention is drawn to understanding the setting:

> *For the correct understanding of what the sacred author wanted to assert, due attention must be paid to the customary and characteristic styles of perceiving, speaking, and narrating which prevailed at the time of the sacred writer, and to the customs men normally followed at that period in their everyday dealings with one another. (Abbott, 1966: 120)*

WHERE AND WHEN DID IT ALL HAPPEN?

Because a people's customs and characteristic styles of thinking, speaking and acting (i.e. their culture) grow out of the interaction between people and their physical environment, it is important to study history and geography. Not that these two subjects are the only relevant ones to study, but they will at least give one a good start. Other subjects like—archeology (the study of a culture through its material remains), paleontology (the study of extinct animals and plants), osteology (the study of bones), sociology, ancient Oriental languages, literary forms—all help in the search to gain a more complete understanding of the setting. This accumulative understanding is ever capable of growing and being revised as new discoveries are made, for example in archeology or historical documents such as the Dead Sea Scrolls or the Nag Hammadi manuscripts.

We are going to concentrate on the New Testament and more specifically on the Gospels. It is obvious that the well-known story of the Good Samaritan (Lk 10: 29–37) loses much of its impact if one does not know something of the ethnic origins of the Samaritans and the strong anti-Samaritan feelings of the Jews. Likewise a knowledge of the mountainous and lonely terrain between Jerusalem and Jericho, which was notorious for its robbers, is necessary for a full grasp of the parable. Without this knowledge the story would fall flat. It would be like someone in Australia at the time of Ned Kelly failing to realize why being a teller in a Glenrowan bank could be such a risky occupation. Or like an American at the time of Billy the Kid failing to realize why travelling in a stagecoach through remote Western regions could be so dangerous.

Much of the public ministry of Jesus centers around the Sea of Galilee in the north of Palestine. The physical surroundings of the sea (or lake) are conducive to sudden squalls arising, as mentioned in Mk 4: 37. Again

Caves at Qumran where the Dead Sea Scrolls were found.

if one notes that Tyre is outside the political boundaries of Palestine, one has grasped a point of profound significance in Mark's account 7: 24–30— the point being that salvation is universal, i.e. salvation is also for the Gentiles. There are many such examples one could quote where the geographical position or history of a place is important in terms of reading and understanding the New Testament. Corinth, for example, was an infamous port in ancient Greece, associated with all sorts of sexual perversion and prostitution. The early Christian community in Corinth had to live out their Christian lives amid all this corruption. Hence Paul's frequent cautions and reminders that the Kingdom of God was not for idolaters, adulterers, catamites, sodomites, thieves, usurers, drunkards, slanderers and swindlers! (cf. 1 Co 6: 9–20)

These are some instances that show the obvious relevance and importance of the historical and geographical background if one is not to remain superficial in reading the Bible. As we proceed further in a more systematic overview of some geographical and historical facts, constant reference will be made to the New Testament.

Geographical Background

SIZE

The country of Palestine (from Greek *Syria Palaistine*, i.e. Syria of Philistines), or "Israel" to the Jews, was very small by our standards. From Dan in the north to Kadesh-barnea is only 200 miles (320 km); from Dan to Elath (on the Gulf of Akaba) 250 miles (400 km). If however, the classical southern boundary of Beersheba is taken, the north-south distance is only 150 miles (240 km). The width of the country varies from 30 miles (48 km) in the north to 50 miles (80 km) at the Dead Sea. The total area of Palestine, taking Beersheba as the southern boundary, is only about 7000 sq. miles (17,920 sq. km). This is only slightly smaller than the State of Massachusetts in the U. S. A., or Wales in the U. K., and less than a third of the size of Tasmania, Australia. Travelling in such a small country today is very swift. Leaving Jerusalem by car in the morning one would make Nazareth comfortably by lunch including a stop at Jacob's Well in Samaria. Bethlehem is only about 5 miles (15 km) south of Jerusalem (cf. Map p.10).

NATURAL REGIONS

The following five regions can be clearly distinguished:
(cf. Map. p.9).

The Coastal Plain

This is a narrow belt stretching all along the Mediterranean seaboard. At Mt. Carmel the limestone promontory reduces the coastal plain to only a few hundred metres. North of Mt. Carmel are the Plains of Acco and Phoenicia, south the Plains of Dor, Sharon and Philistia. These latter two are marshy, luxuriant plains once thickly covered with oak forests. The coastline south of Mt. Carmel has but few natural harbors and as the coastal belt stretches further south, rainfall decreases and the plains merge into steppe and desert.

The Western Hills or Central Highlands

In Palestine the highest peak is Jebel Jermaq in Upper Galilee (4800 ft.; 1219 m; cf. Mt. Everest 29,028 ft.; 8848 m). Lower Galilee consists of a number of east-west ridges descending to the coastal plain and the Jordan. Further south in Galilee is one of the most fertile plains of Palestine, The Great Plain or Basin of Meggido drained by the Kishon River. The Plain of Esdraelon or Jezreel stretches west into the Jordan Valley. Yet further south again the Central Highlands are known as the Hill Country of Ephraim (Samaria) and the Hill Country of Judah (Judea), which consist of hills, stony outcrops and sparse vegetation. Occasionally there are fertile east-west valleys producing olives, sycamore trees, grain, figs and vines. Mt. Gerizim 2860 ft. (889 m) in Samaria is of importance as the "high place" of worship for the Samaritans. (cf. Jn 4: 20)

Beyond the Valley of Beersheba, going south, is the Negeb, a barren steppe merging gradually into harsh desert. To the west are sand dunes and loess hills, in the center limestone and sandstone ridges.

The Rift Valley

This impressive geological fault runs north-south through Palestine, through the Red Sea and reappears in Africa. In Palestine, the River Jordan ("that which goes down") rises in the mountains of Lebanon, near the snow-capped Mt. Hermon 9232 ft. (2841 m) and flows south through the Sea of Galilee, and by way of a very meandering course (about three times the air distance) into the Dead Sea. The Sea of Galilee is also known as Lake Chinnereth (Hebrew for "harp") as it is heart- or harp-shaped (John speaks of Lake Tiberias, a name given to it later in the first century A.D. after the Roman Emperor). It is truly a beautiful lake, about 7 miles (13 km) at its widest, where Jesus spent much of his time with his disciples. Because it is surrounded by hills it is susceptible to sudden storms as winds rush into the basin formed by the lake and swirl around (Mk 4: 37). The Dead

Sea is 1290 ft. (395 m) below sea level and is super-saturated with salt (Salt Sea). One can easily float on the water as it is so thick with salt. It was on the north-western tip of the Dead Sea that the Essenes had their monastery at Qumran. It is flanked by mountains.

The Eastern Hills (Transjordan)

This tableland has a number of rivers running east-west and is considerably fertile with rainfall decreasing eastwards. It produced grain, wine, olives and was famed for its oak and pine.

The Desert

East of the Eastern Hills, the plateau slopes quickly into the wastes of the Syrian desert.

CLIMATE

There are basically two seasons in Palestine: the hot, dry summer and the cool, wet winter. The coast is warm with an average of 50–60°F (10–16°C) in the winter and between 80–90°F (27–32°C) in the summer with considerable humidity. The mountains are, however, 18°F (10°C) cooler than the coast. The rain bearing winds (winter) come from the Mediterranean whereas the hot sirocco or khamsin sweeps in from the desert in Spring (May) and Autumn (Oct.). Jesus knew of both kinds of winds (Lk 12: 54–55). In winter, we read too that Jesus walked up and down in the Portico of Solomon in the Temple—the only porch that offered protection from the prevailing wind (Jn 10: 23).

RAINFALL

As one would expect, the western slopes are much wetter than the leeward side of the Highlands. The Plain of Sharon would get 20–24" (500–600 mm) per annum but Jericho only 4–8" (100–200 mm); Jerusalem about 24" (600 mm) which is not really much; sections of Upper Galilee between 32–35" (800–900 mm); Beersheba only 8.6" (220 mm). Palestine was thus overall a very dry country.

Snow is not unusual in places like Jerusalem, Bethlehem, Hebron or the Transjordan. Mt. Hermon has snow all the year round.

Because of the generally dry conditions and the seasonal nature of rain, water was (and is) very precious in Palestine. It was frequently stored in cisterns. Fortunate were those who had river water, a well or spring—"living water" (Jn 4: 10–14). Jacob was forever blessed for discovering the well in Samaria known in the Gospel as Jacob's Well.

The "wadi" is a very common phenomenon in Palestine. It is a valley, used as a road when dry but subject to flash flooding and strong streams in the rainy season. The wadi is common because few valleys in fact carry permanent streams.

Historical Background

The Jewish people who inhabited Palestine in the time of Jesus had a long history which they kept alive initially through an oral tradition and subsequently in written form. Their history as found in the Old Testament is not history in the modern scientific meaning of the word. It is popular history which likes to dwell upon personal anecdotes and family details and makes no attempt to situate narratives in a wider historical context. It is also, and above all, history as written from a religious standpoint where the hand of Providence is seen in each event. However, earlier suspicions that the narrative history of the Old Testament might not ever have occurred have been refuted by the data collected by historians and archeologists of the Near East.

The Jews were indeed proud of their long and eventful history. In Matthew's Gospel we note, for example, that the author, writing for a Jewish audience, tries to show how we can trace a genealogy of Jesus back to Abraham, the founder of the Jewish people. Luke's genealogy goes to Adam, as he is intent on emphasizing universal salvation—we are all children of Adam. It is thus important for us to try and enter into an understanding of who the Jews were and their unusual history if we are to appreciate the society into which Jesus was born.

The history of the Jews prior to Jesus is found in written form in the books of the Old Testament. However, as we are primarily concerned with the New Testament, we will only sketch in the main periods in that history with some emphasis on the time immediately prior to the time of Jesus.

The main periods in Jewish history in the Old Testament (cf. p. 11) are as follows:

THE PATRIARCHS (c. 1850 B.C.)

This period covers the origins of the Jews and their great patriarchs. Abraham from Ur "of the Chaldeans" was called to found a people and lead them into a land (Canaan) promised them by Yahweh their God. Other patriarchs followed: Isaac, Jacob and then Joseph, who was sold into slavery in Egypt (c. 1700 B.C.) and later joined by most of Jacob's other sons.

PALESTINE: NATURAL REGIONS

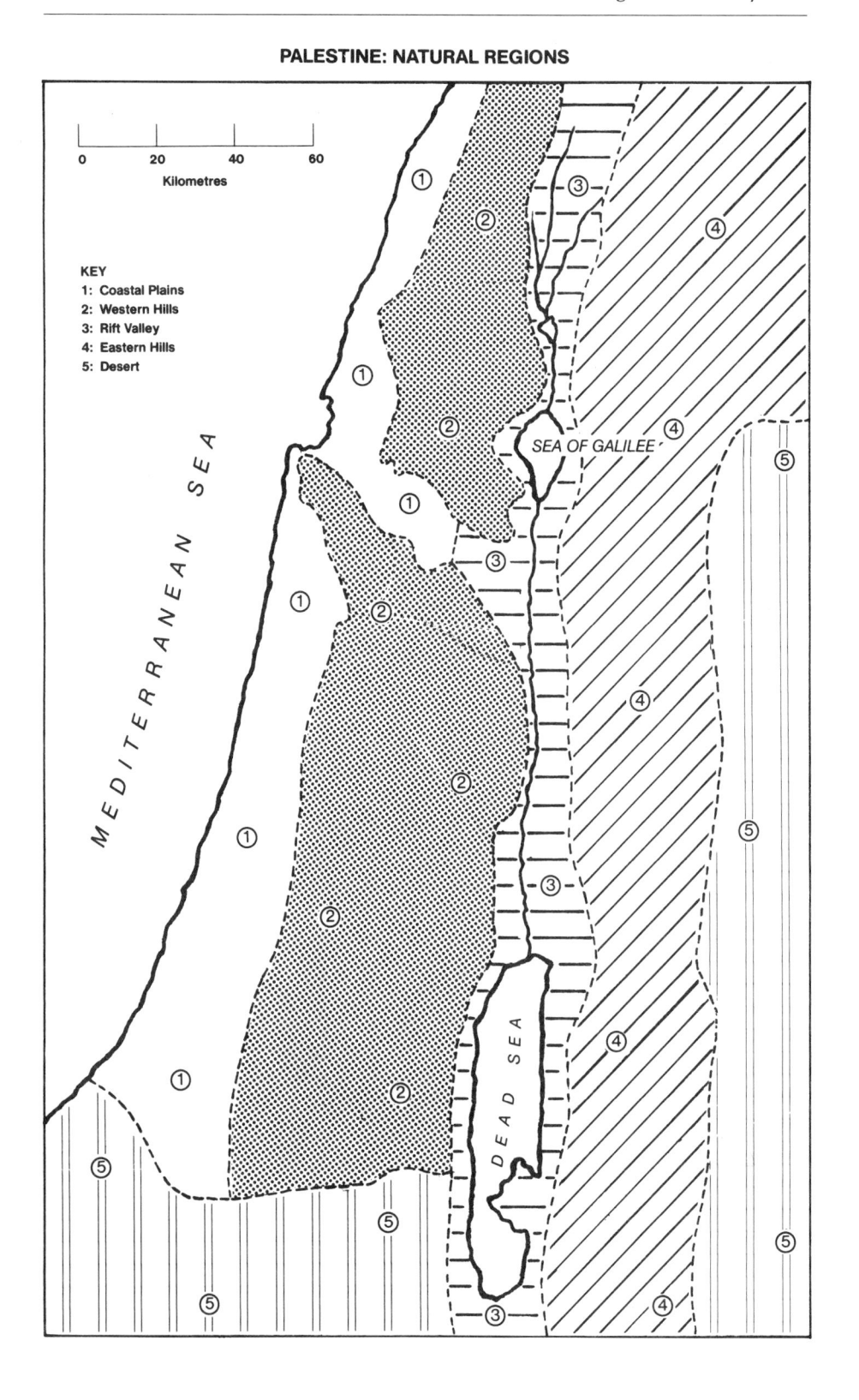

PALESTINE IN NEW TESTAMENT TIMES

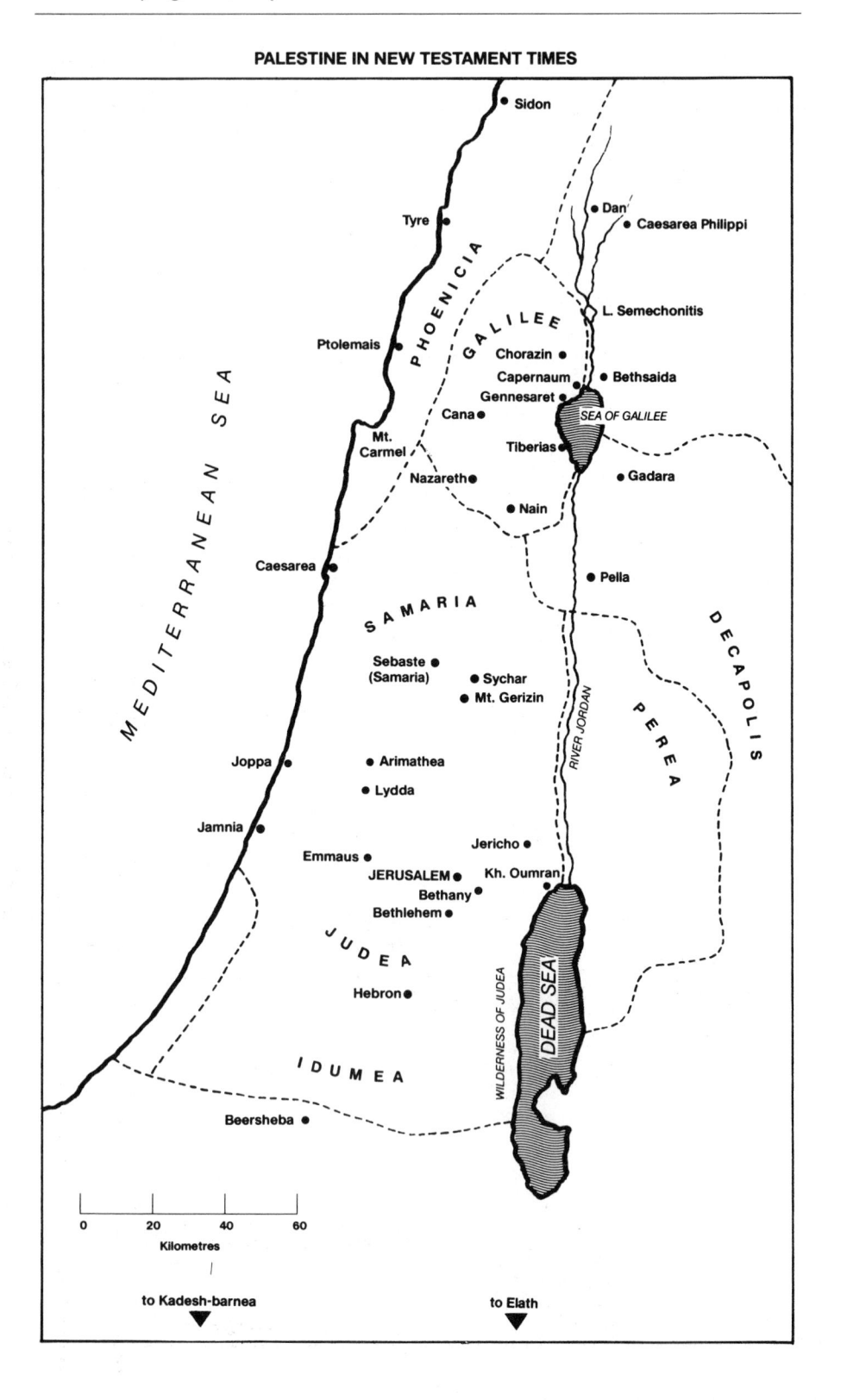

PEOPLE	RULERS	TIME	PERIOD

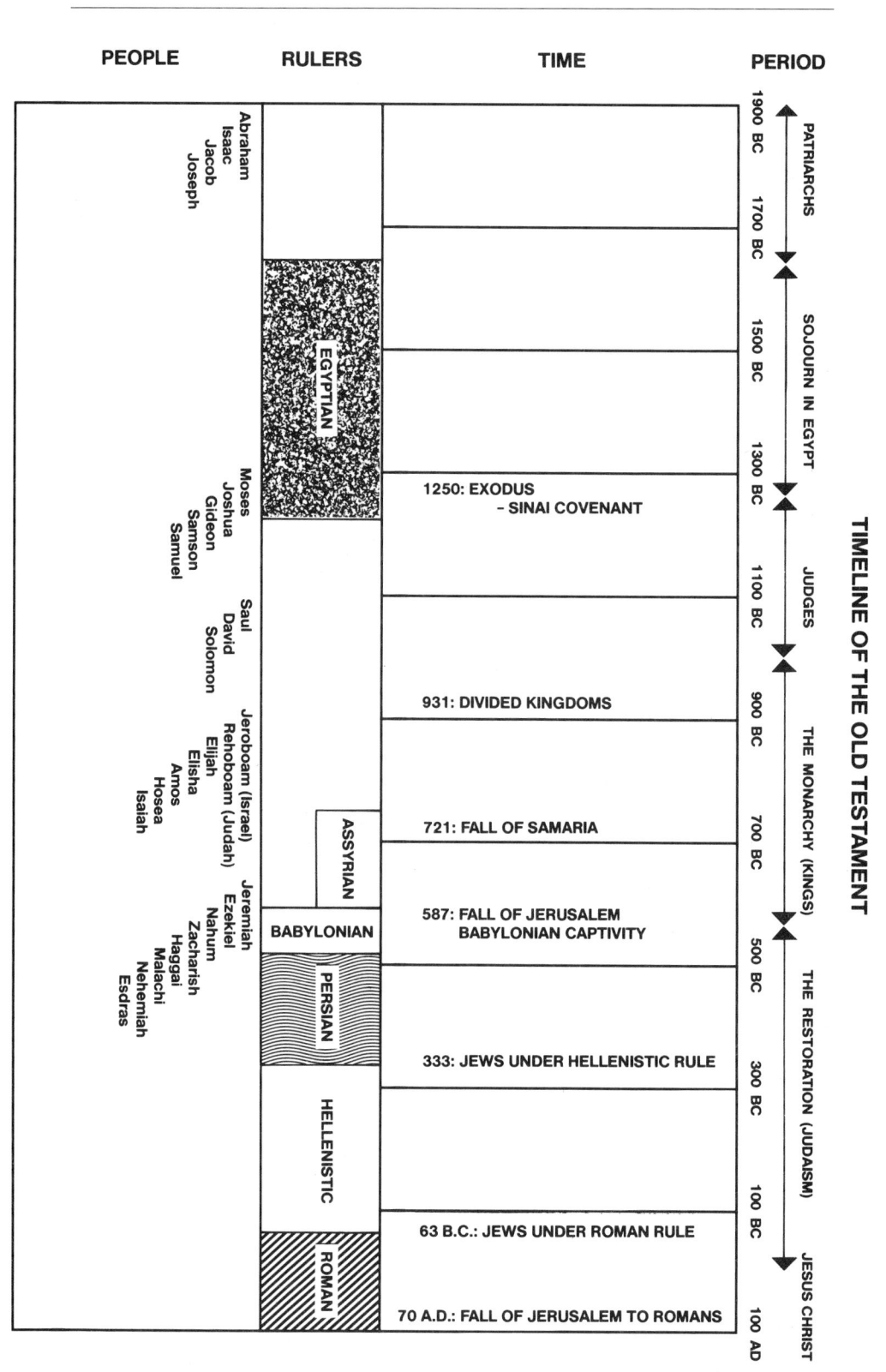

TIMELINE OF THE OLD TESTAMENT

PEOPLE:
Abraham
Isaac
Jacob
Joseph

Moses
Joshua
Gideon
Samson
Samuel

Jeroboam (Israel)
Rehoboam (Judah)
Elijah
Elisha
Amos
Hosea
Isaiah

Jeremiah
Ezekiel
Nahum
Zachariah
Haggai
Malachi
Nehemiah
Esdras

RULERS:
EGYPTIAN

Saul
David
Solomon

ASSYRIAN

BABYLONIAN

PERSIAN

HELLENISTIC

ROMAN

TIME:
1250: EXODUS
  – SINAI COVENANT

931: DIVIDED KINGDOMS

721: FALL OF SAMARIA

587: FALL OF JERUSALEM
  BABYLONIAN CAPTIVITY

333: JEWS UNDER HELLENISTIC RULE

63 B.C.: JEWS UNDER ROMAN RULE

70 A.D.: FALL OF JERUSALEM TO ROMANS

TIME SCALE:
1900 BC
1700 BC
1500 BC
1300 BC
1100 BC
900 BC
700 BC
500 BC
300 BC
100 BC
100 AD

PERIOD:
PATRIARCHS
SOJOURN IN EGYPT
JUDGES
THE MONARCHY (KINGS)
THE RESTORATION (JUDAISM)
JESUS CHRIST

Moses by Michelangelo in the Church of St Peter's in Chains, Rome.

EXODUS AND THE SINAI COVENANT (c. 1250 B.C.)

This period is at the heart of Jewish religious experience. The Jews, who had lived in slavery under the Egyptians, were liberated by Moses, who led them out of Egypt, through the desert of the Sinai peninsula into Canaan. While in the desert they experienced the nearness of Yahweh in a special way and entered into a pact or covenant with Him. The pact was that Yahweh would be their God and look after them and they would be faithful to Him and keep the commandments. The Ten Commandments were accepted by the Jews as the articulation of Yahweh's will for them.

The Jews under Joshua entered the Promised Land by conquering the local tribes one by one about 1200 B.C. They were ruled for about two hundred years by leaders known as Judges (cf. Jg, Ch).

THE MONARCHY (c. 1020 B.C.)

This period marks a highpoint in Jewish history. The people decided they wanted a king and thus a monarchy came to be instituted. Saul was the first king, followed by David, the boy-king who led the Israelites to victory over many an enemy, and then Solomon the Wise, who built the Temple at Jerusalem (I K 6: 1) and established commercial contacts with neighboring Phoenicia and Arabia.

DIVIDED KINGDOMS (931–721 B.C.)

After Solomon the kingdom split up into a northern one, Israel, and a southern kingdom, Judah. Each kingdom was ruled by separate kings and

Site of the temples in Jerusalem where the mosque, the Dome of the Rock, now stands.

during this period many famous prophets lived—among them Elijah, Elisha, Amos, Hosea, Isaiah and Micah.

FALL OF THE KINGDOM AND THE CAPTIVITIES (721–538 B.C.)

Northern Kingdom, Israel

Samaria was besieged and conquered by the Assyrian, Shalmaneser V in 722 B.C., who deported the inhabitants to Assyria (capital: Nineveh on the Tigris River), and replaced them with foreign colonists.

Southern Kingdom, Judah

Judah resisted various attempts at conquest but prophets like Jeremiah warned the people of the impending doom. In 587 B.C. Jerusalem fell to the Babylonian Nebuchadnezzar (the Assyrian power had been broken in 612 B.C.) and the Jews were deported to Babylon in Mesopotamia (the Babylonian Exile).

THE RESTORATION (538–333 B.C.)

When Cyrus, the Persian, conquered Babylon in 538 B.C., he freed the Jews and allowed them to return to Jerusalem and rebuild their Temple.

This was the period of the prophets such as Haggai, Zechariah, Nehemiah and Malachi.

THE JEWS UNDER HELLENISTIC RULE (333–63 B.C.)

The dominance of the Persian Empire came to an end with the conquest of Syria by Alexander the Great in 333 B.C., which event also marks the formal beginning of the Hellenistic period for the Jews.

On Alexander's death in 323 B.C. the Middle East, including Palestine, fell to two generals, Seleucid and Ptolemy and subsequently to their successors. Initially the Jews in Judea were benevolently ruled by the Ptolemies based as they were in Alexandria in Egypt. (During this time the Jewish Law was translated into Greek.) Galilee, during this same period, came under Seleucid rule (based at Antioch) and because the local Jews proved so susceptible to Greek influence, the country earned the title of "Galilee of the Gentiles".

In 198 B.C., however, all Israel came under Seleucid rule. At this time Roman military strength was growing and proving a threat to the Greeks. In order to finance military campaigns against the Romans, the Greeks had to increase taxation of the Jews, which only exacerbated the already deteriorating relationship between the Jews and their Greek rulers.

In 170 B.C. Antiochus IV, a Seleucid, attacked Egypt and had himself crowned king of Egypt. On his way back to Antioch (169 B.C.) he sacked Jerusalem and desecrated the Temple (cf. 1 M 1: 16; 2 M 5: 15; Dn 11: 24–28). Israel revolted in reaction to this treatment, led by the Hasmonean family of Mattathias and his warrior sons. One of them, Judas, was nicknamed Maccabeus ("the hammer"), because of his ferocity in battle (cf. the two books of the Maccabees).

Surprisingly the revolt succeeded and the Seleucids, preoccupied with fending off Roman power to the West and Persian might to the East, allowed the Hasmoneans to rule their fellow Jews. This period of Jewish independence lasted only until the Romans, who had been waiting for the right moment, conquered Israel and with that conquest independence was lost for centuries. It was only in 1948 A.D., with the emergence of the modern State of Israel, that the Jews were to regain independence and a homeland.

ROMAN RULE (63 B.C.)

In 63 B.C. the Romans conquered all Palestine and established local subjects to rule on their behalf, thus ending the Hasmonean dynasty. The Romans chose Antipater as ruler of Galilee. He was from Idumea, south of Judea, an area annexed during the Hasmonean era. Antipater had two sons, Herod and Phasael, who shared in their father's power. On the death of Antipater and Phasael, the Romans in 40 B.C. recognized Herod as king of the Jews and placed him as ruler over all Jewish territory, i.e. Judea, Samaria, Galilee, Perea (Greek word for "beyond"—beyond the Jordan), and lands east and northeast of Galilee.

Herod died in 4 B.C. but prior to his death, Jesus was born in Bethlehem (Mt 2: 1). Herod would naturally have been "perturbed" about news of any rival king of the Jews (Mt 2: 3).

Herod was an Idumean as regards his ethnic origin. Although he had espoused Judaism, he was in fact non-Jewish and had aligned himself as far as possible with the power of Rome. Being chosen by Rome to be king of the Jews would certainly have resulted in being seen as a Roman collaborator by some Jews. Nevertheless he did build the harbor at Caesarea (the seat of Roman power in Palestine) and many public buildings in Jerusalem and Samaria. He was also responsible for changing the name Samaria (the town) to Sebaste, after the Greek "Sebastos" for Caesar Augustus.

On Herod's death, the kingdom was divided as follows among his three sons, called tetrarchs or rulers (cf. Lk 3: 1–2 and map on p. 10):

(i) Archelaus: Judea, Samaria (Capital: Jerusalem).
(ii) Herod Antipas: Galilee, Perea (Capital: Tiberias, after Emperor Tiberias, 14–37 A.D.).
(iii) Philip: Iturea and Trachonitis (Capital: Caesarea Philippi; cf. Lk 3: 1).

Archelaus was deposed in 6 A.D. and his territory placed under a Roman governor, who happened to be Pontius Pilate (26–36 A.D.) at the time of Jesus' crucifixion (cf. Mk 15: 1, Lk 3: 1–2). He had Roman troops at his headquarters at Caesarea (on the coastline) but also at the praetorium (Mk 15: 16) in Jerusalem.

When the Romans conquered Palestine in 63 B.C. their leader was Pompey. Only in 48 B.C. did their leader become a Caesar—Julius Caesar. Antony (41–30 B.C.) followed him but it was Caesar Augustus (31 B.C. –14 A.D.) who was Emperor at the time of the birth of Jesus. Tiberias followed (14–37 A.D.) and after the death of Jesus it was Caligula (37–41 A.D.); Claudius followed (41–54 A.D.), then Nero the first persecutor of Christians (54–68 A.D.) and Vespasian (69–79 A.D.), who continued to persecute the early Church.

Claudius is said to have expelled the Jews from Rome, according to the writer Suetonius, because of disturbances caused by one "Chrestus". Aquila and Priscilla, mentioned in Ac 18: 2, both natives of Pontus (Asia Minor), were the victims of this expulsion order. They fled to Corinth.

The seven-branched candlestick on the Arch of Titus in Rome.

Nero blamed the Christians for a fire in Rome he himself may well have started. Peter and Paul are thought to have died in this persecution.

Under Vespasian the Jews in Palestine tried to revolt (66 A.D.) and did indeed hold out for a while, but were then savagely crushed by Titus, who laid siege to Jerusalem with four legions. An arch in the ancient Forum in Rome, the Arch of Titus, commemorates this Roman victory in 70 A.D. On the arch is a relief of the seven-branched candlestick which Titus is said to have brought back with other spoils of war. Titus himself became Emperor in 79 A.D.

Persecution of Christians continued under later Roman emperors. It was only with the peace of Constantine in 313 A.D. that Christians were allowed to practice their religion freely. Nevertheless there were certain benefits for the emerging Church in the Roman Empire. There was the advantage of unimpeded travel between countries within the Empire. This was of enormous benefit to Paul and others in their missionary work. Because of the "Pax Romana" (Roman Peace), people from neighboring countries were able to be present in Jerusalem at Pentecost: Parthians, Medes, Elamites; people from Mesopotamia, Judea, Cappadocia, Pontus, Asia, Phrygia, Pamphylia, Egypt, Cyrene, and Rome; Cretans and Arabs (Ac 2: 9–11).

EXERCISE 1:   Draw a relief map of Palestine, not less than 6"x8" (15x20 cm) indicating:
— the rivers Jordan and Kishon;
— the Sea of Galilee; the Dead Sea; the Plain of Esdraelon;
— the hill country of Judea, Samaria and Galilee;
Include in your map the towns or districts mentioned in the following texts:

Mk 2: 1	Mk 8: 27
Mk 3: 7	Mt 17: 1
Mt 5: 1	Mk 10: 46
Lk 4: 1	Jn 2: 13
Jn 2: 1	Lk 2: 4

For this exercise consult maps such as those in a Bible, biblical commentary, or biblical atlas (cf. Bibliography).

EXERCISE 2:   Draw a political map of Palestine, indicating the division of territories under Herod's three sons.
Also indicate the capital towns of each territory.

WHAT KIND OF MESSIAH DID THE JEWS EXPECT?

Every society looks for a savior, messiah or guru of some kind or another. Today with high inflation, unemployment and industrial troubles, people might long for an economic savior who will have the magic formula for curing all the economic ills of society.

During the last century, with the growth of nationalism in Europe, each country looked for a leader who would unite the people and forge them into a powerful nation. Cavour and Garibaldi in Italy, Bismarck in Germany (and later Hitler), Napoleon in France, and Gandhi in India—all fulfilled this role to a greater or lesser extent. They were political or national saviors or messiahs ushering in a new era—or so it seemed to the masses. Gough Whitlam would have been seen by some Australians in this light in 1972 and Paul Keating in recent times. In the United States, Bill Clinton in 1993 held promises for a different and better future for Americans. Marx-Leninism also speaks of a future, glorious, classless society after a period of class warfare, although this vision was debunked in Eastern Europe in 1989 with Boris Yeltsin becoming the savior figure for the Russians.

Thus the idea of someone, or some system providing all the answers and introducing a "new deal" is not foreign to human experience. When we look at Judaism however, we find expectations that bear similarities with the above examples, but also sharp differences. It is these Jewish expectations that we will examine now.

In reviewing the history of the Jews above, we noted how frequently they were oppressed by other peoples. One could list their oppressors as follows: Egyptians, Canaanites, Assyrians, Babylonians, Persians, Greeks, Ptolemies, Seleucids and Romans! With this record of oppression it is not surprising that they dreamt of someone leading them to better times, to freedom, to salvation from their foes. With every new prophet the vital question was asked: are you the one to come, or have we got to wait for someone else? (Mt 11: 3) (The evangelist, John, gave symbolic expression to his belief that Jesus was the Messiah by starting his Gospel with the Wedding Feast at Cana—a symbol of the Messianic Age.)

When one speaks of messianism in Judaism, one must firstly bear in mind that it was an idea that grew, developed and changed in emphasis with the long history of Judaism. Within the idea of messianism are a number of different strands of thought which are distinct yet tied up with each other at the same time. Messianism includes, for example, the following ideas:

1. the expectation of salvation in general;
2. the expectation of a new, wondrous era;
3. the coming of an individual messiah who will
   save his people.

If we look for a definition of messianism, the one given by Ellis (1976: 342) is a good starting point:

Messianism may be defined in the broadest sense of the word as Israel's expectation, based on revelation, of a great and glorious destiny. More narrowly, messianism may be defined as Israel's divinely founded and firm expectation of a reign of God over Israel in which Israel will enjoy spiritual regeneration, complete freedom, and continual happiness, and be the vehicle for the same for the rest of humanity.

No explicit mention is made of a personal messiah in this definition. When the expectation of a personal messiah did take hold, the Jews looked forward to him not so much as the object of their expectations, but rather as a person who would introduce the reign of God. The messiah would be God's agent.

Tracing the development of these ideas through Jewish history we gain a clearer picture of the variety of expectations among the Jews at the time of Jesus.

The Period of the Patriarchs

There was a tradition that went right back to the earliest time that Yahweh would save his people. This is sometimes called soteriological messianism (from the Greek, *soteria*, meaning salvation). It includes the curing of both spiritual and physical ills, i.e. total salvation.

This hope was nurtured within the context of Abraham's call and the promises made to him. Yahweh had promised that he, Abraham, would be the father of a great people and through his descendants there would be mediated to the world great blessings. Within this conviction it is understandable how the soteriological hope was projected into the past. After the Fall, Yahweh curses the serpent and promises:

> *I will make you enemies of each other;*
> *you and the woman,*
> *your offspring and her offspring.*
> *It will crush your head*
> *and you will strike its heel. (Gn 3: 15)*

In this verse "it" is taken to refer to the woman's descendants, and this promise of victory over the forces of evil (salvation) is referred to as the proto-evangelium or proto-gospel. The Gospel is the Good News (of salvation); Gn 3: 15 is the pre-gospel, or proto-gospel, the first vague inkling of salvation.

The theme of salvation is again touched upon in the Noachic Covenant (Gn 9: 8–17) where Yahweh promises salvation from material destruction.

In Exodus and Joshua there are sections which summarize Israel's past history as a basis for her future hope. Read for example Ex 2: 24; 3: 6; 15: 16; 6: 2–8; Jos 24: 1–4.

The experiences of Sinai and the Covenant confirm and reassure Israel that she has indeed been chosen by God for a great destiny and a glorious future.

The Period of Dynastic Messianism

The period centers around King David and the establishment of his dynasty as the vehicle through which the Messianic Age would come. The scriptural reference is that of the prophet Nathan who promised to David on Yahweh's behalf that his dynasty will never end. Read 2 S 7: 8–16 (in Ac 2: 3 this text of Samuel is taken to refer to Jesus); 1 Ch 17: 7–14; Ps 88: 20–38.

The Period of a Personal Messiah

This period marks the further development in Israel's understanding of messianism. From the idea of the Davidic dynasty as the means of bringing about the glorious future, the concept of a personal, individual messiah develops.

With the Fall of the Southern Kingdom (587 B.C.) and the Babylonian Captivity, Israel was forced to reconsider its future. If the Davidic dynasty was eternal, it would need to be restored and ideally a personal messiah could do this.

From the period of the Monarchy down to the Exile there was a certain tension in Israel's hope. On the one hand there was the firm faith in the promise of the perpetuity of the Davidic House and on the other hand, as their experience showed, the kings were incapable of bringing about the realization of a glorious era. Out of this tension Israel's expectations became more sharply defined, centering around a person, a messiah filled with the spirit and power of Yahweh who would usher in the reign of God, a reign that would go beyond this world, a final reign, an eschatological reign.

Jeremiah, disillusioned with the Davidic kings and predicting the downfall of Jerusalem, forecasts a new David who would rule with success. Read Jr 23: 1–6; 30: 8–9, 21; Ezk 16: 60; 17: 22–24; 21: 32; 34: 23–24; 36: 25–38; 37: 24–27.

The following is a list of further texts that refer to a personal messiah. Read these texts in the Bible with the help of any explanatory footnotes.

Is 7: 14 predicts a maiden will conceive and bring forth a child Immanuel, i.e. God-with-us. Mt 1: 23 uses this text as messianic.

Mi 5: 1: from Bethlehem will come the one to rule over Israel.

Hg 2: 23: the election of Zerubbabel, a successor of David, is now associated with traditional royal messianism and the messianic expectation takes shape about his person.

Ps 110: 4: this psalm represents Melchizedek (Gn 14: 18) as a figure of the Messiah who is both king and priest.

Further psalms agreed upon as messianic in character are Pss 2, 16, 22, 45, 72, 89, 110, 132; there is less general agreement as to the messianic character of Pss 8, 20, 21, 40, 48, 68, 118.

Is 52: 13; 53: 12: *ebed Yahweh*, the Servant of the Lord. This figure of the Servant of Yahweh is taken to refer to the Messiah. It represents quite a different picture from that of the glorious king insofar as it details his

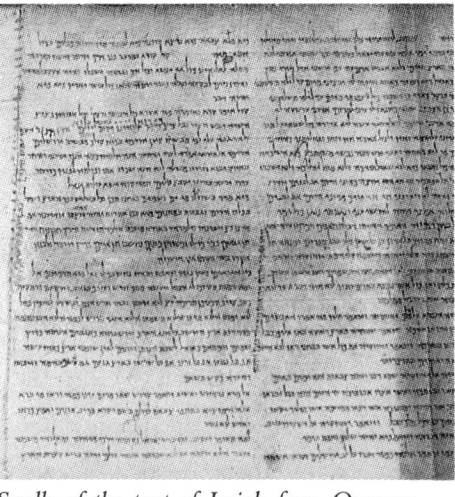

Scrolls of the text of Isaiah from Qumran.

sufferings. (This text is used in the liturgy of Good Friday.) At the same time, after his sufferings he will be feared as an irresistible royal figure, alluded to in anticipation in 52: 13.

Is 61: this is also taken as a messianic reference and was referred to as such by Jesus himself (Lk 4: 16–19); Mark (1: 1–3) and Matthew (3: 1–3) both refer to Isaiah 40: 3 as messianic.

Dn 7: 13–14: this well-known messianic text refers to the Son of Man on whom were conferred "sovereignty, glory, and kingship". Jesus applied this text to himself: cf. Mt 8: 20.

Summary

The first ideas of messianism were in broad soteriological terms: the promise of salvation, spiritually and bodily to Israel and through Israel to all humankind.

With the Davidic dynasty promise, a period when Israel would be restored to its full authority and glory as a nation was uppermost in Jewish minds. They idealized the age of David. Israel's hopes were mainly political and national. This outlook was not concerned with the renewal of the world but with Israel's greatness. It was more nationalistic and expansive than spiritual. It was directed at the past rather than future. However, the covenant belief that they were God's people remained.

During the Isaiahan period the vision of a new people and a new kingdom that would embrace the whole world began to take shape. This new kingdom rests on the spiritual forces of Yahweh. In Deutero-Isaiah the vision is further refined: the world is going to be changed, Israel is called upon to be the light of the world. The figure of the Messiah, although still a king, is also a suffering servant, for spiritual purification is necessary for Israel before it can enter the messianic era. Future salvation can only be realized through atonement for sin, through purification of the people and the suffering of the guiltless servant whom God calls to this task. The Kingdom so inaugurated is eschatological in nature: it is the final Kingdom, it goes beyond this world and lasts forever.

EXERCISE 3:   Read Matthew, Chapters 1–4 and note down all the Old Testament references Matthew has made of a messianic nature. Simply write down the Old Testament text and then a sentence stating briefly what it is about.

SOCIETY IN THE TIME OF JESUS

Groups Within Jewish Society

As we have already seen, one of the primary facts about life in Palestine in the first century A.D. was that it was an occupied country. The Romans did, however, allow the Jews to be administered by the regime to which they were accustomed. There was a superimposition of authorities, and the complicated situation which this produced can be seen in the story of Jesus' trial and execution.

The situation in Palestine was probably more complex than in, say, Gaul or Greece, because the Jews had pronounced ideas about the relative importance of God and Caesar. Furthermore, at least from the time of the monarchy, they regarded the land as the promise and the gift of God to God's own people. Their land was now, as it had so often been in the past, occupied by foreigners and governed according to their terms.

The situation was further complicated by the fact that there was a complexity of political attitudes and parties, as religious and political issues crisscrossed and became entangled. So we find political parties and religious sects ranging all the way from the conservatism of the Sadducees to the militant messianism of the Zealots. Furthermore, the presence in the Jewish community of such officials as tax collectors (Jews employed by the Romans) heightened tension and highlighted divisions.

One further factor, at the very heart of Jewish life, which underlined differences between groups, was attitudes towards the Law, or *Torah*. The

English word "Law" does not convey the richness of the Hebrew word. To the Jews, *Torah* referred to all that their God had revealed about God's self, their history, and the conduct and practices that were required of them, as outlined in the Pentateuch (what we know as the first five books of the Bible). They saw the Law as God's gift to them:

> You yourself have made your precepts known,
> to be faithfully kept . . .
> Explain to me how to keep your precepts,
> that I may meditate on your marvels.
> (Ps 119: 4, 27)

The Law was central to Jewish life and practice, and groups within Judaism could be categorized according to their attitude to the Law and its interpretation.

EXERCISE 4: In order to understand something of the Jews' devotion to the Law, read Ps 119.

SADDUCEES

The name Sadducees, "sons of Zadok", is thought to derive from Zadok, who succeeded Abiather as priest in the days of Solomon (cf. 1 K 1: 8, 32ff, 2: 35). To Zadok's descendants the Jerusalem priesthood was secured by legislation proposed by Ezekiel (40: 46; 44: 15; 48: 11).

The Sadducees seem to have been mainly the aristocratic priestly families, who held a monopoly of the High Priesthood and were powerful in the Sanhedrin. They jealously retained their rights and privileges at all costs, and were more disposed to Gentile tastes and sympathies than other Jewish groups. Thus in the struggle with the Seleucids in the second century B.C. they had supported the pro-Hellene group, and now they were anxious to stay on peaceful terms with Rome, since the preservation of the status quo was to their advantage.

Though overtly faithful to the letter of the Mosaic law in their political pursuits, they lacked the devotion to it which characterized the Pharisees. They rejected the concept of oral law, taking a conservative, even rigid approach to the *Torah*.

As the priestly class, their leadership position in the community had become very important when the Jewish community lived in exile after the destruction of the first Temple. In the Jerusalem of Jesus' time, they were concerned with the temple cultus and the proper administration of the sacrificial rites. Their jealous guarding of the status quo reinforced their conservative outlook, their opposition to innovation, and their fear of any hint of possible insurrection. Hence their closed attitude towards Jesus, their resistance to apocalyptic and eschatological thought, and their disapproval of the popular belief in angels, evil spirits and the hope of the resurrection. An interesting sideline underlines their conservatism: they could act as priests only in their vestments. The cunning Romans at one stage stole the vestments, thus effectively paralyzing them!

The Sadducees, as a group, were so closely aligned with the temple cultus that when the Temple was destroyed in 70 A.D. they disappeared from history.

EXERCISE 5:   Read Mk 12: 18–27.
Here we see Jesus in discussion exposing the errors of the Sadducees. What underlies the Sadducees' question in verse 23? What position does Jesus take in his response to them?

PHARISEES

The origin of the Pharisees is thought to be linked with the Hasidim of the Maccabean period (cf. 1 M 2: 42–48). The Hasidim emerged as a group strongly opposed to the adoption of Greek ways, because to them these customs were bound up with idolatry and immorality. They joined the Hasmoneans in fierce revolt against the desecrating Seleucid, Antiochus IV, but once religious freedom was restored they gradually separated from the politically ambitious Hasmoneans. It is this break-away group which is thought to be the forerunner of the Pharisee party ("the separated"), though some scholars relate the term to their desire for ceremonial purity, their particular attitude to the Law as the guarantee of piety, and their avoidance of Gentiles and sinners.

They were essentially a lay movement, and, as the "popular" party (in contrast to the aristocratic Sadducees), controlled the Synagogue and eventually made it, rather than the Temple, the center of Judaism. However, their influence should not be confined only to the synagogue.

Unlike the Sadducees, they accepted the validity of oral tradition (Oral Torah), and thus sought to make the Law fit changing circumstances. Though this had its liberalizing aspects, it also led them to that casuistry and hairsplitting that has sometimes caused them to be regarded as hypocrites who stressed outward observance whilst neglecting the inner spirit. Matthew presents the Pharisees as very hypocritical (e.g. Mt: 23), but most scholars argue that his indictment reflects the later controversy between the early Christian community and the Synagogue rather than an authentic statement from Jesus. Though there were, no doubt, those Pharisees who were opposed to Jesus, especially in his teaching on the Law, there were also those who allowed him to teach in the synagogue (Mk 1: 21), invited him to dine in their homes (Lk 11: 37, 14: 1–24), warned him that Herod Antipas was out to kill him (Lk 13: 31), and who arranged for his burial (Jn 19: 38 ff.).

They believed in the existence of angels and spirits, and held that after death a person would be judged and accordingly would be happy or punished.

Because of their belief in the religious destiny of Israel and their adaptability to new circumstances, they were able to meet the new situation after the destruction of Jerusalem, and led the Jewish community to recovery.

SCRIBES

These were the professional class of copyists and teachers of the Law (hence in the New Testament they were also called lawyers). They were addressed as *Rabbi*—"my master". The method of teaching the Law was usually by way of a running commentary on the biblical text—*Midrash*. There were two types of *midrashim*: (a) *Midrash Halakah* (or *Halachah*), a legal commentary on the biblical text; (b) *Midrash Haggadah*, a compilation of traditional and devotional narratives (cf. Chapter 3 where Matthew's "Infancy Narrative" is discussed).

Every scribe followed some occupation in addition to his teaching. Most of the scribes seem to have belonged to the Pharisee party (cf. Mk 2: 16: "the scribes of the Pharisee party"), though the Sadducees also had their scribes.

In order to be admitted into the body of professional teachers, the aspiring student had to become the pupil of some distinguished Rabbi. Thus the student Paul went to the famous Rabbi Gamaliel (cf. Ac 22: 3).

Differing schools of opinion or interpretation grew up bearing the name of famous Rabbis. In the time of Jesus there were two such opposed schools: that of Hillel (c. 50 B.C.–10 A.D.) representing those of more moderate view, and that of Shammai representing the stricter elements.

EXERCISE 6:   An instance of the differing schools of thought can be seen in Mt 19: 3ff, where the Pharisees present Jesus with a question on divorce, hotly disputed by the two schools. What position on the question was held by (a) Rabbi Hillel, (b) Rabbi Shammai?

ZEALOTS

The Zealots (or Home Rule party) reflected the religious and political expectations of some of the Jewish people at the time of Jesus. They were probably an extremist offshoot of the Pharisee party, and did not emerge as a definite group until after the census taken in 6 A.D. when Quirinius was governor of Syria. They were characterized by their militant zeal for national independence and eventually (around 66 A.D.) their recourse to armed resistance. They appear to have adopted the Maccabees as their model.

Of Jesus' chosen twelve, at least one was probably a Zealot (cf. Mk 3: 18).

A hair-raising incident occurred in the life of Paul (Ac 21: 38) when he was mistakenly identified as being the leader of an extremist group of Zealots, the Sicarii (from the name of the dagger they used—with precision! The Jerusalem Bible translates the word as "cutthroats"). This very active branch of the Zealots was engaged in the work of secret assassination.

The Zealots were instigators of sporadic uprisings which eventually ended in revolt against the Romans under Zealot leadership in 66–73 A.D. Titus (later Emperor) brutally suppressed the uprising and destroyed the Third Temple. The last pocket of resistance ended with the mass suicide of the defendants of Masada. This marked the disintegration of Judaism as a geographically established nation for nearly 2,000 years.

ESSENES

Though not mentioned in the New Testament, the Essenes were an important group in the Jewish community around the time of Jesus, since they embodied yet another form of response to the religious and political situation. They probably emerged around 150 B.C. as a recognizable group, and were essentially an ascetic sect who lived in groups in the villages or in isolated communities. They followed a strict rule of life, believing themselves to be the community of the new covenant, the "remnant" of God's people who alone lived according to the true understanding of the *Torah*, the correct interpretation of which had been made known to their Teacher of Righteousness. A three-year probationary period was imposed on anyone who wished to join them, and members were bound to keep secret their doctrines and practices.

In 1947 A.D. a remarkable discovery was made in the Dead Sea area by shepherds looking for a lost goat. In caves at Khirbet Qumran they came across fragments of ancient manuscripts, the famous Dead Sea Scrolls or Qumran Scrolls. A steady stream of discoveries has been made in the area since then, throwing much light on the doctrines and practices of the community which probably flourished from about 100 B.C.–68 A.D. It is still too early to establish the exact connection between the Qumran community and the Essenes, but it seems that Qumran may well have been a branch of the Essenes.

The Qumran Scrolls indicate that the community was eschatological in its outlook, awaiting a Messiah and the triumph of the Kingdom of God. Their belief that they alone lived according to the true understanding of the *Torah* brought them into conflict with the Pharisees, and their spiritualized understanding of sacrifice set them at odds with the Sadducees.

The Qumran discoveries have caused much interest and speculation, quite apart from the light they throw on a particular branch of Jewish society of the time. There have been suggestions that John the Baptist was an Essene and perhaps connected with the Qumran community, though this theory has not been proven. Most of the speculation has centered around the question of the relationship between the Qumran community and the early Christian Church, because of similarities in the area of:

a) the eschatological outlook of the two communities;
b) their method of organizing their communities;
c) their liturgical practices.

It may well be, however, that they are parallel contemporary movements growing out of a common sociological milieu, common religious background, and a common heritage rooted deep in the Old Testament.

ETHNIC GROUPS

Deep in the consciousness of every Jew was the conviction that the Jewish people were the chosen people of the covenant to whom God had given this land. This conviction was written into their liturgy, their Law, the very fabric of their lives, and was expressed in their attitude to non-Jews (Gentiles).

In New Testament times, Jews lived side by side with Greeks, for there were in the area Greek cities set up in the post-Alexandrian times of the Ptolemies and Seleucids. These formed the Decapolis or league of ten cities, most of them to the east of the Jordan (Transjordan) (cf. Mt 4: 25, Mk 5: 20). There were other cities, mostly along the coast, which had a predominantly Greek population (e.g. Gaza, Caesarea, Ptolemais), as did the inland cities of Shechem (Herod's Sebaste) and Tiberias. There was constant tension between the two ethnic groups in these cities, and at times rioting broke out.

During its long history, the land of Israel had absorbed a number of ethnic elements, particularly during the Exile. While most of the Jews were living in Babylon, their land was resettled by a mixture of ethnic groups:

Aramaeans, Canaanites, Phoenicians etc., who intermarried with what remained of the tribes of Israel. When the Exiles returned, they were obliged to live side by side with these groups. Later, during the Hasmonean era, attempts were made to convert these people to Judaism, though this conversion did not obliterate diversity of origins. So the Idumeans were regarded as half-caste and of doubtful faith (as we have seen in the case of Herod), and the people of the northern areas, including even Galilee, as not far removed from being Gentile.

The Samaritans in particular were despised, and Samaria was a real tension point in the Jewish world.

Samaria was located between Judea and Galilee. When many of the Jews who lived there were deported to Babylon in 721 B.C., the Assyrian conquerors settled in their place colonists from other parts of their empire. These Gentile settlers intermarried with the remaining Jews. The resulting population considered themselves to be Jewish and followed the *Torah* in their own way. However, not only was intermarriage between Jew and Gentile considered an abomination by the Jews, but it also seems that when the returning Jews were rebuilding the Temple in Jerusalem (about 500 B.C.), the Samaritans tried to prevent the rebuilding. Friction and hostility between the Jews and Samaritans continued into New Testament times.

EXERCISE 7: Note on your map the position of Samaria in relation to Galilee and Judea:
(a) Read 2 K 17: 24–41 and Ezr 4. What do these texts, written from the Jewish perspective, tell you about the Samaritans?
(b) What is the significance of the Jews' question in Jn 8: 48?
(c) What is the significance of Jesus' use of the example of the good Samaritan in the parable of that name?
(d) Read Jn 4: 5–42. Say why it is significant that:
(i) the protagonist is a Samaritan;
(ii) the protagonist is a woman;
(iii) many believed in him on the strength of a woman's testimony (v. 39).

EXERCISE 8: Identify some of the groups that constitute our society today, perhaps in terms of the issues they stand for. Are there any modern equivalents for the groups that constituted Jewish society at the time of Jesus?

Which group do you fit into?
From your knowledge of the Gospels where would you place Jesus in relation to the society in which he lived?

The attitude of the Jews towards the Samaritans highlights a characteristic which developed among the Jews returning from Babylon to Judea: their tendency towards "exclusivism" (or "particularism"), regarding all non-Jews as "the Gentiles", those "others out there". This grew partly out of their conviction of being Yahweh's Chosen People, but also out of their interpretation of the Babylonian Captivity as the result of their turning to "foreign" gods and practices—their failure to keep their covenant with their God. Henceforth, they would separate themselves from anything or anyone that might taint their allegiance to Yahweh. Thus they were forbidden to marry foreigners, and those who were already married to non-Jews were asked to leave them (cf. Ezr 9). At times their resistance to the Gentiles was to reach the level of fanaticism, but at its best their exclusivism was a sign to "the nations" of the reality of their God and the way of life that followed from this reality.

Jewish Religious Institutions and Worship

Jewish worship centered around the Temple and the Synagogues. Religious practice stressed "the works of the Law" (such as Sabbath observance, fasting, almsgiving). The Sanhedrin was concerned with the interpretation of the Law in concrete situations.

TEMPLE

The Temple in existence during the period covered by the Gospel was the third, built by Herod. (For the history of the first two Temples, see Fallon, 1981: 315–317, and NJBC 76: 48–50.)

EXERCISE 9: Find a diagram of the third Temple and draw a ground plan. (There is a diagram in the Jerusalem Bible on the map headed "Jerusalem of the New Testament".) Notice that the temple itself is surrounded by three courts or roofless enclosures. On the outside was the large court to which Gentiles as well as Jews were admitted. Gentiles were not allowed to pass beyond the outer court on pain of death. It is to this that Paul alludes in Ep 2: 14.

The actual temple which stood on rising ground within the third court, the Court of the Priests, was divided into two sections, the Holy Place or Sanctuary, and the Holy of Holies. Only priests were permitted to enter the Holy Place, while the High Priest alone entered the Holy of Holies, and that only on one day of the year, the Day of Atonement (*Yom Kippur*).

Temple worship centered around the sacrificial offerings (the daily burnt offering presented at dawn and in the evening), and the more elaborate rituals of the Day of Atonement and the great festivals of Passover, Tabernacles, Dedication, Weeks and Purim. Private offerings were also made by individuals in accordance with the requirements of the *Torah*. Thus the Temple area was constantly crowded with priests, worshippers, sacrificial animals and those who sold them, and moneychangers who provided the special type of coin required by the *Torah* for financial transactions. Sacrifice was not offered anywhere else but in the Temple in Jerusalem. Thus, once the Temple was destroyed, sacrifice was no longer offered by the Jews.

The High Priest originally held the position for life, but under Roman rule he could be appointed or deposed by the secular authority (Herod the Great's habit of deposing the High Priest at whim made him unpopular with the Jews). In addition to the Sadducees or "upper class" clergy, there were the ordinary priests who came from throughout Palestine, and served for a week on a rotating basis (cf. Lk 1: 8). There were also the Levites, the lowest order, who served as cantors, doorkeepers, etc.

The priesthood (as we have already seen in regard to the Sadducees) was a position of importance and power, but after the destruction of the Temple its power waned rapidly.

The Temple's destruction in 70 A.D. left only part of a wall standing— the Western Wall, a shrine which is still sacred to the Jewish people.

SYNAGOGUE

These were centers of Jewish activity, worship and education, formed wherever there were at least ten men. They appear to have originated after the time of the destruction of the first Temple in 586 B.C., but whether in Palestine or Babylon is not known.

Synagogues were (and still are) basically centers of worship and the study of Scriptures, and were instrumental in nurturing the Jews' deep reverence for the *Torah*. Services were held every Sabbath, on Festival days and sometimes daily. Schools and libraries were often part of the Synagogue. Synagogues were to be found not only in the towns of Palestine, but also wherever communities of Jews lived throughout the Roman Empire. In places where the Jewish people were largely independent, the directors of the Synagogue (Elders) also administered civil affairs (since the Jewish people made no distinction between sacred and secular). In strong Gentile centers, however, the Elders were distinct from the civil authorities. Elders exercised discipline over the Synagogue members and had the power of

The Western Wall, Jerusalem.

punishing by temporary or permanent exclusion, a dreaded penalty (cf. Jn 9: 22, 12: 42, 16: 2).

In some areas sympathetic Gentiles attended Synagogue services. Some of these (the "God-fearers" of Acts, cf. also Jn 12: 20) were particularly ready to become Christians.

The Synagogue service centered round readings from the Scriptures. The first reading was from the *Torah* or Pentateuch (Genesis, Exodus, Leviticus, Numbers, Deuteronomy). The *Torah* was divided into fifty-four portions, one to be read on each Sabbath (sometimes two, to complete the cycle). The *Torah* was handwritten on parchment scroll in Hebrew.

The reading of the *Torah* was followed by a reading from the Haftorah ("completion"), a section of the prophets whose content was closely connected with the reading from the *Torah*.

The psalms were also an integral part of the Synagogue service. All services began with a psalm. The Hallel psalms (113–118) were used on festival days. The psalms were often said verse by verse alternately.

EXERCISE 10: Turn to Lk 4: 16–30. Here Jesus is asked to read from the Haftorah. He then gives a reflection or teaching. Note the response of the congregation. If you compare the reading with Is 61: 1–2, from which it is taken, you will notice that Jesus left out the last line. One could guess that there would have been Zealots among the congregation who would have been waiting eagerly for that line, and who would have been enraged by its omission. Why?

EXERCISE 11: If there is a Synagogue in your area, visit it and find out all you can about it.

SANHEDRIN

The functions and general nature of the Sanhedrin are somewhat obscure, but it appears to have been a type of council or senate. Both the Jewish historian Josephus and the New Testament writers present the Sanhedrin as a political and judicial body, with authority over Jews outside Palestine as well as within (e.g. Ac 9: 2). Roman officials could apparently bring accused Jews before it (cf. Ac 22: 30). Its jurisdiction covered every aspect of daily life (since Jews made no distinction between civil and religious law); the one limit to its power was the death sentence which only the procurator could pronounce (cf. Jn 18: 31). It had no authority over Roman citizens except in the case of trespassing upon the inner courts of the Temple.

In Jesus' time, the Sanhedrin consisted of Chief Priests, Elders and Scribes (cf. Mk 14: 53; 15: 1; Mt 27: 41). According to the New Testament, the presiding officer was the High Priest.

SABBATH

The Sabbath was central to Jewish religious observance. Because the Jews reckoned a day from the previous evening, the celebration of the Sabbath began just before sunset on Friday with family prayer and a meal, and concluded at sunset on the following day.

The Old Testament does not record the institution of the weekly Sabbath, but everywhere reflects its observance. The Sabbath assumed particular importance during and after the Exile, when the ruined Temple was no longer the symbolic center of the Jewish religion.

Ex 20: 9–11 associates the Sabbath with Creation. Israel's observance of the day is grounded in Yahweh's example and Yahweh's authority. It is a sign of the covenant and Israel's fidelity to the covenant. The Jewish liturgy presented their covenanting God as resting on the seventh day and thereby blessing it (cf. Gn 2: 2–3).

The earliest Pentateuchal and prophetic texts present the Sabbath as a day of rest, a joyful festival day, sacred to Yahweh. It took on a greater significance during exilic times; the Sabbath observance was presented as symbolic of Israel's national destiny. Post-exilic writers stressed the Sabbath as the distinguishing mark between Jew and Gentile (Ne 10: 31, 13: 15), regarded its observance as a supreme religious duty and as a condition of messianic fulfilment (Is 56: 2ff.; 58: 13 ff.; 66: 22–23), and introduced rigid prohibitions (Jr 17: 21–22; Ne 13: 19–22). As time progressed, rules became stricter, and by New Testament times there were numerous prohibitions (cf. Jn 5: 10; Mk 3: 2, 12: 2; Ac 1: 12).

R. de Vaux summarizes the significance of the Sabbath thus:

> . . . the Sabbath took on a particular meaning which made it an institution
> peculiar to Israel. Its characteristic feature lies not in the regularity with
> which it recurs, not in the cessation of work, nor in the various prohibitions.
> . . Its distinctive trait lies in the fact that it is a day made holy because of
> its relation to the God of the Covenant. (de Vaux, 1961: 480)

EXERCISE 12: Read Mk 2: 23–28. Compare with Mt 12: 1–4, Lk 6: 1–5. Also read Mk 3: 1–6. Compare with Mt 12: 9–14, Lk 6: 6–11. What was the point at issue in these two scenes? Why do you think the Pharisees chose the topic of the Sabbath on which to challenge Jesus? How does Jesus challenge the Pharisees?

EXERCISE 13: In what ways do our contemporary use of church buildings and celebration of Sundays show continuity with the ancient Jewish tradition? In what ways not?

FESTIVALS

The main Jewish festivals are as follows:

a) The three pilgrim festivals: Passover, Shavuot, Sukkoth;
b) Rosh Hashanah, the ten days of penitence, Yom Kippur;
c) Purim and Hanukkah.

They appear to have had two distinct sources:

• agricultural festivals; and
• theological–historical celebrations.

The Jewish calendar differs from the Gregorian calendar to which we are accustomed. The following chart shows the modern Jewish calendar with the major festivals listed, so that we can better situate particular feasts:

Gregorian Calendar	Jewish Calendar	Main Festivals
September/October	Tishri	Rosh Hashanah (New Year) Teshuvah Yom Kippur (Atonement) Sukkoth (Tabernacles)
October/November	Chevan	
November/December	Kislev	Hanukkah (Dedication)
December/January	Tevet	
January/February	Shevet	
February/March	Adar	Purim
March/April	Nisan	Pesach (Passover)
April/May	Iyar	
May/June	Sivan	Shavuot (Pentecost)
June/July	Tammuz	
July/August	Av	
August/September	Elul	

Jewish festivals were characterized by three factors:

a) Rejoicing, including ceremonial meals (except Yom Kippur), and pro-
   hibition of work;
b) Liturgy (and in Temple times special sacrifices);
c) Special ceremonies (e.g. eating unleavened bread at Passover, or lighting
   of candles at Hanukkah).

EXERCISE 14:   What is your favorite feast in the liturgical cycle?
Find out if it has any connection with an ancient Jewish
festival. If so, in what ways is its focus different from the
Jewish festival?

Lifestyle

OCCUPATIONS

The Palestine of Jesus' time was basically an agricultural and pastoral land. It is not surprising, therefore, that there are many references in the Gospels to farmers sowing and reaping their crops, fallow ground, vineyards, sheep etc. Jesus moved about the countryside and spoke about what he and his listeners knew and understood from daily experience.

It seems that the oldest occupation in the area was shepherding. Long before the Jews had settled as farmers, they had driven their flocks from one pasture to another. In Jesus' time this was still an important occupation, since there were often large flocks of sheep and goats which had to be moved to the best pastures, according to the season. The shepherd's life was lived in the open air for most of the year, and his occupation was often a lonely one if he was not able to band together with other shepherds in the evening. There was need for constant vigilance against wild animals and thieves, and sometimes shepherds would make huge "sheepfolds" with stone walls and a watchtower in order to make the work of protecting their flocks easier (cf. Jn 10: 1–16).

Many of the people worked in the fields, growing wheat and barley and other cereal crops. A primitive plough was used, drawn usually by oxen. The work of ploughing was difficult, for the soil was hard and rainfall scarce, except in the more fertile Galilee, where water was not such a problem. Reaping was carried out with a sickle. The Law gave the poor the right to glean and pick up forgotten sheaves. A husking-sledge drawn by oxen was used for threshing. Men with three-pronged wooden forks then carried out the winnowing process. The mixture of cut straw, husks and grain was tossed into the air; the grain fell straight down, while the chaff was blown away in the wind.

Most families grew a few vines, but there were also the large vineyards, each with its watchtower for protection against thieves. Sometimes the vines were allowed to run at ground-level, but more often other fruit trees (such as figs and olives) were planted and the vines allowed to trail from tree to tree. There was scarcely any pruning done, as we know it, and the life of the vineyard owner was considered comparatively leisurely, except at vintage time.

Fishermen were also an important part of the economic scene, and it seems that they were generally held in high esteem. Some of them lived along the Mediterranean coast, but many lived round the Sea or Lake of Galilee, for its waters were full of fish. The fishermen used two kinds of nets: the round throwing net, about 13 feet (4 m) across with weights all

Fisherman by the Sea of Galilee.

round the edge, which trapped the fish by dropping over them; and the "seine". The latter was a band approximately 1600 feet long and 13 feet deep (500 m by 4 m), with floaters above and sinkers below. When using this net, some of the crew stood on the shore holding one end of the net, while the boat took the other end out as far as it would go. Then the boat travelled in a huge semicircle to the shore, and the net was hauled into shore "enclosing fish of every kind". (Compare Mt 4: 18–21, Mk 1: 9, 16; Lk 5: 2; Jn 21: 6; and Mt 13: 47).

Though most of Jesus' contemporaries were farmers or fishermen, the towns had craftsmen such as carpenters, dyers, tailors, sandal-makers, tent-weavers, potters and goldsmiths. The crafts were usually hereditary, and often carried out at home. Women ground their own corn, turning two millstones against each other. Bread was baked at home. Clothing, too, was often made at home.

In addition, there were the professional class (the scribes, priests etc., already mentioned), and, in the busy coastal centers, a growing merchant class.

The Jews were not, on the whole, a wealthy people, particularly in the country areas, for the soil was not generally productive. However, though the peasant was generally poor, excessive poverty was scarcely known in the area in the time of Jesus. One of the rankling burdens of the day was Roman taxation. Some of the Jews acted as agents for the Romans in this, and they were despised for their occupation. For the Roman tax, the denarius or silver penny was used. In addition to the Temple tax of a tenth of one's produce annually, there was also the annual monetary tax of a half-shekel, which had to be changed into the trusted coinage of Tyre (hence, as we have seen, the presence of moneychangers in the temple precincts).

HOMES AND HOMELIFE

The ordinary Jewish home was a one-room, mud-brick dwelling, roofed with mud-covered reed mats spread across wooden beams. It was not essentially different from older homes found in the area today.

The diet in the average Jewish home consisted of a kind of porridge of wheat or barley, plus vegetables such as beans, lentils and cucumbers, seasoned with onions, garlic and olive oil. Dates, figs and pomegranates were popular, and in some areas fish was plentiful. Watered wine was the universal drink.

Water, a precious commodity in most of the area, was usually drawn from the village well.

The family would gather round a common bowl, dipping in with their right hands.

At night, they unrolled mats and huddled near the fire.

Part of synagogue mosaic (4th Century A.D.) showing woman crowned with pomegranates and grapes.

MARRIAGE

Boys married at eighteen, girls at puberty (officially twelve and a half). They usually married within the clan. The betrothal was celebrated first. The groom stated before witnesses: "She is my wife and I her husband, from today and forever". These words officially bound the couple, though they did not yet live together. During the betrothal year that followed, the girl could not be dismissed except by divorce, and if the boy were to die, she would be considered a widow.

After the twelve-month betrothal period, the bride was brought to the groom's house, the parents pronounced a blessing, and everyone joined in a great celebration of singing and dancing and feasting, lasting a week. (Recall the wedding scene from *Fiddler on the Roof*, and the wedding feast at Cana—it is no wonder that the wine ran out, at the end of the week's celebrating! (Cf. Jn 2: 1–10.)

CHILDREN

Children were highly valued by the Jewish people and considered a blessing and favor from the Lord, since one's descendants were the inheritors of the Covenant (cf. Gn 17: 9). (Leon Uris' *Mila XVIII* emphasizes the extent to which children are still considered to be the precious hope of the Jewish nation.)

When a child was born, narrow lengths of cloth, or bandages, were wrapped round his/her limbs to prevent movement.

On the eighth day after his birth, a male child was circumcised. In Jewish society this was an important religious ceremony, since it was considered a mark of the person's belonging to the chosen people of God. The ceremony of giving the child his name usually took place on this day. The name had a special significance in Jewish society. It was considered to be an integral part of the person, closely associated with his/her characteristics and fate. The right of choosing a name belonged to the father (cf. Lk 1: 59–66).

After the birth of her child, the mother was considered unclean, so she went to the Temple at Jerusalem forty days after the birth (or eighty days if the child were a girl), for the purification ceremony. This included the offering of a sacrifice of a lamb and a pigeon, or, in the case of the poor, two pigeons or turtledoves. Because the firstborn son belonged to the Lord, he had to be "bought back" for the considerable sum of six shekels (cf. Lk 2: 22–24).

EDUCATION

When the boy was six or seven, the father began the work of educating him in the Hebrew traditions and customs. He took the child to the Synagogue to learn the precepts of the Law. If the Synagogue had a school (and many of them did by Jesus' time), he learned to read and write, using the Torah as text.

From his father the boy learned a trade, or perhaps studied with some scholarly Rabbi in order to become a teacher.

By age thirteen, he was expected to know the whole of the Law and to practice its requirements, and many children finished school at this age. At thirteen the boy's Bar Mitzvah ceremony was held in the Synagogue to celebrate his coming of age. He was expected to show publicly that he knew the Torah.

Though education was held in high esteem for boys, it was considered unnecessary for girls, since they had no official place in religion. However, it seems that women did in fact learn the Scriptures at home. Daughters remained with their mothers till they married, performing domestic tasks, carrying water from the village well, spinning wool and, in the country, reaping the crops and shepherding during the daytime.

DEATH AND BURIAL

The death of one of the villagers was announced by a solemn drumbeat. The Jews had a profound respect for the body of the dead person, based on their belief that it was very directly the work of God. It was "anointed" with various perfumes, of which nard was the most common. Myrrh and aloes were also used (cf. Jn 12: 3–8; 19: 39–40). The body was wrapped in a shroud, the face veiled and the feet tied with linen strips.

Burial followed soon after death, either the same day or the next. The village stopped work and walked in two groups to the burial place. Women walked ahead of the open bier on which the body was carried, wailing ritually and clapping rhythmically. Official flautists (at least two) and a mourner were hired for the occasion. Close relatives, according to the ritual, tore their clothing. The men recited the ritual prayer for the

Tombs in the Kedron Valley.

deceased, possibly the Kaddish, which is still known today (cf. Lk 7: 12–15; Mt 9: 23–25).

The typical burial place appears to have been an excavation or cave cut into a cliff or rock, which was later walled up or, in the case of more wealthy people, sealed with a large round rock rolled into a kind of groove (cf. Jn 19: 42; 20: 1).

LANGUAGE

The language spoken at this time was not Hebrew, but one not unlike Hebrew: Aramaic. Aramaic was spoken by semi-nomadic peoples as far back as the end of the second millennium B.C. Under Babylonian and especially under Persian rule it became the main diplomatic and business language, and eventually the native language of the whole region, including Palestine, where Arameans settled while the Jews were in exile in Babylon. Hebrew as the vernacular of the Jewish people began to decline during and after the Exile, and for ordinary usage Aramaic gradually took its place.

PSAL. XXII. כב

כב

א לַמְנַצֵּחַ עַל־אַיֶּלֶת הַשַּׁחַר מִזְמוֹר לְדָוִד:

2 אֵלִי אֵלִי לָמָה עֲזַבְתָּנִי רָחוֹק מִישׁוּעָתִי דִּבְרֵי שַׁאֲגָתִי:

3 אֱלֹהַי אֶקְרָא יוֹמָם וְלֹא תַעֲנֶה וְלַיְלָה וְלֹא־דוּמִיָּה לִי:

4 וְאַתָּה קָדוֹשׁ יוֹשֵׁב תְּהִלּוֹת יִשְׂרָאֵל:

ה בְּךָ בָּטְחוּ אֲבֹתֵינוּ בָּטְחוּ וַתְּפַלְּטֵמוֹ:

6 אֵלֶיךָ זָעֲקוּ וְנִמְלָטוּ בְּךָ בָטְחוּ וְלֹא־בוֹשׁוּ:

7 וְאָנֹכִי תוֹלַעַת וְלֹא־אִישׁ חֶרְפַּת אָדָם וּבְזוּי עָם:

8 כָּל־רֹאַי יַלְעִגוּ לִי יַפְטִירוּ בְשָׂפָה יָנִיעוּ רֹאשׁ:

The Death of Jesus
(Mt 27.45–56; Lk 23.44–49; Jn 19.28–30)

33 Καὶ γενομένης ὥρας ἕκτης σκότος ἐγένετο ἐφ' ὅλην τὴν γῆν ἕως ὥρας ἐνάτης. 34 καὶ τῇ ἐνάτῃ ὥρᾳ ἐβόησεν ὁ Ἰησοῦς φωνῇ μεγάλῃ, Ελωι ελωι λεμα σαβαχθανι; ὅ ἐστιν μεθερμηνευόμενον Ὁ θεός μου ὁ θεός μου, εἰς τί ἐγκατέλιπές με⁸; 35 καί τινες τῶν παρεστώτων ἀκούσαντες ἔλεγον, Ἴδε Ἠλίαν φωνεῖ. 36 δραμὼν δέ τις καὶ γεμίσας σπόγγον ὄξους περιθεὶς καλάμῳ ἐπότιζεν αὐτόν, λέγων, Ἄφετε ἴδωμεν εἰ ἔρχεται Ἠλίας καθελεῖν αὐτόν. 37 ὁ δὲ Ἰησοῦς ἀφεὶς φωνὴν μεγάλην ἐξέπνευσεν. 38 Καὶ τὸ καταπέτασμα τοῦ ναοῦ ἐσχίσθη εἰς δύο ἀπ' ἄνωθεν ἕως κάτω. 39 Ἰδὼν δὲ ὁ

Et facta hora sexta, ténebræ factæ sunt super totam terram usque in horam nonam. Et hora nona exclamávit Jesus voce magna, dicens: Eloi, Eloi, lamma sabactháni? quod est interpretátum: Deus meus, Deus meus, ut quid dereliquísti me? Et quidam de circumstántibus audiéntes, dicébant: Ecce, Elíam vocat. Currens autem unus, et implens spóngiam acéto, circumponénsque cálamo potum dabat ei, dicens: Sínite, videámus si véniat Elías ad deponéndum eum. Jesus autem, emissa voce magna, exspirávit.

Examples of Hebrew, Greek and Latin.

It is Aramaic that Jesus and his contemporaries would have spoken. By this time, Hebrew was almost a dead language, though used perhaps in parts of Judea still, and in the Temple and Synagogue and for prayer in the home.

Greek was also commonly used. After the time of Alexander, it gradually became almost a universal language—not in the original form used in Greece, however. It adapted and changed as it spread till it was virtually a new language, the common language understood and used in varying degrees throughout most of the known world by the first century A.D. Hence its name, *Koine* or common Greek.

Mention has already been made of the fact that the Hebrew Scriptures had been translated into Greek. The Jewish historian Josephus represents Ptolemy II as obtaining from the High Priest in Jerusalem the services of seventy-two Elders to make such a translation—hence the name *Septuagint* (LXX). It is more likely that the various parts of the Hebrew Scriptures were translated into Greek over a period of years, and with unequal merit, to meet the needs of Jews in Alexandria.

Irrespective of how the Greek version, the Septuagint, came into being, it was of great importance. Except among the Scribes and professional students of the Law, Hebrew disappeared as the vernacular of the Jews during the *Diaspora* (the dispersion or scattering of the Jews as a result of the Exile, and the consequent growth of Jewish communities in various parts of the world). Thus the LXX became the form of the Scriptures most familiar to the ordinary people. It was from the LXX that the New Testament writers usually quoted.

The language of the New Testament itself is this unliterary Koine Greek, even though the Gospels are partly based on earlier Aramaic sources, either written or oral.

Latin, the language of the Roman officials, would also have been familiar to the Jews, especially in the busy cosmopolitan cities.

Note the reference to the cosmopolitan language situation in Jn 19: 20.

CHAPTER 2

THE GROWTH AND DEVELOPMENT OF NEW TESTAMENT STUDIES

THE QUESTION OF THE GOSPELS AS BIOGRAPHY

The word "gospel" has a long history. The equivalent Greek word *euangelion* (good news) acquired religious significance in the Roman Empire in the cult of the Emperor, in which public appearances of the Emperor, his accession to the throne, and his decrees were known as good news or gospels. It has been suggested that the New Testament usage derives partly from the "good news" of freedom from captivity which Isaiah proclaimed to the Israelites emerging from the Babylonian Exile (Spivey, 1982: 61). In the New Testament, "gospel" also signifies the good news of salvation (e.g. Mt 11: 5, Mk 1: 1). Early usage of "euangelion" in the Christian community referred to the oral nature of the news; however, with Mark, Matthew, Luke and John, the Gospel became a specific literary category.

Until the last century, the Gospels were generally regarded as four biographical accounts of the life of Jesus, written in much the same way as any modern biography. So it could be imagined that one day Mark, for example, decided that it was time that he wrote a biography of Jesus for the Christian community. He looked around for any letters, reports or other documents. But there were none; Jesus wasn't a letter-writer, and no enterprising journalist was there to interview him, nor did anyone, apparently, keep any records. So Mark contacted as many eyewitnesses of the events as he could (including Peter, who knew Jesus better than most people), and made notes of their impressions. Eventually, he put it all together in chronological order and wrote a small book: "Jesus Christ. A biography by John Mark."

This popular impression of the Gospels as biography presupposed a direct link between the events as they were witnessed, and the first written accounts of them. However, biblical scholarship in the last hundred years or so has radically challenged this view.

The roots of modern biblical scholarship can perhaps best be located in the eighteenth century Enlightenment, with the development of new

45

scientific and philosophical systems and, early in the nineteenth century, new views on the nature and methods of historical enquiry. It was inevitable that the methods of the scientific school of historians should come to be applied to the Bible.

The first critical approach to the story of Jesus was given systematic expression in Germany by Hermann Reimarus, whose work was published posthumously in 1778 (just two years after the American Revolution). Reimarus' thesis was that John the Baptist and Jesus were political insurrectionists out to overthrow Rome; after the failure of their political ambitions their followers invented the story of the resurrection and the figure of Christ. Reimarus' book provoked an immediate outraged response, and it could be said that modern New Testament studies were to some extent born of the effort to refute Reimarus' allegation that Jesus was a political revolutionary.

This effort produced a whole series of "lives of Jesus". Two facts soon emerged:

(1) These biographies of Jesus tended to reflect the spirit of the age and the theological viewpoint and temperament of the particular writer; and
(2) the Gospels do not always agree in their accounts.

EXERCISE 15: **(a)** (i) When did Jesus begin his ministry:
— while John the Baptist was still preaching;
— after John the Baptist was arrested?
(Read: Mk 1: 14; Mt 4: 12–17; Jn 3: 22–27)
(ii) Did Jesus turn the sellers out of the Temple at the beginning or end of his ministry?
(Read: Mk 11: 15–17; Mt 21: 12–13; Lk 19: 45–47; Jn 2: 13–17)
(iii) How many times did Jesus go to Jerusalem:
— according to Mark or Luke or Matthew (look up one)?
— according to John?
(Read: Jn 2: 13, 23; 5: 1; 7: 1–14)
(iv) Words attributed to Jesus himself by the evangelists: Read the Lord's Prayer in Mt 6: 9–13 and Lk 11: 2–4. Comment on similarities, differences.
(v) Where was Jesus on Passover Preparation Day? Compare: Jn 19: 12–16; Mk 14: 12–17.
(b) In the light of your findings in (a), what conclusions do you draw?

Why, for example, does Matthew recount a saying of Jesus in circumstances different from those in which Luke records the same saying? Even attempts at harmonization of the Gospels did not satisfactorily resolve the question of discrepancies and inconsistencies. In fact, the attempt at connecting sections of the four Gospels into a "harmony" tended to raise more questions than it answered; for example, it revealed that the Gospel of John has a different chronological and geographical framework from the Gospels of Matthew, Mark and Luke. The latter three are called "Synoptics" (from the Greek *synoptikos*, "seeing the whole together") because they have many elements in common in their presentation of the story of Jesus. In John, Jesus sets out from Galilee to Jerusalem three times (2: 13, 5: 1, 7: 10), but in the Synoptics Jesus makes only one journey to Jerusalem. In John, Jesus' final stay in Jerusalem lasts about six months, from the Feast of Tabernacles to the Feast of Passover (￼ Chapter 1, p. 33, on festivals), but in the Synoptics he is there only about one week. John's Gospel implies that Jesus' ministry covered a period of nearly three years, but in the Synoptics his ministry lasted scarcely one year. Is it, then, simply a case of choosing between John or the Synoptics for an accurate biographical account? If so, then how does one explain the nature of the "inaccurate" account?

Attempts to reconstruct Jesus' life and teaching from the sources available, viz. the Gospels, and the difficulties to which this effort led, finally raised the question of the nature of these sources. That John's concern was primarily theological was recognized early. D. F. Strauss in his *Life of Jesus* (1835) underlined this point, and went on to point out that because this Gospel was written from a primarily theological perspective, it was not a suitable source for the historical understanding of Jesus. Attention then shifted to the Synoptics as possible sources for the reconstruction of the life of Jesus.

EXERCISE 16: Does the fact that the Gospels are different and even contradictory in some cases, change your thinking and feeling about the Gospels? Does it make any difference to your faith?

SOURCE CRITICISM

That there are literary relationships between the Synoptics had been recognized long before the nineteenth century. There is a great quantity of material common to all three Gospels (the triple tradition); some material common to Matthew and Luke that is not in Mark (double tradition), and yet other material that is peculiar to one Gospel and not found in the others (single tradition). This close relationship between the three Gospels and the questions it raised is called the Synoptic Problem.

EXERCISE 17:

(a) The first example of the interrelatedness of all three Gospels is the Baptism of Jesus (Mt 3: 13–17; Mk 1: 9–11; Lk 3: 21–22).

Draw up three columns, and write down the three versions of the story in parallel form. Then underline in red all the words common to the three versions.

Using a different color, underline any words which are common to two, but not the third account.

What do you find?

(b) In the same way, compare: Mt 8: 1–4; Mk 1: 40–45; Lk 5: 12–16 (Cleansing the Leper).

(c) Compare: Mt 12: 1–8; Mk 2: 23–28; Lk 6: 1–5 (Plucking Grain on the Sabbath).

Source critics make careful comparison of these sorts of parallels. Some of their findings on the areas common to all three Gospels are:

(1) Almost all of Mark's Gospel is reproduced in both Matthew and Luke, or in one of them.

(2) Not only do Matthew and Luke reproduce most of Mark's Gospel, but they do so largely in Mark's order. Furthermore, when either Matthew or Luke diverge from Mark, they later take up again at more or less the point in Mark where they left off.

(3) The triple tradition usually reproduces the same grouping of stories and events.

(4) There is often a remarkable similarity in language and in arrangement of words and phrases used in the narrative. This verbal correspondence is most evident in the record of Jesus' teachings.

Though there are marked similarities, there is also a certain freedom in the handling of common material—additions, omissions, adaptations. You would have noted in Exercise 17, for example, how Matthew diverges from the common account to emphasize to the pro-John group in the community that John was not superior to Jesus.

Over the last 150 years there has been considerable work done in attempting to explain similarities and differences in the Synoptics. Obviously there must have been a common outline and material to which all three evangelists had access. What was this common ground?

1) The Oral Theory or Tradition Theory (J. L. Gieseler, 1818) claimed that the Synoptics were the written products of an oral Gospel tradition given by the Apostles to the earliest Christians for teaching purposes. But this theory did not explain the divergencies in the single and the double traditions. Was there more than one oral tradition at work?

Moreover, the identity of phrases and expressions in two or three accounts suggests a written source of some kind.

2) Was there then, behind the Synoptics, a primitive Gospel written in either Hebrew or Aramaic which the three evangelists used independently? But this theory presupposes that in the rendering from Aramaic to Greek three independent writers arrived at exactly the same translation—an extremely unlikely happening.

3) The Priority of Mark: this theory was neglected for a long time because most scholars followed Augustine (fourth century) in his theory that Matthew is the earliest Gospel, Mark an abridged version of Matthew, and Luke and John are dependent on these two. The theory of the priority of Mark is, very briefly, based on the following observations:

(a) the consistent pattern in the verbal relationships among the three Gospels;

(b) the order of events and the fact that, as regards this order, Mark is the common denominator;

(c) the reproduction in Matthew and/or Luke of most of Mark's 661 verses. There is nothing of significance in Mark that is not found in Matthew and/or Luke. If Mark wrote later and added only approximately 50 verses of little consequence, why did he bother to write at all? It seems more logical to suggest that Mark wrote first, and that Matthew and Luke used his Gospel as one of the sources for their own writing.

EXERCISE 18:   Check out 3(a) above (the consistent pattern in verbal relationships) in the three parallel versions you wrote down in Exercise 17.

The theory of the priority of Mark and of the use of Mark by both Matthew and Luke accounts for the triple tradition, but does not explain the double tradition in which there are striking similarities between Matthew and Luke (completely lacking in Mark). These similarities between Matthew and Luke suggest that they are using a common written source not used by Mark, and probably not even known to him.

EXERCISE 19: (a) Read the Sermon on the Mount (Mt 5–7). It contains both the beatitudes and the Lord's Prayer. Neither of these appears in Mark. Now read Luke's Sermon on the Plain (Lk 6: 17–49). You will find some parallels to the Sermon on the Mount. In two columns record the parallels you find (similarities only).

(b) Note that Luke's version of the Our Father does not appear here, but further on in Chapter 11. Compare Luke's version with Matthew's. Can you suggest, from your reading of Lk 11: 1–13, why he might have held over the Our Father to this point?

Because of the different order and different use of the same material, scholars have concluded that Matthew and Luke did not copy from each other, but that they were using a common written source consisting of sayings of Jesus plus some narratives explaining the circumstances of the sayings. Scholars designate this collection Q (German *Quelle* meaning "source"). Q is a hypothetical source; we do not have copies from which to compare Matthew and Luke, as we do in the case of Mark.

The Four Document Hypothesis

In addition to the sources they have in common (the Gospel of Mark and Source Q), both Matthew and Luke present a good deal of special material of their own (as you will have already noted in your comparison of the Sermon on the Mount with the Sermon on the Plain). This suggests that

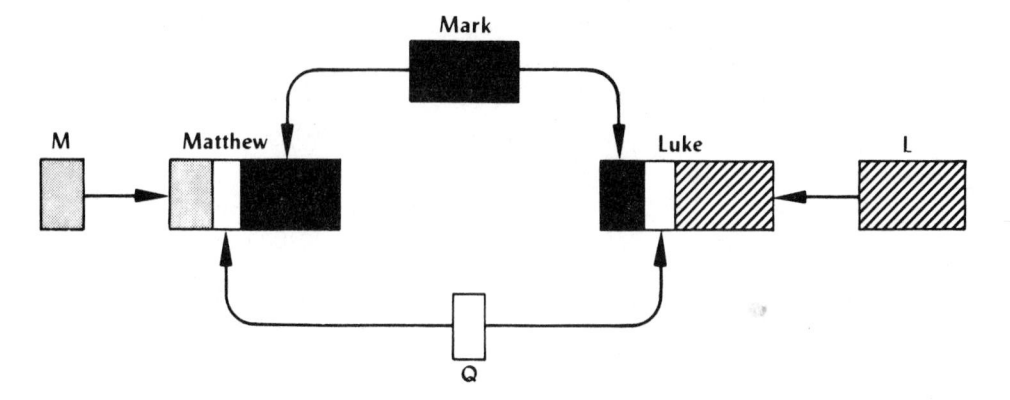

Source: Spivey (1982)

both Matthew and Luke had access to particular sources, either oral or written, of their own (Lukan source L, and Matthian source M).

Source criticism attempts to explain the interrelatedness of the Synoptic Gospels, which can be represented as follows:

(For examples of interrelatedness, see the tables of Parables and Miracles at the end of Chapter 4.)

The Formation of the Gospels

In their study of the sources, scholars had initially been urged on by the conviction that, once the earliest of the documents (i.e. those closest to Jesus' lifetime) had been isolated, it would be possible to write a biography of Jesus. But by the early 1900s a number of scholars (Wilhelm Wrede, Albert Schweitzer, Johannes Weiss and Julius Wellhausen) had begun to recognize that even Mark (on whom they had pinned their hopes) had written his Gospel, not with a view to presenting the life-story of Jesus, but from a theological perspective. Wrede, writing at the turn of the century, summed up the situation thus:

> Present-day study of the Gospels starts from the assumption that Mark had more or less clearly before his eyes, though not without gaps, the real circumstances of Jesus' life. It presupposes that Mark thinks in terms of the life of Jesus, bases the various features of his story on the real circumstances of this life, on Jesus' real thoughts and feelings and that he links the events which he describes in a historical and psychological sense. . . This view and method must be recognized to be false in principle. It must be plainly stated that Mark no longer has any real picture of the historical life of Jesus. (W. Wrede, cited by R. Pesch, 1975: 743)

It had also been recognized that the Gospels were all written several decades after Jesus' death, and that the Gospels as we know them were the end result of a long process of development. This development can be divided into three stages (cf., for example, Appendix C: "Instruction on the Historical Truth of the Gospels", Section 2):

I. The words and actions of Jesus during his lifetime.

II. The oral proclamation of the Apostles, disciples and early communities (preaching, teaching, liturgy). This stage was characterized by a sense of urgency and expectation of the imminent Second Coming of Jesus; in view of this there was neither time nor need to write down the good news.

III. The writings themselves (as can be seen from the diagram below, there was some overlap between stages II and III). Stage III was a time of reflecting in faith on the communities' experience of Christ Jesus and of recording this (in Epistles and Gospels) from and for the communities of faith.

Thus it can be seen that the written Gospels were the end product of a long process of development, and not biographies of Jesus written shortly after his death. In McBrien's words:

> *What we have (in the Gospels) are testimonies of faith, constituted from fragments of the oral and written traditions which developed after Jesus' death and resurrection. It was Jesus as he was remembered by the earliest Christians and as he was experienced in their communities of faith whom we meet in the Gospels. (McBrien, 1980: 403–4)*

(*We are inclined to agree with scholars who date the final version of Mark's Gospel during or after the fall of Jerusalem in 70 A.D. Note also

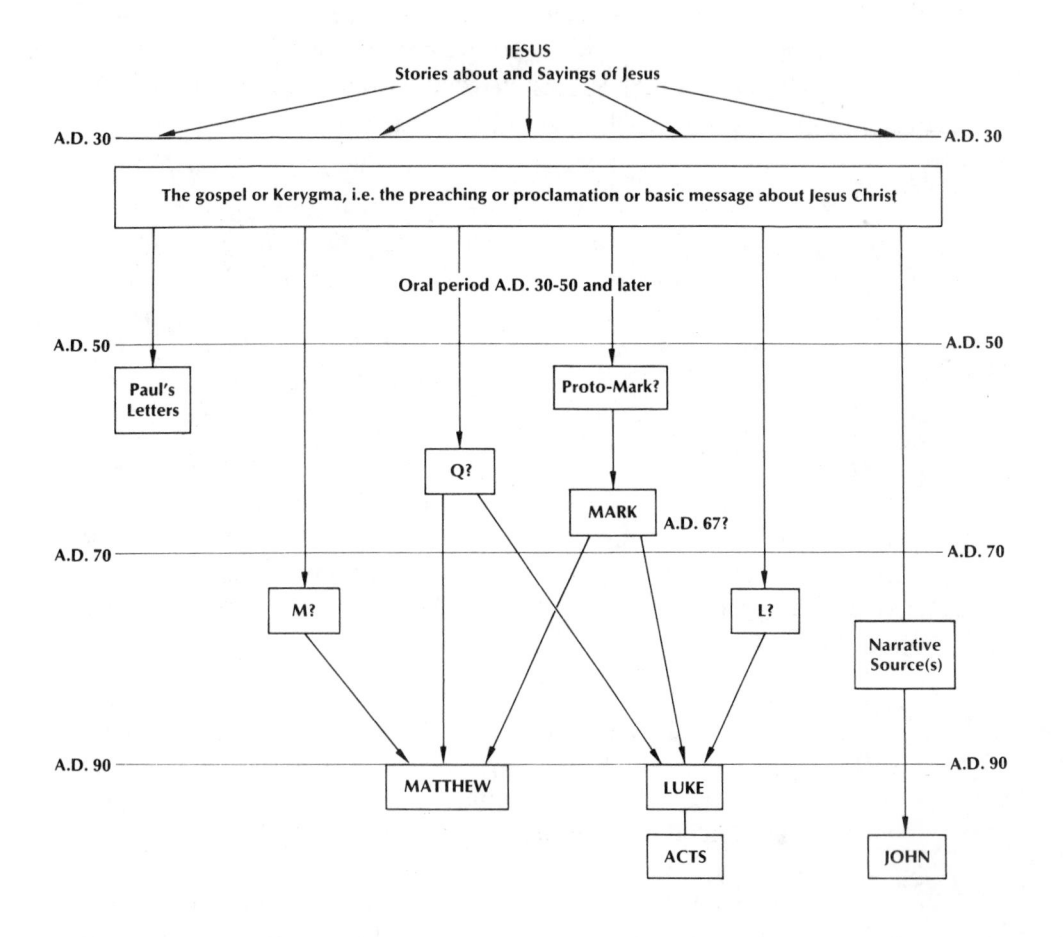

(Spivey, 1982: 66)

that many scholars today would date Matthew, Luke and John slightly earlier than Spivey—cf. Chapter 3.)

EXERCISE 20: What understanding of the Gospels did you have from primary and secondary schooling? How do you react to the idea that the Gospels are not biographies but faith documents?

FORM CRITICISM

After World War I an important new development in New Testament scholarship took place in Germany with the publication of Martin Dibelius' *From Tradition to Gospel* (1919), K. L. Schmidt's *The Framework of the Story of Jesus* (1919) and Rudolf Bultmann's *The History of the Synoptic Tradition* (1921). The method they employed came to be known as "form criticism". Form criticism classifies parts of the biblical text into literary forms or genres (in much the same way that we might classify parts of a newspaper according to their literary forms: editorial, reports, letters to the editor, advertisements etc.). It is a method which goes behind the written unit (a parable or a miracle, for example) to trace its history back to the period of oral tradition about Jesus.

Having examined and classified the form of the text, the form critic asks how this story or saying was passed on or modified in oral and written stages until it reached its final form. What was the function of the story in the Christian community? He/she is not trying to get to the earliest version but is looking at the *Sitz im Leben*—the setting in life—in which the story or saying was told, and which shaped the telling and the order of the story. For the form critic holds that the needs and interests, the circumstances and beliefs of the early Christian community had a direct bearing on the oral transmission and the eventual fashioning of the written material.

The written Gospels were the end product in a long process, more than a generation away from the actual events, written from the context of the community's lived faith and historical situation. Some obvious factors which shaped the process were:

a) the transference of the good news from a Palestinian to a Hellenistic situation;

b) the translation from Aramaic to Greek (much of this had been done before the tradition was written down);

c) changes of audience (e.g. from opponents to disciples);

d) a change in the eschatological emphasis;
e) the influence of the Church's situation, e.g., the delay of the *Parousia* (second coming), and the developing missionary situation;
f) the influence of the Old Testament, folk legends, allegorization;
g) theological concerns and liturgical influences (cf. Beare, 1968).

Form critics proceed from definite assumptions about the nature of the oral tradition. These may be summarized as follows:

1) Before the Gospels were written there was a period of oral tradition (Stage II on the diagram above).
2) As in any oral culture, the material being transmitted was cast into set language and patterns or forms in order to make it easier to recall accurately.
3) During this oral stage the narratives and sayings, with the exception of the Passion Narrative, circulated mainly as single, isolated units, each complete in itself. (These units are called pericopes.)
4) These single units can be classified according to their form.
5) The practical needs of each Christian community (devotional, apologetic, controversial) determined the selection and preservation of the forms found in the Gospel.
6) The material of the tradition has little value for the ordering of events, nor can its geographical locations be accepted as exact. We have the early Church's tradition about Jesus but little that is reliable in the historical account of Jesus himself.
7) A knowledge of the forms of the tradition, therefore, will help us to distinguish the history of the tradition itself from the history it claims to convey (cf. E. Redlich, 1939, and R. Busch, 1975).

Form criticism studies the patterns into which the biblical material has been set, and classifies the material according to its forms, endeavoring to see each unit or pericope in the *Sitz im Leben* which shaped it (the situation in life of the early Christian community, not of Jesus).

The main forms which have been identified and used by form critics in their study of the Gospels to date are as follows:

1) *Pronouncement stories* (sometimes called biographical apothegm): stories from the life of a wise person which culminate in a striking saying. The story framework is usually simple, brief and lacking in biographical detail. Such stories were very popular in ancient world cultures, including the world of the New Testament with its stories of Jesus.

EXERCISE 21: (a) Identify the "situation in life" or actual setting for the following literary genres: postcard, editorial, creed, weather chart, menu, encyclical, summons, government document, pastoral letter.

(b) Look up Lk 11: 27–28; Mk 2: 15–17; 3: 31–35; 12: 13–17, and identify the pronouncement or striking saying in each.

2) *Short sayings* without any story framework: some are in the form of a proverb (e.g. Mt 6: 24); others are judgment sayings, declaring what will happen if a person does not follow Jesus' teaching (e.g. Mk 8: 38; Mt 7: 1–2; Mt 6: 14–15).

EXERCISE 22: (a) Look up the sayings listed above. Note the lack of story framework for the sayings. Can you identify a basic pattern in the judgment sayings?

(b) Look again at the Sermon on the Mount and that on the Plain—at the beatitudes, for example. What is the pattern in these sayings?

(c) Look up Mt 7: 1–14, which is a collection of short sayings. Name the two kinds of short sayings in this passage, and locate examples of each.

3) *Parables:* The most characteristic form of the teaching of Jesus. A parable is a similitude, comparison or short story drawn by Jesus from daily life to make his message plain and vivid. We will return to the topic of parables in much greater detail in Chapter 4.

4) *Miracle stories:* This story form was popular in many cultures of the New Testament world, and was structured according to a specific pattern. We will examine miracle stories in the Gospels in detail in Chapter 4.

5) *The Passion Narrative:* most form critics agree that the story of the Passion was a connected narrative from the beginning of the tradition (rather than a series of pericopes later strung together to form a whole).

(For a list of literary forms identified in the Gospels, see Appendix B.)

Form criticism stresses not only the form of the traditional material, but also the *Sitz im Leben* in which these units of tradition originally functioned—the community life of the Church in a particular time and place and culture. The history of the transmission of the tradition is also studied (for example, J. Jeremias in his *Parables of Jesus* traces the complex process by which the parables reached the form that they did by the time they were written down).

Form critical research has underlined the complexity of the Gospels in

their "intrinsic interweaving of report and confession of faith", an interweaving which "prevents direct access from the individual pericope to the
historical, earthly Jesus" (Maisch and Vogtle, 1975: 731). What the Gospels
present is both Jesus of Nazareth and the Christ of faith. The two are
intrinsically interwoven, for the early Church completely identified the
risen Lord of her experience with the historical Jesus of Nazareth.

So what looks like an account of Jesus instructing his Galilean disciples
may well be the voice of the risen Christ instructing the early Christians
in a Hellenistic world. When we hear Jesus claiming to be the Messiah, it
may well be the faith and understanding of the early Church that we are
hearing, rather than a specific claim by the historical Jesus.

> The faith in God's action in Jesus evoked by the appearances of the
> risen Lord led, in a long process of reflection, inspired to some extent
> by passages from the Old Testament, to the interpretation of the death
> of Jesus as redemptive. As this understanding gradually became more
> explicit. . . the whole of Jesus' earthly life was drawn into the
> post-paschal proclamation of Christ (Maisch and Vogtle, 1975: 734).

Some form critics arrived at a different conclusion, seeing not an
interweaving of report and proclamation but complete discontinuity
between the "earthly Jesus" and "the Christ of faith". Bultmann, for
example, claimed that the proclaimed Christ of the *kerygma* had no
particular link with the Jesus of history beyond the fact that Jesus did exist.
There has been strong reaction to Bultmann's view: Jeremias and
Bornkamm, for example, have recognized that if the continuity between
the Jesus who preached and the Jesus who was preached is not maintained,
then we may end up with a docetic Christ who is little more than an idea.
(The Church rejected this view of Christ in the early stages of its history.)
Bornkamm (1960: 24) writes that "though detailed description of the course
of his (Jesus") life biographically and psychologically is not possible, none
the less the Gospels do bring before our eyes. . . the historical person of
Jesus with the utmost vividness".

REDACTION CRITICISM

The earliest form critics regarded the Synoptic writers as editors (redactors)
rather than authors—editors who systematically strung together or arranged
the pericopes with which they were familiar. But after World War II
another method of enquiry developed—the analysis of the editorial work
of the writers in relation to their sources, or redaction criticism. Attention
was focused on the way that the writers handled the material; they were
not simply stringing the pericopes together, but were arranging their
material in creative ways. In the selection and omission of material, in the

arrangement and editing, in the alteration of the pericopes, in the connecting links constructed between pericopes, they revealed their particular theological perspective.

Redaction criticism assumes that the work of form criticism on the material and its history has already been done, and goes on to enquire into the use of the material by the final author of the text and what it reveals about the author's particular theological stance. The final writer was in fact an author, engaged in a much more creative task than merely stringing together bits of material.

Redaction critics use two types of analysis in order to discover the unique perspective and theological insights of a particular evangelist:

(a) comparison of an evangelist with his sources to identify a consistent pattern of changes to the material;
(b) analysis of the evangelist's arrangement of his material, which reveals his perspective and insights (cf. Perkins, 1978: 77–78).

In Chapter 3 we will discuss the particular theological perspective and concerns of each evangelist. In Exercises 40 and 41, we will compare the Synoptics' redaction of particular pericopes.

SOCIOLOGICAL CRITICISM

There are two main meanings for this term, sociological criticism. The first refers to the readers of the text and enquires about their sociological status, with their particular socio-historical characteristics, and how these have possibly influenced their interpretation of the text.

The second and more commonly used meaning refers to the analysis of the social world of New Testament times. This criticism, which has become very popular in the last couple of decades, uses knowledge about international politics of the times, wars, the structures of society, forms of government, economic factors and lifestyles to gain greater insight into the social world of the New Testament. It sees religion as a social entity. It assumes there is reciprocal interaction between economic, ecological, political, cultural and religious factors in society. It also tries to use and develop social theories to interpret these interactions, often drawing on the work of the famous sociologist, Max Weber. Scholars who have contributed much to this study include G. Theissen, A. Malherbe, W. Meeks, J. Stambaugh, D. Balch, B. Holmberg, E. A. Judge and J. Gager.

To cite one instance of this kind of sociological criticism, Gerd Theissen examines the social groups within Palestine at the time of Jesus—such as the John the Baptist group, the Essenes, the Resistance fighters (Zealots and Sicarii)—and how they interacted. As regards the followers of Jesus, he finds that the synoptic tradition is concerned with a band of wandering charismatics who have been freed from their everyday jobs and constitute a movement of outsiders with a strong expectation of an imminent end to the world. The local communities which supported this movement helped these wandering charismatics with material things. For both groups (the wandering charismatics and the settled local communities), the figure of the Son of Man is central.

In trying to understand society, Theissen makes use of a theory called functionalism which sees society as always striving for equilibrium and harmony.

Other authors examine the phenomena of house churches, the roles of women in early Christianity, the social class of early Christians, institutionalization in the early Church or the ways in which political events of the times may be reflected in the Gospels (e.g. the interpretation of Mk 13: 7–8, 14–16 in the light of the Caligula Crisis of 35–42 A.D.).

One of the weaknesses of sociological criticism is that the data one has to work with is very limited. Often there are not sufficient cases to be able to draw firm conclusions. Another problem is the danger that the sociological interpretation may become the dominant model for the interpretation of a text. Sociological criticism is best used together with other criticisms to shed light on a given text.

EXERCISE 23: Look up the following references and note the work and status in society/stratum of society, of those involved:

Mt 4: 18–22	Lk 5: 27–28
Mt 27: 57–61	Lk 7: 36–50
Mk 2: 15–17	Lk 8: 1–3
Lk 19: 1–10	

In the light of these references, what suggestions could you make as to the possible sociological background of Jesus and his followers?

You might find the following information useful as a guide. It is anachronistic to speak of "classes", but society at the time of Jesus could be divided into three strata as follows:

High stratum: civil and religious leaders; those with education and power; people of noble birth; those who could travel and owned a large house.

Middle stratum: artisans; fishermen; tax collectors; landowning peasants with small holdings.

Low stratum: tenant farmers; day laborers; servants; slaves.

EXERCISE 24: In the following references, what clues are there about the lifestyles of the disciples from a sociological point of view?

(i)   Mk 6: 4
(ii) Mk 6: 7–13
(iii) Lk 14: 26

(iv) Mt 10: 7–10
(v) Mt 6: 6

CANONICAL CRITICISM

This is a criticism which is not of any great consequence today but is worth mentioning by way of information. It is a methodology based on Brevard Childs', book, *Introduction to the Old Testament as Scripture* (1979), which takes the text as a completed entity and is not concerned with how the text arrived at its present form. It looks beyond the final redaction to a point when the faith community accepted the text as canonical. It is concerned with the accepted text, not the historical evolution of the text.

Canonical criticism focuses on the final form of the text because it sees it as alone bearing witness to the full history of revelation. The final form is the only valid basis for a biblical theology. In this sense it is rather rigid and restrictive as it does not allow for the insights gained from the historical-critical methods.

LITERARY CRITICISM

Before talking about literary criticism as such, some introduction to contemporary criticisms is necessary because they are quite different from the historical-critical methods (source, form, redaction, sociological) in their approach to the text.

The kinds of criticisms that we have been considering up to now are often referred to as those concerned with the text-world "behind the text" examining the way the text was compiled, or how it was shaped by redactors, or how other sociological factors influenced its expression—that is, historical-critical methods. These methods originated, as we saw, in the nineteenth century and eventually dominated biblical interpretation in the first half of this century.

Now we want to outline contemporary criticisms that have arisen in the latter half of this century, and that are concerned with the text-world "in front of the text", so to speak. In other words, they are concerned with readers and how they respond to the text. These contemporary criticisms have arisen, as Thiselton indicates (1992: 57), out of influences on hermeneutics such as the development of literary theory, especially reader-response theories, the areas of semiotics (the study of the system of signs) and deconstructionism, as well as new ways of understanding how knowledge is acquired (the sociology of knowledge).

Having briefly introduced contemporary criticisms, we are now in a position to examine the term "literary criticism" and other criticisms associated with it (narrative, structuralist, rhetorical). By literary criticism is meant the method of viewing the text as a literary creation. The text is explored as literature to discover its vitality. As an artistic pursuit, literary criticism is neither opposed to, nor isolated from the religious interest of the text.

The last ten to fifteen years has seen a growing emphasis on the study of the Gospel texts as story, as unified texts, complete in themselves. Contemporary study often focuses on the Gospels as *narratives*, a type of literary criticism known as "narrative criticism". It involves "a study of the content of these [Gospel] narratives and of the rhetorical techniques by means of which they are told" (Kingsbury, 1986: 1).

Narrative criticism is not primarily trying to gain insight into the historical or theological realities that lie behind or beyond the text (as in source, form and redaction criticism); it assumes that that work has already been done. The narrative critic focuses on the unified narrative, the story a particular Gospel tells and the means by which it is told. He/she draws on the methodology of the literary critic (for example, of the English Literature critic). It is interesting to note that Rhoads and Michie's *Mark as Story: An Introduction to the Narrative of a Gospel* (1982) is the result of the combined effort of a biblical scholar and an English scholar.

In looking at the content of the story, the narrative critic (as also the critic of any literature) studies plot, events, characters, settings. In looking at how the story is told (variously called "the rhetoric", "rhetorical technique", or "discourse"), he/she examines such things as implied/real author, point of view, style, implied /real reader and the narrator. Throughout, emphasis is placed on the unity of the text as a whole.

Sometimes the expression "rhetorical criticism" is used in the context of literary criticism. This is simply a form of literary criticism in which the text is criticized using clues given in the text itself. The major clue to interpretation is the text seen as an organic unity of interlocking words and motifs. This method is not only cognitive and rational but meant to be emotive and imaginative as well. Whereas formerly readers were seen as passive, this form sees them as active, creative and productive of meaning. From being judges of texts they are now validators. Phyllis Trible uses this method in her book, *Texts of Terror* (1984).

"Structuralism" is the name given to a kind of literary criticism which studies the biblical text in terms of recognizable patterns of thought and experience. It owes its inspiration to F. de Saussure's book *Course in General Linguistics* (1978). Structuralists assert that language does not refer to the world in any understandable way at all; language is autonomous and meaning is conveyed through a system of relations and oppositions internal to the language itself. The meaning therefore of language is relational rather than essential. De Saussure made a distinction between the underlying structure of the language (in French, *langue*), and instances of its use (*parole*). In short, structuralism seeks the underlying structure of the text in terms of binary oppositions such as inversion which have nothing to do with the content of the text.

The viewpoint that texts have only a relational, not an essential meaning was developed further by a form of literary criticism known as "Deconstructionism". J. Derrida and R. Barthes are the scholars associated with this form of textual criticism, an involved form which sees texts as a collection of metaphors and meanings systems. When in the process of being actively read, this collection becomes a living text of intertextual meanings which go on forever in their cross-referencing. The point is that no final meaning is ever reached.

In deconstructionism, the reader needs to be alert to what is *not* expressed in the text and what the shape of the text excludes from discussion. For example, the Gospels give a theological view of the world and largely exclude any psychological insight. Thus a partial view prevails. Deconstructionists would say that this process of discovering partial views signifies the collapse of the structure of the text.

In deconstructionism, therefore, all meaning is open ended and deferred. There is a never-ending network of intertextuality which denies any embedded meaning in the text as such.

LIBERATIONIST CRITICISM

This criticism springs from the Latin American experience of life as a struggle against oppression and for freedom and is typified by G. Gutiérrez's book, *The Theology of Liberation* (1975). Other theologians who have written on liberation theology include J. Comblin, J. Miguez-Bonino, J. Segundo, L. Boff, H. Assmann and R. Alves. Liberation criticism basically attempts to read the Gospels from the point of view of the poor. The Gospel is put in the hands of the ordinary powerless person who reads it and relates it to everyday life and especially to the power structures in and out of the Church. Liberation criticism applies the "hermeneutic of suspicion" insofar as it questions previous explanations of the Gospels as perhaps trying to protect vested interests of groups in positions of power and influence. It operates in small groups called basic communities, who meet, read the Gospel and relate it to their lives.

EXERCISE 25:  What was Jesus' attitude to individuals or groups of people in positions of power in society, such as the Roman rulers, Herod, publicans, Sadducees, Scribes and Pharisees, the Sanhedrin, the rich and powerful?

Give examples from the Gospels. Use these references as starters: Lk 13: 32; 16: 14–15; 18: 9–14, 18–27; Mk 12: 18–27; Mt 5: 23–24; 23; 25: 31–45; 27: 57–60.

Without being fundamentalist in your use of the Gospel texts, what conclusions can you draw?

EXERCISE 26: Read the song of Mary called the *Magnificat* in Lk 1: 46–55, which has become the song of the people gathered in Christian basic communities in Latin America. From a *political* viewpoint, what could the meaning be of phrases like "he has looked on his lowly handmaid", "he has shown the power of his arm", "he has pulled down the princes from their thrones and exalted the lowly", "The hungry he has filled with good things, the rich sent away empty"?

How does this meaning fit into the meaning of the Gospel as a whole?

Now look up 1 S 2: 1–10. What do you notice?

FEMINIST CRITICISM

Over the centuries, women writers have raised questions about the Bible, recognizing that it is a "male-centered account of male experience for male purposes with women relegated to the margins of salvation history. . . patriarchal in its assumptions and often in its explicit teaching, and at times deeply sexist, i.e., anti-woman. Its God-language and imagery are overwhelmingly male" (Schneiders, 1991A: 38).

Women have also raised questions about the way in which the Bible has been interpreted/used by patriarchal authorities to define women as inferior and to reinforce their secondary role in society. Most notable of the early women critics were Hildegard of Bingen (1098–1179) and Christine of Pizan (1365–c. 1430). But their work was until recently ignored or forgotten and there was no continuity in women's biblical writing, so that individual writers, unaware of earlier women biblical critics, frequently covered the same ground.

All that was changed with the work of Elizabeth Cady Stanton who, in the U.S.A. in the 1880s, established her own group of scholars to critique sections of the Bible that deal with women or in which women are conspicuously absent. Their aim was to refute the use of the Bible to enforce the subordinate role of women. *The Woman's Bible* Vol. I was published in 1895 (Vol. II in 1898) and was an immediate best-seller, but then was lost until its rediscovery by contemporary feminists.

Feminism in Schneiders' definition is "a comprehensive ideology which is rooted in women's experience of sexual oppression, engages in a critique of patriarchy as an essentially dysfunctional system, embraces an alternative vision for humanity and the earth, and actively seeks to bring this vision to realization" (1991A: 15).

Feminist scholarship has, over the last twenty years, developed principles for what Fiorenza calls a "critical rereading of the Bible in a feminist key" (1984: 1). The main scholars of feminist criticism are: E. Schüssler Fiorenza, S. Schneiders, C. Newsom, S. Ringe, C. Osiek, L. Russell, M. Tolbert, P. Trible, D. Hampson, E. Johnson, and E. Wainwright.

Feminist biblical hermeneutics explores the Bible as the product of patriarchal culture and in the process arrives at interpretations alternative to those that, for over two thousand years, have legitimated the secondary role of women. Not surprisingly, feminist hermeneutics embodies the main features of liberation theology (cf. Thiselton, 1992: 438–439):

(1) it begins with women's experience—not only the experience of oppression but also of claiming self-definition and autonomy;
(2) this consciousness-raising is itself part of the process of developing new tools to critique the socio-political context;
(3) the texts are themselves freed in the process so that they may become tools of liberation;
(4) feminist hermeneutics is not, as Russell points out, simply about particular stories of women or particular female images of God, but is part of a larger process and vision of a New Creation (1985: 138).

There is, however, a significant difference between feminist hermeneutics and liberation theology: while the Bible does provide sources of hope for the poor and the stranger, that same text not only does not generally recognize the oppression of women but it is itself "a major source and legitimator of women's oppression in family, society, and Church" (Schneiders, 1991B: 181).

Those engaged in feminist biblical hermeneutics do so in a variety of ways. Some feminist scholars explore neglected texts and reinterpret familiar ones in order to "discover and recover traditions that challenge the culture" (Trible, 1990: 25). In *Texts of Terror*, through a careful exploration of Old Testament texts from the woman's perspective, Trible retells the stories of abused women "in memoriam". She is engaged in the "depatriarchalizing" process of revealing "counter-voices within a patriarchal document" (1978: 203).

Fiorenza takes a different approach in *In Memory of Her: a Feminist Theological Reconstruction of Christian Origins*. Her goal is to reconstruct early

Christian history "in order not only to restore women's stories to early Christian history but also to reclaim this history as the history of women and men" (1983: xiv). She examines the text to find what is behind it. In order to do this, she must apply a *hermeneutic of suspicion* to the text and its interpretation. The text is not neutral; the picture of women that it gives is that created by men; the reader must presume that it is a distorted record; interpretation of the text, up until the last twenty years, has been by men.

Starting from a presumption of bias in the text and its interpretation, the feminist scholar's task is then one of *retrieval*. Schneiders (1991B: 184–186) lists some of the strategies commonly used by feminist scholars in this process:

(1) challenging translations that render women "textually invisible";
(2) focusing on texts with liberating potential;
(3) raising women to visibility;
(4) revealing the text's "secrets";
(5) rescuing the text from misinterpretation.

EXERCISE 27:   If you have access to S. Schneiders' *The Revelatory Text,* work your way through her exploration of Jn 4: 1–42 in Chapter 7, "A Case Study: a Feminist Interpretation of John 4: 1–42". It is a very good illustration of a feminist critical hermeneutical approach.

Jesus healing the woman with a hemorrhage. Third century lunette.

EXERCISE 28: Read the stories of Mt 9: 18–26. For the purpose of this exercise, we will focus particularly on the woman with a hemorrhage; a closer look at her story may reveal details we had not seen before.

Notice that this story is framed by the story of the curing of a synagogue official's daughter. They must be looked at together.

(a) Compare the two people who approach Jesus: how are they identified/named? how does each approach Jesus? who has a (public) voice?

(b) What taboos are broken by (i) Jesus? and (ii) the woman?

In the parallel stories in Mk 5: 21–43 and Lk 8: 40–56, there is detail about the girl which Matthew omits. Can you identify the detail? Why do you think this detail was included by Mark and Luke?

(c) Compare the endings of the stories.

(d) What might have been the significance of the story of the woman with a hemorrhage in the early communities?

(Based on E. Wainwright, 1992: 13–20)

THE EMERGENCE OF CATHOLIC CRITICAL SCHOLARSHIP

A glance through the names of the best New Testament scholars in the first half of this century reveals that Catholic scholarship was conspicuously absent. This was the result of an historical circumstance which virtually paralyzed scriptural investigation for forty years.

In his encyclical *Providentissimus Deus* in 1893, Leo XIII encouraged scientific research into Scripture, and in 1901 a Commission and Biblical Institute were set up in Rome. This Institute was the only Catholic faculty which could grant degrees in exegesis. But during the next few years the so-called Modernist crisis caused Church leaders to react against the progressive work going on at the Institute, because they thought that some scholars were destroying the idea of inspiration in the Scriptures. The Commission and the Institute were both used to restrain, in a quite drastic way, biblical scholarship, which receded into the background until Pius XII's *Divino Afflante Spiritu* in 1943. This encyclical encouraged biblical scholarship and the use of scientific methods in studying the Scriptures:

> Let the interpreter therefore use every care, and take advantage of every indication provided by the most recent research, in an endeavor to discern

the distinctive genius of the sacred writer, his condition in life, the age in which he lived, the written or oral sources he may have used, and the literary forms he employed. He will thus be able better to discover who the sacred writer was and what he meant by what he wrote. For it is evident that the chief law of interpretation is that which enables us to discover and determine what the writer meant to say. . .

But frequently the literal sense is not so obvious in the words and writings of ancient oriental authors as it is with the writers of today. For what they intended to signify by their words is not determined only by the laws of grammar or philology, nor merely by the context; it is absolutely necessary for the interpreter to go back in spirit to those remote centuries of the East, and make proper use of the aids afforded by history, archeology, ethnology, and other sciences, in order to discover what literary forms the writers of that early age intended to use, and did in fact employ. For to express what they had in mind the ancients of the East did not always use the same forms and expressions as we use today; they used those which were current among the people of their own time and place; and what these were the exegete cannot determine a priori, *but only from a careful study of ancient oriental literature. . .*

At the same time, no one who has a just conception of biblical inspiration will be surprised to find that the sacred writers, like the other ancients, employ certain arts of exposition and narrative, certain idioms especially characteristic of the Semitic languages, and certain hyperbolical and even paradoxical expressions designed for the sake of emphasis. "In the divine Scripture," observes St. Thomas, with characteristic shrewdness, "divine things are conveyed to us in the manner to which men are accustomed." (Pius XII, 1943: No. 38, 39)

This encyclical provided the impetus for renewed and outstanding efforts among Catholic biblical scholars, such as Alexander Jones, Raymond Brown and Joseph Fitzmyer. Of particular note is the ecumenical nature of much of biblical scholarship today.

Vatican II gave further encouragement to responsible biblical scholarship in its *Dogmatic Constitution on Divine Revelation (Dei Verbum)*. The task of the biblical scholar is seen as one of "working toward a better understanding and explanation of the meaning of Sacred Scripture, so that through preparatory study the judgment of the Church may mature."

EXERCISE 29:   Read the Vatican II statement on revelation, *Dei Verbum*, in particular Nos 12, 13, 17–20. List the main points.

CHAPTER 3

THE GOSPEL STORIES

INTRODUCTION

At a meeting of local parishioners the topic of youth ministry came up for discussion. It was agreed that the young people were vital to the future of the Church and that nothing was being done for them. All agreed that a youth minister should be engaged. However then the differences in the way people saw the problem emerged. Naomi, who was concerned with establishing a variety of ministries to meet various needs in the parish, spoke strongly from the viewpoint of meeting a well-identified and urgent parish need. Jack, whose teenage son and daughter find church services boring, saw the proposal as helping the growing disaffection of his teenagers with the institutional Church. Jane, the representative of the junior school parents, said the proposal was going to benefit a large number of young children as they grew up in the parish. The Pastor also had his view. He wanted to know how the proposal was going to be financed. He was disenchanted with some parishioners who often received but seldom gave. He wanted the parents of the young people to assume some financial responsibility for the proposal.

If Naomi, Jack, Jane and the Pastor all had to report to people outside the group what happened at the meeting, you can imagine what points they would understandably emphasize.

It is to some extent the same with the Gospel stories. We have four accounts and each one brings a richness and diversity of concerns while telling essentially the same story of the life, ministry and death of Jesus. There is only one Gospel of salvation, but it is told in four different ways by Matthew, Mark, Luke and John. Hence we say, "the Gospel *according to* . . ."

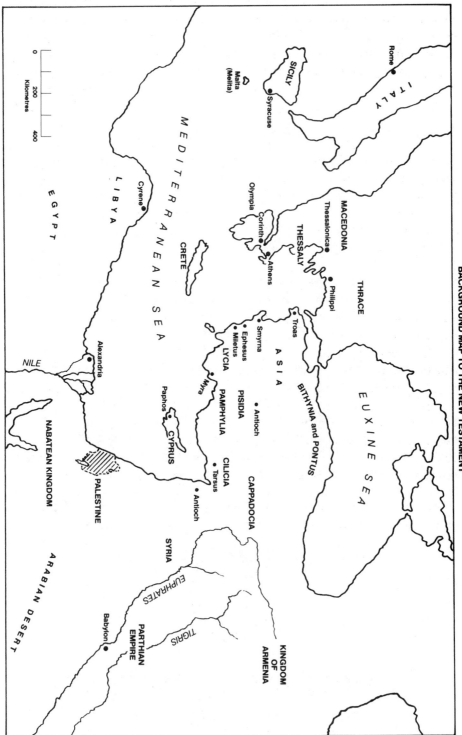

BACKGROUND MAP TO THE NEW TESTAMENT

MARK
A Gospel in a Hurry

Author:

We do not know who wrote the Gospel which bears the name of Mark. Early Church tradition, based on the somewhat unreliable historian Papias, thought it was the John Mark of Acts, the disciple of Peter (1 P 5: 13), but internal evidence does not support this view. In fact, the differences in the background and situation of John Mark, when compared with the impressions the Gospel gives us of its author, are too marked for an identification of Mark the evangelist with John Mark of Acts (cf. Brown & Meier, 1982: 191–197, and Doohan, 1986: 10–11). The most we can say is that Mark was writing for a community that may have known the influence of Peter until his martyrdom sometime between 64 and 67 A.D.

Date:

Internal evidence suggests that the Gospel was probably written between 65–70, after the death of Peter and towards or at the end of the four-year war between Israel and Rome which resulted in the destruction of Jerusalem in 70. Mark 13 has echoes of this struggle and of the destruction of Jerusalem, as well as mentioning earthquakes (there were three in Nero's reign, which came to an end in 68) and famine (the collapse of Jerusalem was accompanied by famine).

Place:

According to tradition, the Gospel was written in Rome. Some scholars have been puzzled by the lack of urban imagery in the Gospel (compared with the Gospel of Matthew, for example) and have suggested a more rural location to the north of Palestine. However, given the internal evidence of the Gospel, Rome is still the most favored location.

Intended Community:

On internal evidence, it is clear that Mark was writing for a predominantly Gentile community (i.e. Christians of non-Jewish origins). There is little concern to show connections with the Old Testament. Mark explains Jewish customs (cf. 7: 3–4; 14: 12; 15: 42), and translates Aramaic words (cf. 3: 17; 5: 41; 7: 11; 10: 46). There are more Latinisms in Mark's Gospel than in any other, and it would seem that he is writing for people who knew and used Latin.

Background of the Community:

The atmosphere was one of conflict for a community constantly under threat of persecution by the erratic Roman emperors, especially Nero, who had already killed two of their leaders in Rome by 67. The community would have been distressed by the news of the impending destruction, or final destruction in 70, of Jerusalem and its Temple—the place where Christianity had its roots. No doubt some people were asking: is this the end of time? the final event leading to the Parousia? (In Mk 13: 5–6 and 21–22, there are indications that Mark was reacting against "parousia pretenders"—men actually claiming to be the risen Christ returning at the end of time.)

Sources:

Before Mark wrote his Gospel, the words and actions of Jesus had been reflected on, in some instances grouped together, and used as the basis of preaching or teaching for over thirty years. Mark seems to have chosen from among the traditions circulating in his community:

1. Probably an early *passion narrative* (arrest, trial, death of Jesus). This narrative was filled with Old Testament references (as is Mk 15) to help believers understand that Jesus went to his cross "in accordance with the Scripture", and to help Jewish converts (grounded in the Jewish Scriptures) to believe in a crucified Messiah.
2. An *account of the Lord's Supper* (Paul also used a similar account when writing earlier to the Corinthians: 1 Co 11: 23–26).
3. A cycle of *miracle stories* (Chapters 5 and 7).
4. *Controversy stories*. Mark carefully frames these between miracle stories of cures of paralysis.
5. A collection of *parables* (Mk 4).

Papyrus fragment of earliest extant manuscript of Mark's Gospel. Third century. Chester Beatty Library, Dublin.

6. *Apocalyptic writing* (Mk 13)—a style of writing that belonged to the late Old Testament period (e.g. Daniel) and to earliest Christianity.

The author of the Gospel of Mark brought these materials together, imposing a geographical and chronological framework on the "Good News about Jesus Christ"—a framework followed by both Matthew and Luke (but not by John). This framework is more theological than historical, presenting a view of the ministry of Jesus from a particular post-resurrection perspective influenced by his (Mark's) own and his community's faith experience.

Structure:
Preparation for Public Ministry 1: 1–13
The Galilean Ministry 1: 14–7: 23
Journeys outside Galilee 7: 24–10: 52
The Jerusalem Ministry 11: 1–13: 37
The Passion Narrative 14: 1–15: 47
The Resurrection Narrative 16: 1–8; (16: 9–20 later addition)

The structure of the Gospel is inverted parallelism or chiasm in which the first section of the Gospel parallels with the last, and the second with the fourth, with the journey to Jerusalem as the center or hinge of the chiasm:

a. Preparatory events
b. Ministry: Galilee

c. Journey to Jerusalem
b. Ministry: Jerusalem
a. Concluding events: burial

Style:

Mark's Gospel has been called "a Gospel in a hurry". It is sprinkled with expressions such as "straightaway" Jesus did this and "at once" he did that (there are forty such expressions). Mark is an accomplished storyteller, with an eye to detail and a directness which has emotional impact and draws the reader into the experience. Mark's Jesus is a vivid, human Jesus.

Mark does not use the polished Greek of Luke, but rather everyday, colloquial Greek. As has been said, he translates Aramaic words and uses more Latinisms than any other Gospel. His Gospel has only two speeches or discourses (4: 2–34; 13: 5–36). He repeats particular words or phrases within an episode to emphasize the point (e.g. forgiveness of sin 2: 5, 7, 9, 10).

Mark also uses a repetition pattern of three: three commissioning stories (1: 16–20; 3: 13–19; 6: 7–13), three passion-resurrection predictions (8: 31; 9: 31; 10: 33–34), three episodes of Jesus at prayer (1: 35; 6: 46; 14: 32–42), three episodes on the mountain (3: 13; 6: 46; 9: 2). He uses parallelism, too, including inverted parallelism or chiasm (e.g. the arrangement of the five controversy stories 2: 1 to 3: 6).

Theological Slant and Concerns:

Past, present and future all flow together in the Gospel of Mark: the past of the ministry of Jesus in Galilee, outside Galilee, and going to Jerusalem; the present of the ministry of Jesus in and through his Church; the future of the ministry Jesus will exercise when he comes soon as Son of Man. The writer thinks in terms of a drama that began in the past, continues in the present which the community is experiencing, and will reach a climax in the near future with the imminent coming of the end. Thus past, present and future tend to merge in his story.

Mark is concerned for *Gentiles*, e.g. 13: 10; 13: 27; 14: 9. There are references to Gentiles in the miracle stories in Mk 5 and 7 (the Gerasenes are Gentiles). The centurion in 15: 39 is a Gentile; he confesses Jesus as Son of God.

Mark uses *geography* for theological purposes. Galilee is a key place for Jesus' preaching and becomes the point of departure for going to Tyre and Sidon to meet the Gentiles. Ultimately, after the Resurrection (16: 7),

Galilee becomes the gateway for spreading the good news. Conversely, Jerusalem is a city shut in on itself that rejects Jesus and puts him to death. In Mark's story, the lake, mountains and wilderness take on rich theological symbolism that goes beyond traditional Jewish understandings of the significance of these places.

The overall image of Jesus is that of the Anointed One, the *Messiah*—a suffering Messiah. The Gospel is of sufficiently early date to reflect the difficulty the Church encountered in its preaching of a suffering rather than a triumphant Messiah. Mark is reminding his readers, constantly faced with the possibility of persecution, that to be a disciple of Jesus means sharing in suffering and rejection before sharing in glory. It is only after the Resurrection that the disciples know who Jesus really is and what discipleship means.

From its very beginning the Gospel moves toward the culminating point of the *Passion*. Mark immediately introduces John the Baptist (1: 4), then records his arrest (1: 14) and later links Jesus with John the Baptist (6: 14ff.), subtly indicating that what happened to John will happen to Jesus. Mark includes a number of controversy stories of conflicts that center around Jewish structures and practices: the Sabbath, cleaning, fasting, almsgiving—the boundaries by which the Jews identified themselves. From Mk 8 onwards, there are indications that Jesus was convinced that his ministry would end in death (8: 32–33; 9: 30–32; 10: 35–45; 14: 34).

Mark presents the Passion as the culminating point in Jesus' experience of rejection and abandonment. It is also the point where, in response to the High Priest's question, "Are you the Christ, the Son of the Blessed One?", Jesus answers "I am" (14: 61–62)—thus turning the trial, says Doohan (1986: 87) into "an epiphany of the Lord to the worshipping community".

At the beginning of the Gospel, Mark introduces Jesus as the *man from Nazareth* (1: 9). Jesus of Nazareth is the man who goes to the cross. From beginning to end, Mark's story is of a very human Jesus with strong emotions.

Mark is quite explicit about the meaning of *discipleship* (8: 34–35). Some have suggested that one of the primary purposes behind the writing of this Gospel was a clarification of discipleship (cf. Doohan, 1986: 93), no doubt prompted by the situation of the Christians in Rome, whose world was collapsing around them. Mark often focuses on the uncertainty and fear that Jesus' disciples experienced, at the same time addressing the need of his community to understand the nature and the challenge of discipleship. It is significant that Mark has Jesus present his main teaching on discipleship on the way to Jerusalem (to his death) and that this teaching is framed between two stories of Jesus curing the blind (8: 22–26; 10: 46–52). He is gradually opening their eyes to see who he is and to understand the true nature of his Messiahship.

The *community of disciples* gathered around Jesus constitutes the Church for Mark. He does not use the word "Church" and is not preoccupied with its organization and structure. He uses simple images to express his understanding of the Christian community, such as boat (3: 9; 4: 1), flock (6: 34, 14: 27), temple—the new temple of God which replaces the old (14: 58; 15: 29).

Mark has Jesus begin his ministry with the words "The kingdom of God is close at hand" (1: 15). His Gospel has been called a history of the *Kingdom:* he speaks of requirements for entry (10: 13–31) and membership (4: 1–34).

The nature of the reign of God and human responses to it are presented in the parable of the sower and instruction on its meaning (4: 1–34).

EXERCISE 30: Almost every chapter in Mark has some reference to the wilderness or the desert. Read the section on the Galilean Ministry, where the wilderness is stressed particularly, and list the various meanings Mark gives it in relation to Jesus' ministry.

EXERCISE 31:  Read 8: 22–10: 52 in the light of the above comments on discipleship. Trace the process by which the people involved come to "see". What do you, personally, learn about discipleship?

EXERCISE 32: Locate and read Markan stories in which women play a part, especially the passion and resurrection stories. Compare the women's actions and responses to Jesus with those of the male disciples. What do you find?

EXERCISE 33: Which follower/disciple/character do you most relate to in Mark's story?
What part does he/she play in the narrative?
How does Jesus relate to him/her?
What is his/her response to Jesus?
What do you learn about discipleship from this person?

MATTHEW
Jesus As the New Moses

Author:

It is generally accepted that the author is not the Apostle Matthew. The reasons for this are that an eyewitness would not have relied so heavily on Mark, and secondly, by 85–90 A.D., the apostle Matthew would probably have been dead. A third reason for rejecting the Apostle Matthew, as author, is that the concerns of this Gospel are of second generation Christians. It could be of course, that the Apostle Matthew was associated with the community in which the Gospel arose. This would explain why the tax collector Levi in Mk 2: 14 becomes the tax collector Matthew in Mt 9: 9 and 10: 3.

The author was probably a <u>Jewish convert</u> who was familiar with the Law, prophets, Jewish traditions and messianic expectations.

Date:

It seems clear from internal evidence that this Gospel was written after the destruction of Jerusalem, which is seen as an event in the past (22: 7; 21: 41). There is also an allusion to the destruction of Jerusalem in the parable of the Great Supper. Ignatius of Antioch (d. 110) in his letters, seemingly refers to the Gospel of Matthew a number of times. Within this framework a date of 85–90 is likely.

Place:

One cannot be certain but Antioch in Syria is suggested by a number of scholars.

The shekel and denarius. One mina equalled 30 shekels.

Intended Community:

His frequent reference to the Jewish Scriptures and traditions suggests that his readers were predominantly converts from Judaism. However he also has a missionary outlook and openness towards Gentiles which argues for a Gentile audience as well. This audience is quite likely an urban community. Matthew uses the word for "city" (Greek *polis*) twenty-six times and the word for "village" only three times. Mark by comparison uses these words eight and seven times respectively.

There is some internal evidence to suggest that the Matthean community was relatively wealthy. Whereas Mark and Luke tend to refer to small change or lesser denominations ("copper coins", Mk 6: 8 or "minas/pounds", Lk 19: 11–27), Matthew frequently uses terms such as gold, silver and talents in his Gospel. A talent, for example, was worth about fifty times the value of a "minas/pound".

Background of the Community:

Matthew reflects a period of consolidation for the early Christian communities. The Parousia, seen as imminent in Mark, is not so pressing in Matthew. The threat of immediate and total persecution has passed, although tensions between Christians and their Jewish and Gentile neighbors are real. Matthew speaks of disciples being "handed over to tribulation" hated by all, and even put to death (10: 18, 22; 13: 21; 24: 9). Jewish Christians were clearly separate from other Jews, however, as can be seen by Matthew's reference to "their" synagogues and his refusal to say anything good about the Scribes and Pharisees.

The time at which Matthew wrote was one of settling down for the Church while attempting to articulate its life and mission. Questions of order, discipline and authority arise. There are also echoes of the Church's liturgy; for example, "Go, therefore make disciples of all the nations; baptise them in the name of the Father and of the Son and of the Holy Spirit . . ." (28: 19) gives us the first trinitarian formula in the New Testament which was most likely used in baptism in Matthew's community.

Sources:

(1) Mark: Of Mark's 661 verses, Matthew reproduces some 606 verses.
(2) Q: Matthew and Luke have 200 common verses not found in Mark.
(3) M: This source provides material not found in Mark or Q.

This source could have been oral or written. The Infancy Narrative comes from this source.

Structure:

The Infancy Narrative 1: 1–2: 23
Preparation for Public Ministry 3: 1–4: 11
The Galilean Ministry 4: 12–13: 58
Retirement from Galilee 14: 1–18: 35
The Journey to Jerusalem 19: 1–20: 34
The Jerusalem Ministry 21: 11–25: 46
The Passion Narrative 26: 1–27: 66
The Resurrection Narrative 28: 1–20

Matthew can also be arranged into five books, possibly to parallel the five books of the Torah. In each book the discourse is introduced by a narrative section:

Prologue: 1: 1–2: 23
Book One: The Proclamation of the Reign 3: 1–7: 29
Book Two: Ministry in Galilee 8: 1–11: 1
Book Three: Controversy and Parables 11: 2–13: 52
Book Four: The Formation of the Disciples 13: 53–18: 35
Book Five: Judea and Jerusalem 19: 1–25: 46
The Passion Narrative: 26: 1–27: 66
The Resurrection Narrative: 28: 1–20

Style:

Matthew uses better Greek and a richer vocabulary than Mark, whom he often abbreviates. He improves upon Mark whenever he can. In keeping with his Jewish background, he uses the rabbinical styles of composition known as Midrash, Halakah (e.g. 17: 24–27) and Haggadah (cf. Infancy Narrative).

Whereas Mark's is a Gospel in a hurry, Matthew's is slower in pace, more reflective, and concerned with the teachings of Jesus rather than his actions. He is a highly skilled writer with an eye to symmetry. There are three divisions in his genealogy, three temptations, three duties (6: 1–18), three sets of three miracles (8–9), three signs, three parables of judgment and three challenges to the Scribes (22). There are seven parables of the Kingdom (13), seven woes, and seven parables of warning (23: 13–33; 24: 32–25: 46). He plans the whole Gospel around five discourses arranged in inverted parallelism (chiasm) with the first and fifth dealing with blessings or woes, the second and fourth with aspects of the life of the new community, and the central third speech dealing with the Kingdom.

Theological Slant and Concerns:

Matthew is a very *Jewish Gospel.* This is firstly shown by the vocabulary used. Matthew refers to the Kingdom of *Heaven,* rather than the Kingdom of God. Other typically Jewish words such as "righteousness", "almsgiving", "prayer", "fasting", "sons of God", "the consummation of the age", and

Fragment of third century manuscript of Matthew's Gospel. Chester Beatty Library, Dublin.

"the day of judgment" are frequently used. Matthew constantly cites Scripture—over 130 times. He often uses the rabbinical style of question (17: 24, 25; 18: 12; 22: 17, 42; 26: 66) and counter question (12: 5; 21: 16; 22: 31). Jesus, in Matthew's Gospel, is initially and primarily concerned with the salvation of Israel (15: 21–28). Matthew is also concerned with the *Law* and how Jesus fulfils it.

Although Matthew's is a Jewish Gospel, he can be anti-Jewish on occasions (12: 6; 21: 28–32; 27: 25). At other times he expresses both pro-Gentile bias (2: 1–12; 4: 14–16; 12: 21; 28: 19) and anti-Gentile prejudice (10: 5). Matthew is very harsh on the *Scribes and Pharisees,* referring to them as a brood of vipers (3: 7–12), as people who cannot read the signs of the times (16: 3), and as murderers of prophets (21: 31). Chapter 23 is likewise very strident in its condemnation of them. This attitude is seen to reflect the strong feelings and tensions between the Jewish Christians and the Orthodox Scribes and Pharisees in the local community in which the Gospel arose.

Another concern of Matthew's is that of the *Church.* He is the only evangelist to use the word *ekklesia* which appears three times (16: 18; 18: 17). It translates the Hebrew "qahal", meaning "gathering of the brethren", which is also Matthew's understanding of the local Church. The Church is a community of the people of God and the disciples of Jesus. Within this community there are "prophets" (some false prophets) and "teachers".

This community had by 85 developed an organizational structure for governing its life. Peter, for example, receives "the keys of the Kingdom of Heaven" (16: 19) as first among the disciples. The power of "binding and loosing" (18: 18) is given to all the disciples and enables them collectively to regulate the difference of doctrine or discipline that may occur in the community. Yet within the group Peter clearly holds a position of special prominence as leader: "Thou art Peter and upon this rock I will build my Church" (16: 18).

Matthew's *theology of salvation* is that the Good News, which was initially directed at the Jews, has been rejected by them and is now to be offered to the Gentiles. Matthew indicates that salvation is initially for the Jews by using geographical boundaries. Jesus' ministry is confined within the borders of Israel (15: 24; 10: 5–6). Matthew has the Canaanite woman "coming out" of the region of Tyre and Sidon so that it is in Israel that Jesus grants his favor (15: 21–28). (Mark has no such qualms about Jesus performing miracles in pagan territory.) Jesus, in Matthew's Gospel, starts his ministry in Galilee, and after his Resurrection he meets his disciples again in Galilee, from whence he sends them out to the whole world (28:19). The movement is clearly from Jewish territory out to the pagan world.

Jesus is seen as the new *Moses,* the *Teacher* and *Law-Giver,* in Matthew's Gospel. Not surprisingly, therefore, much of the Gospel focuses on the teachings of Jesus (as opposed to the actions of Jesus in Mark).

Like Moses on Sinai, Jesus preaches the Beatitudes (the new Law) from the Mount. He is transfigured on a mountain and he meets the eleven disciples, after the Resurrection, on a mountain in Galilee (28: 16). The physical setting of a mountain is thus used to emphasize the image of Jesus as the new Moses, the new Law-Giver on Mount Sinai.

In a way, the end of Matthew's Gospel sums up the author's and his community's understanding of their *mission.* Chapter 28: 16–20 relates how Jesus, after his Resurrection, met with his disciples in Galilee and commissioned them to go out into the world and preach the Good News. In this account a number of significant points indicate how the new religion (to be known later as Christianity) has made a break with the religion from which it sprang (Judaism): Jesus meets with them on a mountain (like Moses on Sinai) and gives them a new Law; he claims "all authority on heaven and earth" (allowed only to Yahweh by traditional Jews); he commands them to go and make disciples of all nations (a new missionary perspective for Jews); they are to baptize followers into the new faith, which rite replaces that of circumcision; Jesus replaces the Torah as teacher, as the one who is to be obeyed; and finally the promise he makes is to be with them always, until the end of time (cf. Moloney, 1986: 118–122).

EXERCISE 34:   Compare Mt 5: 3 with Lk 6: 20
                    Mt 22: 9 with Lk 14: 21
                    Mt 27: 57 with Lk 23: 50–51
                    Mt 19: 23 with Mk 10: 23
Could you suggest why Matthew's account differs from Luke's and Mark's?

EXERCISE 35:   What Matthean preoccupations do the following references suggest?
5: 17–20; 23: 2–3, 23; 12: 46–50; 10: 17, 18; 21: 33–46.

EXERCISE 36:   In Matthew's Gospel Jesus is portrayed as the Teacher. Which teachers do you remember with fondest memories and respect?
Why were they a success in your eyes?
What did Jesus teach people? (Refer to the Gospel passages.)
What has he taught you personally?
Are there any similarities between Jesus as a teacher and your favorite teacher?

LUKE
The Compassionate Savior

Author:

According to Fitzmyer and other scholars, the author of this Gospel is quite likely a Syrian of Antioch, a physician (Col 4: 14) and collaborator of Paul, named Luke. He travelled with Paul from Troas to Philippi in Greece. He was also in Caesarea and later in Rome. According to one tradition he subsequently worked in Achaia (Greece). Early Christian writers such as Irenaeus (178 A.D.), Eusebius and Jerome, all refer to the Evangelist Luke and suggest he lived in Antioch in Syria. Another tradition according to which Luke was a painter originates from the fourteenth century and is thus less reliable.

Date:

It is dated later than 70 because it separates the destruction of Jerusalem from the end of the world. Furthermore it no longer sees the Kingdom as imminent as Mark does. Scholars suggest a date around 80–90.

Place:

Possibly Greece or Asia Minor.

Intended Community:

The author is clearly writing for Gentile Christians. The internal evidence for this is convincing. Luke dedicates Luke-Acts to a person bearing a Greek name, Theophilus (Lk 1: 3; Ac 1: 1). He relates the promised salvation to Gentiles or non-Jews. He seldom quotes the Old Testament and eliminates predominantly Jewish preoccupations from Mark or Q sources, e.g. the Sermon on the Plain omits the discussion on the fulfilment of the Law that Matthew has (Mt 5: 17–48); Luke also leaves out the section from Mark (7: 1–23) which deals with the details of the clean/unclean controversy of the Jewish ritual for purity.

Background of the Community:

Luke is writing in a period of expansion for Christians. The Parousia is no longer seen as imminent and hence Luke prays for bread "each day" and exhorts followers to take up their crosses "daily". The disciples are settling down to a lifetime of work and prayer. In the meantime the Church will expand and grow under the guidance of the Spirit.

Sources:

1) Mark: Luke has 350 verses of Mark's 661 (55%). By and large he follows Mark's sequence.
2) Q: He has 230 verses from this source also found in Matthew.
3) L: This is Luke's own source, which could come from Johannine circles as he shares some motifs with John such as the Temple and Jerusalem. Most of the Infancy Narrative also comes from this L Source.

Structure:

Prologue 1: 1–4.
The Infancy Narrative 1: 5–2: 52.
Preparation for Public Ministry 3: 1–3: 13
The Galilean Ministry 3: 14–9: 50
The Journey to Jerusalem 9: 51–19: 27.
The Jerusalem Ministry 19: 28–21: 38.
The Passion Narrative 22: 1–23: 56
The Resurrection Narrative 24: 1–53.

Style:

The author has a varied style. He writes in good, polished Greek. He is very observant of human behavior, recording the mannerisms of people in his stories as well as giving psychological insight. In 9: 43 Luke comments that Jesus gave the cured epileptic boy "back to his father" (cf. Mk 9: 27); in 18:1 he speaks about the "need to pray continually and never lose heart"; at other times he is able to give insight into the feelings of the crowd—"a feeling of expectancy had grown among the people" (3: 15) and later "they imagined that the Kingdom of God was going to show itself then and there" (19: 11). (Cf. also 4: 14f.; 11: 1, 29; 13: 1; 17: 20.)

Theological Slant and Concerns:

Luke is concerned with projecting Jesus as a *prophet*. Luke uses this title more than Mark (cf. 4: 24; 7: 16; 9: 19).

Luke is concerned for the *Gentiles*. He omits Semitic words like Boanerges, abba, Iscariot, hosanna, Gethsemane, ephphatha, which his audience would not understand. Instead of "rabbi" he uses "didaskale" (teacher); instead of "golgotha" he uses "kranion" (skull), and instead of "amen" he uses "truly". He writes for people who do not know Palestine. Hence he explains, "a city called Bethsaida" or "the feast of unleavened Bread which is called the Passover".

Luke cares for the *poor*. In the Infancy Narrative, the poor and lowly are chosen for the greatest privileges. In the Beatitudes it is "happy are you poor" (not "poor in spirit", as in Matthew). Luke alone has the Isaiahan text about the poor when Jesus appears in the synagogue in Nazareth (4: 18) and refers to it again later (7: 22). The Story of the Rich Man and Lazarus is exclusive to Luke (16: 19–31) as well as the material in Luke 12: 13–21 relating to the poor. With the poor go the marginalized in society such as the *Samaritans* to whom Luke also gives particular attention (cf. 9: 51–56; 10: 29–37).

The *Holy Spirit* and *Prayer* are also emphasized in Luke. He first mentions the Holy Spirit in 1:15. John the Baptist from his mother's womb, is "filled with the Holy Spirit". Thereafter Luke frequently mentions the Holy Spirit (cf. 1: 35, 41, 67, 80; 2: 25, 26, 27; 4: 1, 14, 18; 10: 21). The Acts of the Apostles, also written by Luke, continues this emphasis on the Holy Spirit. *Prayer* is likewise highlighted with mention made of it before all the important steps in the ministry of Jesus; i.e. at his baptism (3: 21), before the choice of the Twelve (6: 12), before Peter's confession of faith (9: 18), at the transfiguration (9: 28), before teaching the "Our Father" (11: 1), and in the Garden of Gethsemane (22: 41). Jesus insists that his disciples be people of prayer too (cf. 6: 28; 10: 2; 11: 1–13; 18: 1–8; 21: 36).

We can also say that Luke's Gospel is one of *messianic joy*. The words used by Luke abound in joyous response to the wonder of what has taken place (our salvation). His disciples are to consider themselves fortunate and blessed.

Luke's Gospel has been called the Gospel of *Mercy* or *Great Pardons*. The theme of compassion and forgiveness pervades the whole Gospel.

One thinks of the stories of the lost sheep, lost coin and lost son (Chapter 15), the sinful woman (7: 36–58), the story of Zacchaeus (19: 1–10). Jesus also forgives his executioners (23: 34). Luke has the injunction "Be compassionate (not "perfect" as in Matthew) as your heavenly Father" (6: 36). This compassion and pardon is *universal* in Luke. His genealogical table (3: 23–38) goes back to Adam showing thus how we are all one human family with one Savior.

Stewardship of wealth is another Lucan theme. Parables such as the Rich Fool, the Dishonest Steward and the Rich Man and Lazarus illustrate the point that the goods of this life are ours to look after and share.

Luke gives greater prominence to *women* than do the other evangelists. In addition to incidents where women play a prominent role which Matthew or Luke have taken from Mark, Luke has his own stories of women and gives them an importance peculiar to his Gospel. It is obvious that Mary plays a central role in Luke's Infancy Narrative (as opposed to Matthew's). In Jesus' public ministry a group of women (Mary Magdalene, Joanna, Susanna and several others, 8: 2) journey with him in his travels and are also present at his Crucifixion (while the disciples flee), at his burial and at the tomb on Easter Day. They become the first preachers of the Easter Message (24: 9). Luke seems to make the point that women are the first to come to Easter faith and the first to proclaim it (Moloney, 1984: 61).

In addition Luke has the story of Martha and Mary (10: 38–42), the Widow of Nain (7: 11–17), the sinful woman who washed Jesus' feet (7: 36–50), the cure of the crippled woman (13: 10–17), the lost coin (15: 8–10) and the importunate widow (18: 1–8). From Luke's projection of women in his Gospel, scholars have concluded that women played a significant role in Lucan communities.

We also note in Luke that the *ministry of Jesus parallels the mission of the Church in Acts*. Jesus is baptized by the Spirit in Luke 3: 21f. Likewise the Church (Ac 2: 1ff.) is "baptized" by the Spirit at Pentecost. Other parallels concern the preaching about the Spirit (Lk 4: 16–19; Ac 2: 17); theme of rejection (Lk 4: 19; Ac 7: 58; 13: 50); cure of the multitudes (Lk 4: 40f.; Ac 2: 43; 5: 16) and glorification (Lk 9: 28–36; Ac 1: 9–11).

EXERCISE 37: Look up the following references in Luke and say what typically Lucan concerns are mentioned:
7: 39; 12: 16–21; 11: 13; 23: 39–43; 23: 55–24: 8.

EXERCISE 38: Read the concluding verses of Luke's Gospel, 24: 50–53. Compare this with the opening scene in 1: 8–10. What do these passages have in common? What do we call this literary technique?

EXERCISE 39: (a) Read and compare/constrast: Lk 8: 2; Mt 4: 23–25; Mk 1: 39.

Can you account for the differences?

(b) Read Lk 24: 9–11; Mt 28: 1–20; Mk 16: 9–11; Jn 20: 11–18. Compare the role of the women in these narratives and try to account for the differences.

(c) What issues concerning the role of women in the Gospels are raised by (a) and (b)?

Application of Redaction Criticism to the Synoptic Gospels

Since you are now familiar with the community for which each evangelist is writing, and with his particular interests and theological slant, you will be able to compare the synoptics' redaction of the Caesarea Philippi incident (Exercise 40) and The Parable of the Great Supper (Exercise 41).

EXERCISE 40: The Synoptics' account of Jesus and his disciples at Caesarea Philippi:

Mk 8: 27–9: 1; Mt 16: 13–28; Lk 9: 18–27

(a) Read Mark's account of this incident. What happened? Summarize in one sentence the main point in Jesus' teaching in 8: 31–9: 1. From what you know of the community for which Mark was writing, what was Mark saying to his readers about Jesus and about them?

What concept of the Messiah is Mark impressing on his readers?

(b) Now read Matthew's account. What happened according to Matthew? In what way does it differ from Mark's account? (Note 16: 17–19; a piece of tradition which has no parallel in Mark or Luke.) It has been said that Matthew's concerns are ecclesiological; his is a "church book".

What is he saying about the Church to his readers?

(c) In Luke's account, the opening verse touches on a peculiarly Lucan interest. Can you identify it? Luke was writing for people who realized that the Second Coming was not going to happen tomorrow, but that the Christian life was for an indefinite time.

Compare Lk 9: 23–27 with Mk 8: 31–9: 1.

What differences have been introduced to show that Luke is thinking in terms of a longer period?

EXERCISE 41:   *The Parable of the Great Supper:* After you have studied
Chapter 3 on Matthew's and Luke's Gospels, read and com-
pare: Mt 22: 1–14 and Lk 14: 15–24.
   (a) Applying source criticism to these texts, what conclusions
   would you draw?
   (b) Draw up two columns and list differences in the plot and
   details of the stories.
   (c) Applying redaction criticism, account for the differences
   identified in (b).

INFANCY NARRATIVES

Having discussed the three Synoptic Gospels and before we go on to John's
Gospel, let us take up in some detail the question of the Infancy Narratives.

   The categories used in form criticism were worked out from the public
ministry accounts in the Gospels. The Infancy Narratives (found only in
Matthew and Luke) do not belong to the Public Ministry section of the
Gospels, and thus are not strictly speaking a form. However, like Passion
Narratives and Resurrection Narratives, they can be seen as a sub-genre of
the Gospels.

   In terms of the development of the Gospel structure over a period of
time (cf. Chapter 2, p. 52), the Infancy Narrative came last. The Passion
Narrative, as we saw above, came first as the basic kerygma. Then the

*Virgin of the Annunciation. A
woodcut from the fifth or sixth
century. Perhaps the earliest extant
representation of Mary.*

Public Ministry accounts (didache = the teachings of Jesus as seen in what he did and said) were prefixed to the Passion Narrative. Finally the Resurrection Narrative was appended to the developing Gospel, and in the cases of Matthew and Luke, an Infancy Narrative placed before the Public Ministry. Diagrammatically, the stages or building blocks of the developing Gospel could be presented thus:

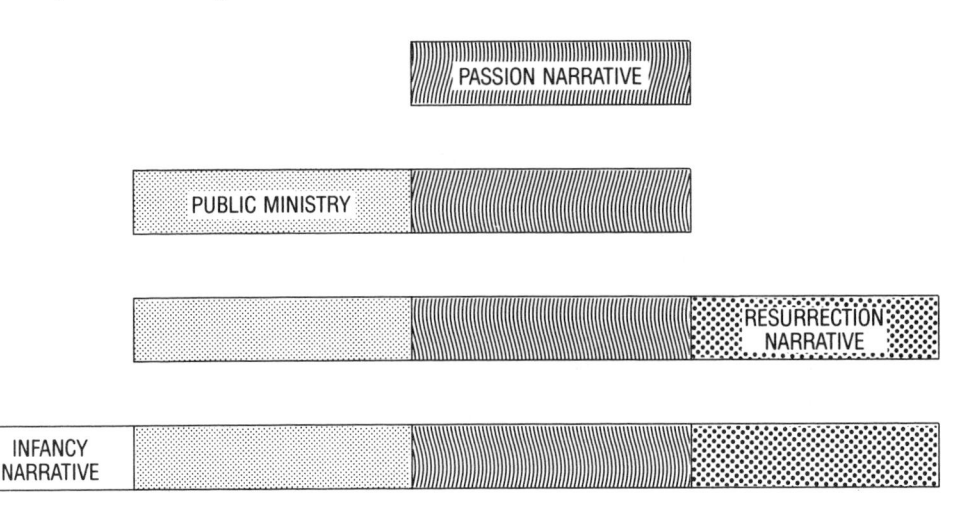

If you look at Mark (without the appendix 16: 9–20, which many manuscripts do not have), it consists basically of the Passion Narrative and the Public Ministry. (The Resurrection is briefly mentioned in 16: 1–8). It does not have the Resurrection or Infancy Narrative. (Compare Ac 10: 36–41 which, in a way, is a miniature Gospel, a summary of Jesus' career.)

The biographical concerns about the birth and early childhood of Jesus were bound to be expressed sooner or later. However, these concerns as expressed in the Infancy Narratives must not be understood in terms of modern historical biography. As Fitzmyer says,

Early tradition tended to take to itself folklore, astrology and the interpretation of the Old Testament. These are known features in much ancient tracing of origins, where the sophisticated modern use of genealogical and historical records was unknown (1981: 305).

EXERCISE 42:   Compare Matthew 1: 1–2: 23 with Luke 1: 5–2: 52 and write down those events that are unique to either Matthew or Luke. Just list the events by way of main headings.

As regards sources, there is no evidence that Matthew used Luke or vice versa. They both seem to rely on traditions in their respective communities that existed prior to their writing. In short, we do not know the sources of these two different Infancy Narratives. Looking at Luke's account, some commentators suppose two sources: (a) a Jewish-Christian source for the canticles (Magnificat, Benedictus, Nunc Dimittis and probably the section, "Jesus among the doctors of the Law") and (b) an early Baptist source for the announcement story of John the Baptist, and the story of his birth, circumcision and manifestation.

EXERCISE 43:   Scholars have identified a list of the details that the two evangelists share in their Infancy Narratives.
Find the appropriate references in Matthew and Luke:

	Matthew	Luke
1. Jesus' birth is related to the reign of Herod.	_____	_____
2. Mary his mother to be, is a virgin, engaged to Joseph, but they have not yet come to live together.	_____	_____
3. Joseph is of the House of David.	_____	_____
4. An angel from heaven announces the coming birth of Jesus.	_____	_____
5. Jesus is recognized to be a son of David.	_____	_____
6. His conception is to take place through the Holy Spirit.	_____	_____
7. Joseph is not involved in the conception.	_____	_____
8. The name "Jesus" is imposed by heaven prior to his birth.	_____	_____
9. The angel identifies Jesus as "Savior".	_____	_____
10. Jesus is born after Mary and Joseph come to live together.	_____	_____
11. Jesus is born at Bethlehem.	_____	_____
12. Jesus settles, with Mary and Joseph, in Nazareth of Galilee.	_____	_____

The term "announcement story" as used above requires some explanation. It is a literary form found mainly in the Old Testament and is used when some important announcement such as the annunciation of the birth of a child, is made to a believer. The usual elements of this particular literary form are as follows:

i)   Appearance of an angel (or the Lord himself)
ii) Fear response of person
iii) The divine message:
    —person addressed by name
    —qualifying phrase describing person
    —person urged not to be afraid

—woman is to have a child
—name by which child is to be called
—phrase interpreting the name
—future accomplishments of the child

iv) Objection of the person

v) A sign to reassure the person

The elements are not always found in this order, nor do individual stories always have all the elements.

EXERCISE 44:   Look up the announcement stories of the birth of Ishmael (Gn 16: 7–12), of Isaac (Gn 17: 1, 3, 16–21) and Samson (Jg 13: 3–23); also read Dn 9: 20–27. Identify the elements used.
Now look up Lk 1: 8–20; 1: 26–37 and Mt 1: 20–21. Whose births are being announced? Identify the elements of the announcement stories that are used in each case.

If we compare Matthew's and Luke's Infancy Narratives we notice that Luke is less obviously structured than Matthew (Fitzmyer). Luke emphasizes the parallel between John the Baptist and Jesus, both of whom are introduced as agents of God's salvation history. John the Baptist is also presented as the precursor of Jesus (as he is in the Gospel proper) and plays a transitional role, being part of the Period of Israel. (Luke-Acts can be said to have three stages: Period of Israel, Period of Jesus, Period of the Church/Spirit.) Luke also imitates Old Testament motifs; for example, his reference to David and his lineage (Lk 1: 26–33) recalls the childhood of Samuel in the Old Testament (1 S: 1–3).

Matthew on the other hand structures his Infancy Narrative around five episodes.

EXERCISE 45:   Look up the following episodes in Matthew's Infancy Narrative:
1: 18–25; 2: 1–12; 2: 13–15; 2: 16–18; 2: 19–23.
How does each conclude?
What do you think Matthew is trying to achieve by this?

Matthew too seems to have used the birth of Moses as a model for his account (compare Ex 4: 19 with Mt 2: 19f.). (This fits in well with Matthew's portrait of Jesus as the New Moses in the rest of his Gospel.) Some scholars have pointed out elements of midrash in Matthew's account:

he uses Old Testament texts as central and then weaves a story around these.

EXERCISE 46: Look up the following references and write down the Old Testament texts to which they refer. You may need to use the notes in your Bible, either in the margin or at the bottom of the page.
Mt 1: 23; 2: 6; 2: 15; 2: 18; 2: 23

Matthew commences his narrative with a genealogy. Luke places one later on (3: 23–38). Matthew is seen to show how Jesus is connected with Abraham and David, the recipients of the messianic promises. Luke goes back to Adam, since his concern is more universal, in keeping with the rest of his Gospel.

Both lists of names are artificial in parts. Matthew has three sets of fourteen (2x7) names (which means leaving out some names). Luke sometimes chooses not to follow the line of the Kings of Judah. Both, on occasions when biblical records fail, have to improvise.

Matthew has four women in his genealogy of Jesus: Tamar, who deceived her father-in-law into an incestuous union (Gn 38); Rahab, the prostitute of Jericho who sheltered spies and was admitted to the Israelite community (Jos 2); Ruth, the Moabite who joined the Israelite community (Rt); and Bathsheba, the wife of Uriah and partner of David's adultery (2 S: 11 and 12).

It is difficult to guess Matthew's interest here. Various opinions have been expressed. Jerome regarded all four women as sinners and their inclusion as a foreshadowing of the fact that Jesus had come to save all sinful humankind. However, it is not at all clear that all these women were sinners, and in fact in Jewish piety at the time of Jesus, they were highly esteemed. Another opinion holds that the women were regarded as foreigners and were included by Matthew to show that Jesus was related by ancestry to the Gentiles. There is doubt, however, about Tamar and Bathsheba being foreigners, as well as other reasons for rejecting this opinion.

A third approach, favored by Brown (1977), is that which identifies common elements the four Old Testament women share with Mary:

(i) there is something irregular or extraordinary in their union with their partners—a union which even though scandalous to outsiders, continued the lineage of the Messiah; and

(ii) they showed initiative or played an important role in God's plan.

It is a combination of these two ideas that possibly best explains Matthew's choice of these women in his genealogy.

Overall, when reading the Infancy Narratives, one should bear in mind that both evangelists use them as overtures to their Gospels, that is, they introduce themes that will be repeated over and over again in the Gospel proper. (In this way they are similar to the function of the Prologue in John's Gospel.) In Matthew's Infancy Narrative we have the themes of the identity of Jesus (raised by the titles used of Jesus), continuity and discontinuity with Old Testament salvation history, and conflict and rejection. In Luke's narrative, in addition to the theme of Jesus' identity as an agent of God's salvation history, we have the following themes: the journey; universal salvation; the simple and poor; Mary the first believer; missionary discipleship; and Jesus and the Temple.

EXERCISE 47:  Taking each theme in the Infancy Narratives of Matthew and Luke mentioned in the paragraph above, cite the incident in the narrative which introduces the theme. (Matthew's Infancy Narrative: 1: 1–2: 23; Luke's 1: 5–2: 52.)

Identify instances in the rest of the Gospels where these themes are further developed.

JOHN
On Eagle's Wings

Author:

The identity of the author remains a mystery. Irenaeus, writing at the end of the second century, identified the apostle John with the evangelist John, and others have speculated that the Gospel was written by disciples of John the Apostle who was the Beloved Disciple.

Today the identification of John the Apostle with the Beloved Disciple is seriously questioned (cf. Brown, 1978: 33–34; Ellis, 1984: 3; Kysar, 1976: 20). Many think that somewhere behind the Gospel is the unnamed "other disciple" or "beloved disciple" referred to in the Gospel; a disciple of Jesus but not one of the Twelve, and the leader in the community that gathered around him. It is thought that a Johannine school or group of scholars developed in this community, who interpreted and expanded the Beloved Disciple's teaching as the years went by until someone wrote the Gospel in the form in which we now have it. The same group is also thought to be responsible for the Epistles of John.

The Gospel shows an insider's familiarity with the Old Testament and with Jewish cultic life, so that we may conclude that whoever was behind the Gospel was of Jewish background. However, there are also indications that he may not have been from mainstream Judaism.

Date:

Internal evidence indicates that the Gospel was written after 85, and probably around 90.

In the 80s, Jewish leaders met at Jamnia to re-establish Jewish identity after the devastating fall of Jerusalem and the confusion caused by the strange doctrines of the followers of Jesus of Nazareth. Probably after 85, another benediction was added to the eighteen benedictions which had to be recited publicly at the daily synagogue morning prayer. This benediction asked that the Nazarenes (Christians) and heretics might suddenly perish (cf. Perrin, 1974: 230; Moloney, 1986: 163), thus placing the Jewish Christians in a dilemma, since they were banned from the Synagogue if they did not recite the benediction. There is clear evidence in the Gospel of the Johannine community's conflict with the synagogue leaders (e.g. in Jn 9). Moreover, the Gospel of John is the only book in the New Testament that uses the technical Greek term for excommunication from the Synagogue: *aposunagogos* (9: 22; 12: 42, 16: 2).

Given this evidence, it seems reasonable to date the final writing of the Gospel around 90 when the results of the expulsion order would have been most felt in the Mediterranean area.

Place:

There is an ancient tradition which says that the Gospel in its final form was written at Ephesus. There does not appear to be any internal evidence either to support or deny this tradition.

Intended Community:

John's primary audience seems to have been a group of Jewish Christians who were in a situation of increasing tension with the Jewish Synagogue (cf., for example, Jn 9 and the aftermath of the healing of the blind man). They were torn between their allegiance to the Jewish Synagogue and their Jewish roots on the one hand and the Christian community on the other, and their faith in Jesus may have been wavering as a result of conflict and persecution (cf. 20: 31).

Background to the Community:

Brown's study of the Johannine community (cf. 1979: 25–58; 166–7) suggests that it was made up of several layers or groups, each of which, over the years, exercised its influence, which was carried through into the Gospel's final written form:

1. The originating group of Jews in or near Palestine, which included followers of John the Baptist. The group also included the Beloved Disciple, who had known Jesus during his ministry.
2. Jews who may not have belonged to mainstream Judaism: they were hostile towards official Judaism, had an anti-Temple bias, and understood Jesus against a Mosaic background rather than the more usual Davidic background (as in the Synoptic Gospels). They made converts in Samaria. (It has been suggested that this group was associated with Stephen in Jerusalem and fled after his martyrdom into Samaria and thence further north (cf. Schillebeeckx, 1980: 315). Under the influence of this group, a "high", pre-existence Christology developed. This was particularly upsetting to the Jews because it seemed to establish Jesus as a second God. (There are indications that it may also have upset some Jewish Christians in the community.) The Jews would eventually have the Johannine Christians expelled from the synagogues. These Christians would have understood very well a Jesus who is portrayed as rejected by his fellow Jews.
3. Gentiles—Greek converts who came into the community after it moved from the Palestine area, and who were seen as fulfilling God's plan in place of "the Jews", who were blind.

   Given the Greek background of some of the community, John cannot assume that all his readers will understand Hebrew, so he sometimes translates Hebrew words (1: 38 and 1: 42), and uses universal symbols, such as the vine and bread.

Sources:

The question of whether John knew the Synoptic Gospels, or any one of them, has long been discussed, and to date there is no conclusive answer. While some of the events in John have parallels in the Synoptics (most notably Mark) and the Passion Narratives have much in common, there are obvious differences in style, presentation and order of events as well as in the chronological framework of the Gospel.

The Gospel consists of narrative material (some of it in common with the Synoptics) combined with long discourses which have no parallel in the other Gospels. There are no parables in John, and his use of miracles ("signs") is different from the Synoptics. Some suggest that John may have used a "signs source" that contained some but not all of the Synoptic miracles and sayings, and that the discourses were developed out of these, or perhaps were based on fragments of homilies by the Beloved Disciple (cf. Ellis, 1984: 3–4).

If John were indeed using some early oral or written source(s) in common with the Synoptics, he has so made it his own that it is impossible to identify distinct sources.

Though John draws primarily on Jewish thought and Old Testament themes, it seems that his background may not have been mainstream Judaism but a branch of Judaism that had been influenced by non-Jewish religious and philosophical thought, especially Hellenism. Note must also be made of the similarities between the themes and language of John and

Fragment of an ancient
manuscript of John's Gospel.
Chester Beatty Library, Dublin.

of the Scrolls of the non-mainstream Essene sect at Qumran. Brown (1979: 30–31) believes that the connection is explained by the presence in John's community in its early stages of some Jews, perhaps followers of John the Baptist, who held the kind of ideas expressed in the Qumran Scrolls, rather than by the Johannine writer's use of the Scrolls themselves. Others suggest that John was influenced by "a broad type of Judaism which embraced a great variety of forms and expressions" (Kysar, 1976: 19).

Structure:

1: 1–1: 18	Prologue
1: 19–12: 50	The Book of Signs (Public Ministry)
13: 1–20: 31	The Book of Glory (Last Supper, Passion, Resurrection)
21: 1–25	Epilogue (regarded by most scholars as a last minute addition)

Sometimes the structure of John's Gospel is seen in terms of the Jewish feasts:

Prologue: 1: 1–19
The First Passover: 1: 19–3: 21
Journeys in Samaria and Galilee: 3: 22–4: 54
The Second Feast at Jerusalem: 5: 1–5: 47
Another Passover: 6: 1–6: 71
The Feast of Tabernacles: 7: 1–10: 21
The Feast of Dedication: 10: 22–11: 54
The Last Passover: 11: 55–17: 26
The Passion Narrative: 18: 1–19: 42
The Resurrection Narrative: 20: 1–24: 25

Style:

The Gospel uses simple, everyday Greek terms whose meaning is never exhausted. In Moloney's words: "It is written in one of the simplest forms of Greek in the New Testament, and yet it carries one of its profoundest theologies" (1986: 168). The writer uses words, images and concepts that a non-Jewish Hellenist would understand ("the way", "living water", "new life"); at the same time, he writes with an insider's knowledge of the Hebrew Scriptures. He typically begins with everyday realities—water, bread, light—and then leads the reader in a reflective way into their symbolism on many levels.

By comparison with the Synoptics, the Gospel has only a small amount of narrative material combined with large blocks of discourse material. The Book of Signs consists of short stories and seven signs, out of which a long discourse or dialogue grows, leading the listener deeper into the meaning of the event and ultimately of his/her relationship with God (e.g., Jn 3: Nicodemus and the discussion about being born again; Jn 6: feeding the multitude and the discourse on the bread of life).

From the very beginning of the Gospel we are struck by John's constant use of dualistic symbols or pairs of opposites (e.g. light/darkness, above/below) which seem basic to the expression of his thought. Other characteristics of John's style are: his use of double-meaning words (words that have one meaning for Jesus and another for Jesus' audience, e.g. 2: 19–22, 3: 3–4, 4: 10–12); explanatory comments (which correct misunderstandings or explain symbolism—e.g. 2: 21, 18: 9, or remind the reader of something that has already happened—e.g. 11: 2); inclusions (what is said at the beginning is repeated at the end, thus serving as a frame for the whole, e.g. 2: 1–12, 20: 1–18; note the repetition of key words such as names of people and/or places). Inclusions indicate the natural divisions of the Gospel; the present division of the Gospel into twenty-one chapters dates only from the thirteenth century and does not always respect John's inclusions (cf. Ellis 1984: 8–10). John (like other Old and New Testament writers) also uses chiasm (e.g. 2: 1–12).

Theological Slant and Concerns:

John leaves us in no doubt as to his purpose in writing his Gospel: "These things are recorded so that you may believe that *Jesus is the Christ, the Son of God*, and that *believing this you may have life through his name*" (20: 31). While he may well have been writing for those who had not yet come to believe in Jesus, he was addressing more explicitly his community which, as has already been noted, was engaged in a traumatic debate with the local Jewish Synagogue.

John's primary intention was to strengthen the community as synagogue opposition grew and they were being cut off from their Jewish roots. Through narrative and theological discourse, John develops his theme of faith. Behind the Gospel is the central question: "What kind of faith is needed to commit oneself totally to all that Jesus has come to reveal?" (Moloney, 1986: 176). The reactions/responses of people in the Gospel to Jesus embody various levels of faith, from rejection of Jesus (the "Jews", that is, the Jewish synagogue leaders who opposed the Johannine community, e.g. 5: 15–16; 6: 41; 8: 59; 10: 31ff.), to complete acceptance of him (e.g. Mary, 2: 1–11, or the royal official, 4: 46–54). Moloney speaks of a journey from no faith to partial faith to true faith (cf. 1986: 175–7).

The signs evoke various responses and decisions—for Jesus or against him. The Book of Glory was written specifically for those who have accepted Jesus as the one sent from God and who can therefore be led further into his revelation of God in his "hour".

Not only does John show Jesus leading Nicodemus or the Samaritan woman or the royal official on this journey of faith. At the same time, the reader, whether in the Johannine community then or the Christian community today, is being nurtured and challenged on the same journey: "These things are recorded so that *you* may believe . . ."

More urgently than any other Gospel, that of John asks the question: "Who is Jesus?" John's attempt to explore the question of *Jesus' identity* is expressed in terms, concepts and symbols that are often quite different from the Synoptics—his thought shaped both by the living faith experience of Jesus in his community and by the opposition encountered in the local Synagogue with its accusation that Christians worshipped two Gods. John's response is to state that Jesus Christ is the Messiah, is divine, but is not a second God. The attempt to hold these two truths in tension accounts for the paradox in some of his writing.

Writing for a community that was being cut off from its Jewish roots, John takes four major Jewish feasts, situates Jesus' ministry within the framework of these feasts (cf. 5: 9ff., 6: 4ff., 7: 2ff., 10: 32ff.), and "develops a Christology that indicates that *the presence of the living God once celebrated in the feasts has now been incarnated in the person of Jesus'* (Moloney 1986: 178). Likewise, John shows that the presence of God in the Temple is being replaced by God's presence in Jesus.

John's view of Jesus has been called "high" Christology. Emphasis is placed on the person of Jesus who comes "from above", is the pre-existent Logos, the unique human presence and revelation of God, one with the Father in being (e.g. 3: 35; 4: 34; 14: 28).

The Prologue to the Gospel uses the term *Logos*, translated as "Word", to express something of John's understanding of the identity of Jesus Christ—a term used nowhere else in the New Testament. Logos had its roots in a number of religious and philosophical systems, and John may well have been influenced by the Stoic and/or gnostic concepts of his time. But the Prologue is also written out of the ancient Hebrew tradition of the Word of God which brought all things into being, and of the tradition of Wisdom literature. However, for John the Logos is not a merely abstract philosophical or religious concept—it is a living, historical person who is both (paradoxically) identical with God and yet distinct from God.

John returns to this paradox of identity and individuality again and again through his exploration of the *Father/Son* analogy. Whoever believes in and responds to Jesus (the Son) believes in and responds to God (the Father) (cf. 5: 23, also 12: 44–50 which is central to Johannine theology). For John the answer to the question "Who is Jesus?" is not a purely speculative one, but a practical one. Beyond the paradox and the struggle to express the Son/Father Jesus/God relationship is the simple reality lived out in the community's experience: to respond to Jesus is to respond to the Father.

John's view of the *Church* is different from that of the Synoptic Gospels. He does not use the word "church", nor is he interested in its institutional structure or authority, as was Matthew. But he does emphasize the community aspect of Church, e.g. in the allegory of the Good Shepherd and the Door (10: 1–18) and the True Vine (15: 1–10). And in Chapters 15–17 he stresses the oneness of Christians—for whom the relationship between Father and Son and between Jesus and the believer is the model. The community is the "locus of the manifestation of God" *now* (Kysar, 1976: 100).

There is no mention of "apostle" or "the twelve" in John's Gospel. The writer uses the word "disciple"—and seems to include in this any believer. We note the prominence given to "the Beloved Disciple", a prominence based on the fact that he loved Jesus and was loved by him (13: 23; 20: 2; 21: 7, 20). John is presenting in the Beloved Disciple a model of the true believer and is suggesting that any disciple can be the "Beloved disciple".

John's interest in the *Spirit* is different from Luke's. He emphasizes the presence of the Spirit-Paraclete in the experience of the Christian community, and is the only New Testament writer to use the word "Paraclete" for the Spirit (cf. Jn 14–16, where he talks of the role of the Spirit). Why the use of this unusual and multifaceted term? Kysar (1976: 93–98) suggests that, locked as they were in a tense situation with the leaders of the local Synagogue, the Johannine community needed to speak of the presence of God among them in a distinctive way. Again, there was the problem posed by the delay of the Parousia. Christ had not returned in the way they had expected he would, but is present in the community in the form of the Paraclete. The return of Christ is not an event in the future, but is the experience of the Paraclete in the community NOW.

EXERCISE 48: (a) As you read the Gospel, note the pairs of opposite symbols used by John, and add to the following chart:

positive symbol	location	negative symbol
light	1 : 5	darkness

(b) The struggle between the powers of light and darkness will not, as in Gnosticism, be fought out in the cosmic arena, but in the life of Jesus (cf. Moloney 1986: 201).

Read the Book of Glory in the light of this comment.

EXERCISE 49: Read the story of Jesus' encounter with the Samaritan woman, Jn 4: 1–42.

What is the Samaritan woman's initial response to Jesus? At what point in the story are there indications of partial faith? In terms of faith, how would you describe the reaction of the Samaritan villagers? Which character or group of people do you most relate to in terms of response to Jesus? (This is a good question to keep in mind whenever you are reading John's Gospel.)

EXERCISE 50: Compare the stories of the Samaritan woman's confession of faith (Jn 4: 25–45), Martha's confession of faith (Jn 11: 27–44), and Peter's confession of faith (Mk 8: 27–33; Mt 16: 13–23; Jn 6: 67–71).

What do you notice? What is Jesus' response in each case? What does the Samaritan woman then say/do? Martha? Peter? From the above exploration, what conclusions do you draw about women's discipleship in the early communities?

EXERCISE 51: Identify the seven signs in the Book of Signs: 2: 1–11; 4: 46–54; 5: 1–9; 6: 1–14; 6: 15–25; 9: 1–8; 11: 1–46.

What is the main point of the discourse or dialogue which follows the third, fourth and sixth signs?

EXERCISE 52: (a) Compare John's story of the Last Supper (Jn 13–17) with that of the Synoptics. In what ways are the telling of the story and the celebration different? What themes is John highlighting?

(b) Reflect on your personal journey. Which aspect of the Last Supper and Last Discourse speaks to you most at this moment?

THE GOSPELS AT A GLANCE

The following pages offer a summary sheet of the four Gospels

	MARK	MATTHEW	LUKE	JOHN
Author	Unknown.	Unknown, but very likely a jewish Christian convert who knew Jewish traditions.	Possibly the 'beloved physician' who accompanied Paul to Philippi (Col. 4:14). He was a Gentile, a Syrian of Antioch.	Unknown.
Date	65-70 A.D.	85-90 A.D.	80-90 A.D.	± 90 A.D.
Place	Rome (?)	Antioch in Syria (?)	Greece or Asia Minor(?)	Ephesus (?)
Intended Community	Gentiles, i.e. non-Palestinian Christians	Predominantly Jewish Christians.	Christian Gentiles.	Christian-Jews and Jews in Diaspora.
Background of the Community	Constant threat of *persecution* under Nero, shocked by the impending or final destruction of Jerusalem, 70 A.D. End of time, Parousia, thought to be imminent.	Period of *consolidation*; conflict with official Judaism. Period of second generation Christians. Questions of order, discipline and authority.	Period of *expansion*. Parousia not imminent. Time of expansion under guidance of the Spirit.	Period of *conflict* with official Judaism and reflection on meaning of Christian discipleship.
Sources	1) An early Passion Narrative 2) An account of the Lord's Supper 3) Parables 4) Controversy stories 5) Apocalyptic writings	1) MK 2) Q 3) M	1) MK 2) Q 3) L	Jn presupposes Synoptics. He may have shared a common oral tradition with Mk. Some association with the Lucan tradition is also possible. However Jn is quite distinctive and most of his Gospel has little in common with the Synoptics.
Structure	Preparation for Public Ministry 1:1-13. The Galilean Ministry 1:4-7:23. Journey outside Galilee 7:24-10:52.	The Infancy Narrative 1:2-2:23. Preparation for Public Ministry 3:1-4:11. The Galilean Ministry 4:12-13:58. Retirement from Galilee. The Journey to Jerusalem 19:1-20:34.	Prologue 1:1-4. The Infancy Narrative 1:5-2:52. Preparation for Public Ministry 3:1-4:11. The Galilean Ministry 3:14-9:50. The Journey to Jerusalem 9:51-19:27.	Prologue 1:1-18. The Book of Signs 1:19-12:50. The Book of Glory 13:1-20:31 Epilogue 21:1-24:25
	The Jerusalem Ministry 11:1-13:37.	The Jerusalem Ministry 21:11-25:46.	The Jerusalem Ministry 19:28-21:38.	
	The Passion Narrative 14:1-15:47.	The Passion Narrative 26:1-27:66.	The Passion Narrative 22:1-23:56.	
	The Resurrection Narrative 16:1-8 (16:9-20 later addition).	The Resurrection Narrative 28:1-20.	The Resurrection Narrative 24:1-53.	

Theological Slant and Concerns			
...a Gospel in a hurry. Not familiar with Palestinian geography. Use of Latinisms.	...Writes in good Greek but also manifests Aramaic and Semitic influences. More interested in teaching than actions. Contrived approach.	...of psychological insights.	...technical vocabulary. Develops themes, eg. truth, light, life, glory, worker, rather than give series of events. Many discourses.
Jesus seen as a suffering Messiah.	Jesus seen as the Teacher, the new Moses, the Law-giver, the Messiah-King.	Jesus seen as a prophet, the savior of the oppressed.	Jesus seen as the Incarnate Word, the Son of Man, the Light of the World. The Way, the Truth, the Life.
Passion and Resurrection is the key to understanding Jesus.	Frequent use of scripture and its fulfilment.	Parallels Jesus' ministry with Church in Ac.	Emphasizes community.
Uses geography with a message.	Jesus has come to fulfil the Law, not destroy it.	Has concern for the Gentiles and marginalized people.	Sacramental approach of signs and symbols used.
Gives a very human portrait of Jesus and the disciples.	Scribes and Pharisees are strongly criticized.	Prominence given to the Holy Spirit, prayer and messianic joy.	'Eternal life' possible for believers here and now.
	Highlights 'Church' and Peter's role.	Emphasizes proper stewardship of wealth.	A theological Gospel that shows period of reflection on Jesus' message.
	Galilee important for Jesus' ministry and after Resurrection is gateway to the world.	Greater prominence given to women than other evangelists.	
		A Gospel of compassion/mercy (or Great Pardons) and universal salvation.	

CHAPTER 4

▼

A PORTRAIT
OF JESUS

Most of us have had the experience of meeting someone who has suffered a severe illness which has physically changed that person. We invariably make comparisons between the way that person is now to the way we used to know him or her. We find it difficult to accept the changed appearance and prefer to retain and cherish the previous, healthy image we had. How often too we hear people say that they dread seeing their parents or friends when an illness or old age has changed them too drastically, because they want to remember them enjoying good health. In other words, they have an image of their parents or friends that appeals to them and they want to preserve that comforting picture.

In a similar vein we can say we all have an image of Jesus. People have a preferred image of Jesus which they unconsciously call to mind whenever they pray or think of him. They might prefer a certain image simply because they grew up with a large picture of Jesus portrayed like that in their bedroom or at school; or because the kind of piety practiced suggested a certain image. Hymns such as *Christ is King of Earth*, *All Glory, Laud and Honour/To Thee, Redeemer King*, and *Thee, O Christ, the Prince of Ages* suggest an image of Christ quite different to that implied in *The Lord's My Shepherd* or *Amazing Grace*. The time comes, however, when one must ask the questions: is my understanding of, and relationship with Jesus dominated and even disadvantaged by a particular image of Jesus? am I aware of other images of Jesus? which of these images reflect aspects of Jesus as found in the Gospels? which do not?

IMAGES OF JESUS

Our image of Jesus is a private one. Other people such as artists and producers have publicly expressed their image of Jesus through the medium of films, musicals or paintings. One thinks for example of films such as *King of Kings*, *The Robe*, *The Greatest Story Ever Told*, where Jesus is portrayed in Hollywood style as some kind of person completely different from ordinary humans. Even in Zeffirelli's *Jesus of Nazareth*—although an

The Miracle of Lazarus. Detail from Sarcophagus Front, c. 290 A.D., Rome.

attempt is made to emphasize the humanity of Jesus (reflected too in the choice of title)— the long hard stares, the significant glances and the good looks of the actor playing Jesus, suggest a superman behind the toga and beard. On the other hand, a film like Pasolini's *The Gospel According to Matthew* portrays Jesus, Mary and Joseph as very average Jews of those times and seeks at every turn to demythologize the Gospel accounts of the miraculous. The actors are not cast in the glamorous Hollywood style, but are ordinary, everyday people. Jesus as a man among men is the image that strikes us. However, too much emphasis on the humanity of Jesus sometimes provokes protests as it did with Scorsese's *The Last Temptation of Christ*. Other instances where the ordinariness and humanity of Jesus come through would be the TV productions *The Son of Man*, *The Passover Plot*, and Jackman's novel, *The Davidson Affair*.

The musicals *Jesus Christ Superstar* and *Godspell* were both great box-office successes. Both these musicals sought out novel ways in which the Gospel story could be presented. Rather than attempting to give a complete theological statement as to who Jesus is, these musicals emphasize some aspects of the Gospel or personality of Jesus that might have been forgotten or neglected—or simply the preferred image of the producer. *Godspell*, for example, conveys an infectious joy about the Gospel message that is often strikingly absent in both our theory and practice of Christianity.

Art is another form of expression that has portrayed Jesus in various ways. One of the earliest portrayals is a wall fresco in the Sacrament Chapel of the Catacombs of San Callistus, Rome, which portrays Jesus as a humble rustic raising Lazarus from the dead. Another presentation from earliest times is that of Jesus the Good Shepherd, the one who looked after the faithful and promised everlasting life. The shepherd image was ideal in many respects since it accurately reflected the close ties between the congregation and the presbyter-shepherd. It is an image that is also faithful to the Gospels. One could say that these early images of Jesus performing miracles or as the Good Shepherd are images of the historical Jesus, i.e. Jesus as experienced in the Gospel stories that were handed down.

After this period, from the fourth century onwards, typological art is frequently used in portraying Jesus. By this term we mean artistic formulas or types. There was the type of the Roman or Byzantine emperor which could be used to show rank, dignity or power. The brilliant mosaics of San Vitale, Ravenna and later of the Cathedral of Monreale, Sicily, show Jesus the Pantocrator, Jesus the Ruler of the Universe, i.e. the Risen Christ as the powerful Emperor—grave, noble and majestic, with the imperial insignia and garments. Later on, under the influence of the feudal king type, Jesus is often portrayed with medieval crown, seated on a throne. The King, before whom one bowed and pledged fealty. Again the image is that of majesty and power.

Another variation of this typological art during the Middle Ages and Renaissance was that of Christ as Judge at the Second Coming. One thinks of Michelangelo's *Last Judgment* on the Sistine Chapel's ceiling as the typical example of this—Christ coming to judge everyone, with either paradise or eternal damnation awaiting all. It clearly reveals an age when faith was riddled with fear.

Another common image was that of Jesus as the suffering Savior. Much attention was given to the instruments of the scourging and crowning with thorns, the physical aspects of the crucifixion and the actual pain suffered. One thinks of Reni's *Head of Christ* (1640, Paris, Louvre), Grunewald's *Christ on the Cross* (1515, Colmar) or Cimabue's *Crucifixion* (13th Century, S. Domenico, Arezzo).

In more recent times we have an image that Elsen refers to as the "Faceless Christ". This era is illustrated by Matisse's *Ave* and *le Chemin de la Croix* (1951, Convent Chapel, Vence, France). In these two murals Matisse shows the Virgin and Child and the Stations of the Cross, without however filling in the facial features. Each viewer is meant to provide his/her own image of Jesus and Mary. Matisse turned to a symbolic rendering of popular themes and thus avoided simply repeating conventions and types from his predecessors. The challenge thrown out to us, the viewers, is to provide our own image of Jesus.

The above refers to classical art if you like. On the level of popular art

Christ Pantocrator. Mural. 12th century. Church of Panagia Tou Arakou, Lagoudera Monastery, Cyprus.

Raphael: *The Alba Madonna* (detail). 1510. Andrew Mellon Collection, National Gallery of Art, Washington.

The Good Shepherd. 6th century. Museo Cristiano Lateranese, Rome.

Jose Clemente Orozco: *Christ and His Cross*. 20th century, Mexico. Baker Library, Dartmouth College, New Hampshire.

Jesus is often portrayed as effeminate and saccharine—one thinks of innumerable holy cards or plastic statues; or as a modern businessman in suit and tie as on some revivalist posters. It is particularly on the level of this kind of popular art that people should be encouraged to be critical of the images of Jesus being portrayed, and to assess whether or not these images have any relationship to the Gospel or tradition.

EXERCISE 53:   Write down your favorite image of Jesus.
Do you know how you came to settle on this image?
What incidents in the Gospels give validity to your image of Jesus?

WHAT DOES WORLD HISTORY SAY ABOUT JESUS?

The search for the true Jesus has been pursued by scholars especially since the nineteenth century. The distinction is made between the historical Jesus and the Christ of faith. Underlying this distinction is, on one hand, an understanding of the Gospels as faith documents and not biographies of Jesus as was discussed in Chapter 2, and on the other, a supposition that there is historical knowledge in the sense of objective factual knowledge concerning the earthly Jesus. For a moment let us set aside these faith documents (Gospels) and examine references to Jesus in other documents.

Jesus in Extra-biblical Sources:

If we disregard the New Testament for a moment and consider world history as such, what is the evidence about Jesus? There is in fact very little mention of Jesus.

As we have seen in Chapter 1, the Latin writer Seutonius, who wrote about 120 A.D., mentions Christ while writing about Emperor Claudius and the expulsion of Jews from Rome in 49 A.D.: "He expelled the Jews from Rome, on account of the riots in which they were constantly indulging, at the instigation of Chrestus". "Chrestus" is believed to have been an incorrect reference to "Christus". The Christians at this early time of their emergence in history were still thought to be a sect of Judaism.

Another Roman writer, Tacitus, writing about 115 A.D., mentions the name of Christ. He does this in his annals when chronicling Nero's attempt to blame the Christians for the burning of Rome in 64 A.D. He says, referring to Christians:

> They got their name from Christ, who was executed by sentence of the procurator Pontius Pilate in the reign of Tiberius. That checked the pernicious superstition for a short time, but it broke out afresh—not only in Judaea, where the plague first arose, but in Rome itself, where all the horrible and shameful things in the world collect and find a home.

Pliny the Younger in a letter written about 111 A.D. refers to Christ. Pliny was appointed legate to the Roman province of Bithynia (Asia Minor) and wrote to Emperor Trajan on how he dealt with Christians. He demanded that they recant by "cursing Christ" and offering worship to the Emperor. He recalled too how Christians sang hymns to "Christ as God".

Another source of information is the famous Jewish historian Josephus. He wrote the *Antiquities* and twice refers to Jesus. In book 20, he speaks of the death of James, the leader of the Jerusalem Church, as a brother "of Jesus the so-called Christ" (*Antiquities*, Book 20, Ch. IX, par. 1). The second reference comes from Book 18:

> Now, there was about this time, Jesus, a wise man, if it be lawful to call him a man, for he was a doer of wonderful works, a teacher of such men as receive the truth with pleasure. He drew over to him both many of the Jews, and many of the Gentiles. He was the Christ and when Pilate, at the suggestion of the principal men amongst us, had condemned him to the cross, those that loved him at the first did not forsake him; for he appeared to them alive again at the third day; as the divine prophets had foretold these and ten thousand other wonderful things concerning him. And the tribe of Christians, so named from him, are not extinct at this day. (Ch. III, para. 3)

This is a most complimentary reference to Jesus and Christians, especially so if we recall that Josephus had deserted his countrymen in the 63–73 A.D. revolt and joined the Roman forces and that the reference in book 20 to "Jesus the so-called Christ" is perjorative. These considerations have led scholars to the opinion that the passage in Book 18 has been favorably edited by Christian writers. It certainly reads like a witness to Christian faith. Note the sentence: "He was the Christ".

The conclusion we are forced to draw from the above is that very little about Jesus can be gleaned from extra-biblical sources. This is not as surprising as it may sound, since we have very little information about any individuals who lived in the first century A.D. The interest in a religious leader such as Jesus would naturally have been centered in his followers. Hence we turn at this stage to the Gospel portraits of Jesus, bearing in mind that they are not historical biographies of Jesus, but faith accounts of his life and death (cf. Chapter 2).

Historical Facts About Jesus in the Gospels

The historical facts about Jesus which we can glean from the Gospels are not many. No mention is made of his appearance or stature and very little biographical detail is given.

It is known he was crucified in or outside Jerusalem at the time of the Jewish Passover, about 30 A.D. He lived and preached throughout Galilee and Judea. He had a small group of followers and often associated with tax collectors and sinners. He antagonized the religious leaders of his day to the point where they were prepared to do away with him. Mary was his mother and Joseph his putative father but very little is known about his birth.

The exact date of his birth is not even certain. According to Matthew and Luke he was born in the days of Herod and of the Emperor Augustus (cf. Mt 2: 1; Lk 1: 5; 2: 1). Herod ruled from 37–4 B.C., hence Jesus was not born in 1 A.D. It was probably about 6 to 7 B.C. The mistake in the calculations of the Christian era, which should have started with the birth of Jesus, was made by a Scythian monk, Dionysius Exiguus, in 525 A.D., and the error has been with us ever since.

Jesus grew up in the Galilean village of Nazareth. He was born in Bethlehem according to Matthew and Luke.

JESUS AS SEEN IN THE GOSPEL ACCOUNTS

We now turn to the Gospel accounts as faith documents of a believing community, i.e. documents about what Jesus did and taught for our salvation as recounted and interpreted by believers.

In order to build up our image of who Jesus was, we will consider in turn what Jesus says, what others say of him and then what he does—his words and actions and how others perceived him.

What Did He Say?
KINGDOM PREACHING

From reading the Gospels it is obvious that the Kingdom theme is central to Jesus' deeds, words and prayers and hence a key to understanding him and his mission.

Before considering what the Gospels say about the Kingdom, it is useful to sketch the Old Testament background to this concept. The idea of kingship or lordship is not foreign to the Jewish world of the Old Testament and is thought to have originated during the period of the wandering in the desert (Ex 15: 11–13, 18), inspired by Israel's notion of herself as the Chosen People. Further to this the kingship of Yahweh was constantly experienced in the historical action of God in Israel's life.

David, when he was made king, was conscious that his kingship was instituted by Yahweh. The judge, Gideon, realized that ultimately not he, nor his son, but Yahweh must rule over the Israelites (Jg 8: 23). Yahweh's Kingdom was not however tied to Jerusalem or the temple: "All the earth is filled with his glory" (Is 6: 3), and as Isaiah declared, eventually all nations will bow before Yahweh (Is 25: 6–8; 56: 7; 60; 66: 19–21).

In later Judaism, as we have seen, a very nationalistic understanding of the Kingdom developed. In reaction to this tendency a totally different kind of thinking arose which expressed itself in what is known as apocalyptic literature (Greek *apocalyptikos* = revelation). This literature envisaged the heavenly Kingdom as arriving through God's intervention and preceded by calamitous signs such as earthquakes, plagues, stars falling from the skies and general confusion resulting from the fall of rulers and princes. The expectations of the Kingdom were described in terms of elaborate and imaginative visions of a future paradise. The Book of Daniel with its unusual imagery is typical of apocalyptic literature (cf. Dn 7: 9–12).

The link between messianism and kingship was emphasized in Chapter 1, but it is worth recalling that the concept of the Kingdom of God would have elicited a whole history of ideas and emotions among Jesus' audiences. Ideas of setting up a political kingdom were still very much alive and fanned by the Zealots. Longings for a Messiah or prophet to lead them out of Roman clutches are evident in the Gospels.

Jesus himself, at Capernaum, refers to his mission in terms of Isaiah 61: 1–2. In contrast to the Zealots, the Essenes expected God to intervene and overthrow the sons of darkness in a cosmic battle and give victory to the sons of light. As we read the Gospels we constantly see how Jesus had to correct and refine the expectations of his audiences and disciples as to the true nature of the Kingdom he was proclaiming.

The expression "Kingdom of God" *basileia tou theou* is a common one in the Gospels, although Matthew sometimes uses the expression "Kingdom of heaven". By so doing Matthew avoids the use of God's name in accordance with Jewish custom, bearing in mind he was writing for a Jewish Christian community. The two terms, "Kingdom of God" and "Kingdom of heaven" can be taken as synonymous. Some scholars have suggested the expression *basileia tou theou* might be better translated as the "reign of God" to avoid the impression that the Kingdom is a material, physical entity with identifiable boundaries such as the Roman Empire. On the positive side, the expression "reign of God" helps us to see the Kingdom as the divine redemptive presence which is active in our midst through the power of the Holy Spirit. It is something dynamic and active. It is God reconciling, renewing, healing and liberating through Jesus Christ.

What exactly did Jesus say about the Kingdom? He said a number of things which, if taken together, give us some kind of initial idea of the Kingdom. He taught that the Kingdom of God is imminent, at hand; that it comes down by divine intervention; it is not the result of human effort; it is a gift from the Father; a reward for faithful followers; one must enter this Kingdom with more virtues than the Scribes; tax collectors and prostitutes will enter it before the chief priests; it will be taken away from those to whom it was offered and given to others who will bear its fruit; trials and sufferings will show who is worthy of the Kingdom; the keys of the Kingdom were given to Peter.

Besides these short statements the concept of Kingdom is further developed and explained by the frequent use of parables. Furthermore, the miracles and acts of compassion are a sign of the Kingdom which has arrived in an incipient way. In this respect McBrien's definition of the Kingdom is most apt:

> *The redemptive presence of God actualized through the power of God's reconciling Spirit.*
> 1980: 1102

Hahn in his book, *The Worship of the Early Church*, makes a distinctive and valuable contribution to our understanding of Kingdom. His perspective is that of worship in the New Testament and Early Church. By worship he firstly means the service of God to the community, and then secondarily, the service of the community before God. This is fundamental to his approach. He speaks of the salvific action of God through Jesus as irrupting into this world. Jesus challenges a number of the religious assumptions of the day. The cult of the Old Testament with its sacred precincts, its ritual regulations and its sacrificial system is overturned. Worship is no longer cultic in nature. Worship will no longer need to take place in a separate realm but in the midst of the existing world. In this perspective the Kingdom means that the proclamation of the word, baptism, and the Lord's Supper are brought to people and thus take the form of service to humankind. In a way, this endorses the definition of McBrien quoted above.

A number of problems arise from what is stated in the Gospels about the Kingdom. On the one hand the Kingdom is said to be "at hand" (Mk 1: 15), "in your midst" (Lk 17: 21), and on the other hand it appears also to be an eschatological event: "I assure you" says Jesus, "among those standing here, there are some who will not taste death until they see the reign of God established in power" (Mk 9: 1). Before we try to solve the problem, a word about the word "eschatological".

The Greek word *eschata* (from singular *eschaton*) means "the last things", i.e. ultimately God, but we would say, the end of life, death, judgment, etc. Scholastic theology spoke about the four last things as being death, judgment, heaven and hell. In general though, an eschatological event is one pertaining to the things at the end of time which are thus definitive events; nothing more will happen after them; the final state of things will have arrived.

The question of whether the Kingdom is at hand or is a future eschatological event has elicited different opinions among scholars. We can briefly identify four different eschatologies:

Consequent Eschatology (also called consistent, futurist, or thorough-going):

This focuses on the Kingdom as a future event which will arrive as a result of God's intervention. The Kingdom is seen as wholly other, as completely the work of God. Among its advocates must be mentioned A. Schweitzer, J. Weiss, M. Werner, A. Ritschl.

Realized Eschatology:

Proposed by C. Dodd, and focused on the past, this opinion sees the Kingdom as having already arrived in Jesus. All we need now are the ethical teachings of Jesus to enable us to reach the Kingdom.

Existential Eschatology:

Here the emphasis is on the present. For those who respond to the Word of God in the daily challenges of their lives, the Kingdom is a present opportunity and reality. Emphasis is placed on the individual decisions made moment by moment either for or against the Kingdom. R. Bultmann is the theologian most closely associated with this eschatology.

Salvation-History Eschatology:

The mainstream of Catholic theologians such as K. Rahner, E. Schillebeeckx, J. Metz, as well as Protestants such as O. Culmann, J. Jeremias and R. Schnackenburg support this understanding of echatology. Here the Kingdom concerns the past, present and future. The history of salvation has a timeline according to which salvation begins in the past, continues through the present and will have a climax in the future eschatological event. The Kingdom which naturally includes salvation, began in an incipient way in the past, grows through the present and achieves its fullness and perfection at the Second Coming.

(Another kind of eschatology called proleptic is sometimes identified. Encouraged by J. Moltmann, author of *Theology of Hope*, it is within the broad boundaries of Salvation-History Eschatology, but emphasizes how hope in the future eschatological event colors our present theology and understanding of the Kingdom.)

EXERCISE 54: What do these references say about the Kingdom in relation to time?

Mk 1: 15	Lk 12: 35–40
Jn 3: 16	Mt 25: 1–13
Jn 5: 24	Mt 25: 31–46

The expression "Kingdom of God" has received many interpretations over the Christian centuries. Origen thought Jesus himself was the Kingdom—which in fact seems supported by comparing Mk 9: 1 with the parallel text in Mt 16: 28, where "before they see the Kingdom of God come with power" becomes "before they see the Son of Man coming in his Kingdom". The early Christians certainly expected the Second Coming of Jesus. It would seem their hopes for the coming Kingdom of God received a focus in the person of Jesus.

In the West the growing Church became more and more identified

Christ in Majesty, c. 1215, Biblioteca Apostolica Vaticana.

with the Kingdom of God. Augustine said as much. Later on under the Franks political power became seen as part of the Kingdom of God. Charlemagne was the New David, and the Pope was Moses holding his arms up in prayer. Boniface VIII however made it clear that political power could not be equated with the Kingdom and at the same time he claimed absolute power over all spiritual and temporal matters.

For others, like Francis of Assisi, the Kingdom was very much of the spirit as also for the great mystics like Meister Eckhart, who saw the Kingdom as God himself (sic!) with all his riches in the depth of the soul. For Luther, God's Kingdom was invisible and spiritual—the reign of the Spirit. However in spite of these valuable insights the domination of the institutional Church over Kingdom in many respects continued into this century. Loisy could say with great conviction and obvious disappointment in 1902 "Jesus proclaimed the Kingdom of God, and what came was the Church" (1902: 111). The relationship between the two obviously needed to be worked out further.

Although there is a close association between the Church and the Kingdom—Peter was given the keys of the Kingdom (Mt 16: 18)—one cannot simply identify them. The Kingdom is more than the Church. The Church is directed towards and belongs to the Kingdom. It is a herald and an anticipatory sign of the Kingdom. "The Church has a single intention: that God's kingdom may come" (*Lumen Gentium,* art. 45).

The Kingdom itself, in the days of Jesus, conjured up a host of ideas and dreams for the Jews. Tied up with the concept of Messiah-king, it signified the fulfilment of many different desires and dreams. Today this aspect has been reinterpreted by Perrin in his book *Jesus and the Language of the Kingdom.* He suggests Kingdom is a symbol rather than a sign or concept. Kingdom can be symbolic of people's dreams for life, their hopes and fears. Every time we feel the call to become "more", to grow, to be liberated, we implicitly long for the Kingdom. In the New Testament these longings, individual and collective, converge on Jesus who becomes a symbol of the Kingdom. Today is no different. We experience longings and hopes, desires for more freedom, for liberation from various kinds of oppression, from sinfulness in all its manifestations—and these desires and hopes will find their fulfilment in Jesus, who symbolizes the fullness of the Kingdom.

The Kingdom is thus a complex sign or symbol which occupied a central place in Jesus' preaching. Closely associated with the proclamation of the Kingdom was the call to enter it, which we will discuss now.

EXERCISE 55: What was your understanding of "Kingdom" as a child? How has it changed? What caused it to change?
How do you see the meaning of "Kingdom" today?
What do you consider as signs of the Kingdom in your daily life?

CALL TO DISCIPLESHIP

It becomes clear in the Gospels that there was around Jesus a very intimate group of disciples as well as a wider circle. The small group certainly seem to see in him the possibility of their dreams and longings, as mentioned above, being fulfilled. Their expectations of Jesus, therefore, had to be refined continually. It was not really until after the Resurrection that they understood how different the Kingdom was. During Jesus' life these disciples are seen as co-workers of Jesus, proclaiming the rule of God, healing the sick and driving out devils (cf. Mk 6: 7–13; Lk 10: 2–12).

The pathway of discipleship invariably starts with a call. In most accounts the story is presented in a stereotype form as follows:

a) Jesus passes by;   )
b) he sees somebody;   )   The
c) a more detailed account is given of the person's   )   Literary
    occupation;   )   Construction
d) the call comes, "follow Me';   )   of the Call
e) the person leaves all;   )   to Discipleship.
f) the person "goes after" Jesus, or is "with him"   )
    or "follows him".   )

Note that this literary construction has its parallels:
the Old Testament accounts of the call of Elisha (1 K 19: 19–21)
Amos (7: 15), Abraham (Gn 12), and David (1 S 16: 17–21). (Read Mk 1: 16–21; Lk 5: 1–11 and Jn 1: 35–51.)

An important distinction is to be made between the kind of discipleship prevalent at the time, and discipleship with Jesus. It was common practice in the Greco-Roman world of Jesus' time for people to choose their teacher according to good reports or interests. Frequently the person would literally sit at the feet of the master and learn until there was nothing more to learn from that particular teacher and then move on in search of another.

Plato we know became a "disciple" of Socrates when twenty years or younger. When Aristotle was seventeen, he went to Athens to study and became a disciple of Plato. Even today when students are thinking in terms of higher study, they sometimes choose a university or faculty or particular person from whom they think they can learn much.

Christian discipleship however is different. In each case in the Gospel the Master calls the disciples; they do not choose him but respond to a call. Secondly the disciple is never in a position to move on, having learned all. The Christian disciple never graduates.

The disciple is thus called to learn from Jesus without ever exhausting the source of that learning.

The call entails a rupture, as with the call of Abraham to give up everything in Haran. Elisha too slaughtered his oxen and ate them with his workers; he even used the plow to cook them on—thus destroying his former life. The disciples in the New Testament "dropped their nets" or "left everything". The model is thus one of *Metanoia*, becoming like a child, which is necessary for entering the Kingdom.

The call is a matter of life and death. Jesus said, "Let the dead bury their dead" in reply to one of his disciples who wanted to bury his father first (Mt 8: 19–22, Lk 9: 57–60). "Dead buriers of the dead" are people in this case who do not at once get themselves involved with Jesus' message of the Kingdom and its summons. The obligation to bury the dead was one of the most solemn of Judaism, so in releasing people from this obligation Jesus is saying that his is the call of the eschatological prophet announcing the Kingdom of God. The call requires total commitment, the burning of one's boats for the Kingdom.

The idea of discipleship includes mission and service. In the Gospels it is clear that disciples are co-workers of Jesus. The relationship with Jesus as disciples is sealed by a share in his mission. ". . . I commissioned you to go out and to bear fruit" (Jn 15: 16). The commissioning is further described in Lk 9, which gives an account of the disciples' first mission, enumerates the conditions of following Jesus (self-renunciation, "losing one's life", not being ashamed of Jesus), and warns finally against feelings of self-importance.

EXERCISE 56:  When do Christians receive their call to discipleship? In what ways can the Christian life be said to entail a break/rupture with society? Is there any distinction made in the call to discipleship between men and women in the Gospels?

EXERCISE 57: Being a disciple includes the idea of mission and service. How do you see your own "mission" in today's world? What service do you render?
Do you feel satisfied with the way you are responding to your "mission" and call to service?

PARABLES

Much of Jesus' teaching and preaching about the Kingdom was done through parables. As the Gospels have come down to us, parables constitute about a third of their total content. It is thus necessary to study them closely in order to gain a deeper understanding of Jesus' message.

The parable is basically a story, but a special kind of story in the same way that myths, satires, and sagas are. In other words, the parable is a literary form that must be understood as such. The origins of the parable can be traced back to the Hebrew word *mashal*, derived from the verb meaning "be like". *Mashal* was a broad term used really for any verbal image from a figurative saying or a proverb to a long involved parable or apocalyptic prediction. In Greek the word *parable* was used to translate the Hebrew *mashal*, and although the word changed, the basic Old Testament connotations remained. Thus in the New Testament proverbs like "Physician heal thyself" and sayings like "The things which come out of a man are what defile him" are called parables equally with the Talents. O'Hagan and Crowe define them thus:

> . . . *parables are images or stories in which Jesus illustrates some point of His message by a concrete or typical case. (1973: 54)*

As a parable is a literary form, we can expect to find certain characteristics. These are rules or strategies of a literary nature that identify a particular literary form and contribute to its success. In parables there are four important such characteristics:

Repetition

This technique always helps to imprint the story on the minds of the audience. In the parable of the Vineyard Laborers (Mt 20: 1–16) for example, note the repetition of the word "vineyard" and the expression "he sent them into his vineyard" or similar expressions. In the Talents (Mt 25: 14–30) there is repetition of the formula "sir, you entrusted me with . . . talents; here are . . . more I have made" and the master's reply: "Well done good and faithful servant; you have shown you can be faithful in small things. I will trust you with greater; come and join in your master's happiness." In The Unforgiving Debtor (Mt 18: 23–35), the theme of compassion for others is stressed by the frequent repetition of expressions such as "feeling sorry", "being distressed" or "having pity on".

Contrast

When opposites and contrasts are used they help to throw elements of a story into sharp relief. In Dives and Lazarus (Lk 16: 19–31) the contrast between rich/poor, well-fed/starving, Abraham's bosom/Hades is strikingly evident. Or in Mt 25: 31–46, the Last Judgment scene, there are many examples: sheep/goats, on right hand/on left hand, Come you whom my Father has blessed/Go away from me with your curse upon you, the Kingdom/eternal fire etc. In the short Parable of the Lamp (Mk 4: 21–23) we have another clear example of this technique: on the lamp-stand/under the bed, hidden/disclosed, kept secret/brought to light.

The Folkloric Threesome

Storytellers throughout the ages have discovered and preserved the importance of three in a tale, be it three characters or three incidents or events. In children's literature, this folkloric threesome is found in the stories of the Three Little Hens, Three Blind Mice, Goldilocks and The Three Bears, Little Red Riding Hood and in Cinderella (three sisters). Jokes, too, often rely on three characters. One thinks of the number that begin: There was an Englishman, an Irishman and a Scotsman . . .

It is not surprising then that parables make use of this technique. In the Talents (Mt 25: 14–30) the man has three servants to whom he gives five, two and one talent respectively. Matthew (21: 33–43) in The Wicked Husbandmen has two groups of servants and then the son coming to collect the produce from the tenants on behalf of the landowner. In the Lost Sheep (Lk 15: 3–7) the ninety-nine, the lost one, and the shepherd make three groups.

The Rule of End Stress

There is often some emphasis, climax or concentration of attention directed to the last character in the series. In Matthew's Wicked Husbandmen, the climax comes with the third attempt to collect the produce from the tenants. In the Talents, the third servant is rebuked.

EXERCISE 58: Examine the following parables and taking one at a time identify the four characteristics of a parable mentioned above.
1. Sower (Mt 13: 4–9)
2. Good Samaritan (Lk 10: 29–37)
3. The Pounds (Lk 19: 12–27)
4. Ten Bridesmaids (Mt 25: 1–13)

Being able to recognize a parable and its literary characteristics is, however, not sufficient. The meaning and nature of a parable must be explored. This interpretative problem has exercised the minds and imagination of scholars for centuries and continues today. A very popular way of interpreting

(N o B)

parables in the past was to see them as allegories, i.e. stories where each item in the narration was important and had special significance. Great ingenuity was employed in finding meaning for each detail in the account. Tertullian (160–220 A.D.) has a typical example of such elaborate allegorizing in his exposition of the Prodigal Son:

> *The Elder Son in the story is the Jew; the Younger the Christian. The patrimony of which the Younger claimed his share is that knowledge of God which a man has by his birthright. The citizen in the far country to whom he hired himself is the devil. The robe bestowed on the returning prodigal is that sonship which Adam lost at the Fall; the ring is the sign and seal of baptism; the feast is the Lord's Supper. And who is "the fatted calf", slain for the feast, but the Savior himself? (Hunter, 1960: 24)*

In a similar vein the parable of the Good Samaritan became an allegory. The man who was attacked was interpreted as being Adam. The brigands were the devil. The Priest and Levite stood for the Law and the Prophets who left mankind (sic!) unaided until the coming of Christ (Good Samaritan). Fallen "man" was subsequently carried to the Church (inn) for his wounds to be healed by the sacraments (oil and wine).

However this way of interpreting the parables was challenged and rejected by Adolf Jülicher and others by the end of the last century. The view today is that many items in the parables are there merely to make the story interesting or more vivid. As a rule the parable presents one or two main points of comparison. The lesson of the parable must be sought in the very specific terms of Jesus' own historical situation and eschatological message. Secondly where the parable concerns a course of action to be taken, we must pass a judgment on the situation depicted. Who was the neighbor to the man who fell among thieves? (Lk 10: 36) Which of the two sons obeyed his father? (Mt 21: 31) Having passed judgment we ourselves are often encouraged to "go and do likewise".

A parable then is designed to make people use their intelligence and imagination and by so doing serve as a spur to spiritual perception and a practical response. Jesus used parables in his preaching to sharpen our understanding and present truth in a vivid and memorable way.

Grouping Parables

Given that the parables are concerned with the theme of Kingdom, attempts have been made to group them accordingly. Thus one could speak of parables concerned with the arrival of the Kingdom, e.g. the Strong Man (Mk 3: 23–27) and the Bridegroom (Mk 2: 18–20); The Growth of the Kingdom, e.g. the Mustard Seed (Mk 4: 30–31), Leaven (Lk 13: 20), Seed (Mk 4: 26–29) and the Sower (Mk 4: 3–8); Good and Evil within the

Kingdom, e.g. the Dragnet (Mt 13: 47) and the Tares (Mt 13: 24–30); or Values operating in the Kingdom, e.g. compassion and love for the poor and lowly in such parables as the Prodigal Son (Lk 15: 11–32), the Lost Sheep (Lk 15: 4–7), the Lost Coin (Lk 15: 8–10) and the Great Banquet (Lk 14: 16–24).

Another way of grouping the parables is that proposed by Crossan. He speaks of parables of Advent, Reversal and Action. They can briefly be described as follows:

(1) *Parables of Advent*: those which develop the theme of the new time and new history for people who are prepared to look and search. These deal with hiddenness and mystery, gift and surprise, discovery and joy, e.g. the Fig Tree, Parable of the Yeast, Sower, the Mustard Seed, the Lost Sheep and the Lost Coin.

(2) *Parables of Reversal*: those in which conventional expectations are toppled or traditional worldviews turned upside down by a sudden new insight or illumination. In the Good Samaritan the conventional expectation was that a Samaritan would not help a Jew, given their history of mutual hatred, and that a Priest or Levite would help the needy. In this parable, however, it is the Samaritan who does help the Jew and the Priest and Levite who do not. Similar reversals are seen in the Rich Man and Lazarus, the Pharisee and Publican, the Wedding Guest, the Prodigal Son, Laborers in the Vineyard and the Wedding Feast.

(3) *Parables of Action*: those which depict crucial or critical situations which demand a prompt decision and firm and resolute action. In some cases the decision is taken, in others not, and in still others the protagonist (main character) succeeds or succumbs under the pressure of the crisis. Examples of these parables are: the Inopportune Friend, the Unscrupulous Judge, the Seed growing by itself, the Burglar, the Darnel, the Tower-builder, Warring Kings, the Rich Fool, the Ten Bridesmaids, the Wicked Husbandmen, the Conscientious Steward, the Unforgiving Debtor, the Crafty Steward etc.

EXERCISE 59: Name three of your favorite parables. Why do you like them? What do you see as the meaning of the stories? In what way does each challenge you to respond in your daily life?

EXERCISE 60: Rather than using Crossan's categories for grouping parables, group them according to parables of (1) growth, (2) celebration and feasting, (3) relationships, and (4) violence. Use the table of parables on pp. 143–145. What difference would this make to your insights into the Gospels? To whom in society would such groupings appeal? Why?

Suggested Method for Interpreting Parables

When one is faced with the problem of analyzing and interpreting a parable in some depth for the first time, it is useful to have a method. The following is suggested as a practical aid.

1. Write down the story in simple language and as far as possible, in its non-allegorical form (e.g. in the Sower (Mk 4: 1–9) verses 13–20 do not form part of the original parable, as they are allegorical interpretations of the parable).

2. Analyze the parable according to:

   (i) *Exegesis.* Go to any standard biblical commentary and read the comments relevant to the parable.

   (ii) *Literary Criticism.* Analyze the story using first of all, the four characteristics of Repetition, Contrast, Folkloric Threesome and End Stress mentioned above. Next consider the structure of the story and its plot. What constitutes the introduction to the story? What events occur that help develop the plot? Where is the turning point in the story? Is there a resolution to the story? Who is the protagonist?

   (iii) *Other disciplines.* Do any other disciplines such as history, archeology, psychology etc. help us to deepen our understanding of the parable. Biblical dictionaries and commentaries are two sources that could assist in filling in the background. A knowledge of the historical facts about the origin of Samaritans and the history of their relationship with the Jews will give a greater appreciation of the impact that the parable of the Good Samaritan must have made on the original audience.

   Much research is being done nowadays on the psychological interpretation of parables. This marks a new and original insight. Examples of how this discipline has been applied to the parables will be given below.

3. Interpret the parable. Come back to the original story and attempt to articulate its meaning in terms of the Kingdom in one or two sentences.

APPLICATION OF METHOD TO THE PRODIGAL SON (Lk 15: 11–32)

Let us now take the parable of the Prodigal Son and analyze it according to the method we have proposed. Without attempting to be exhaustive, the analysis would look something like this:

The Story

The story is about a son who leaves his father and then falls on evil times, realizes his mistake and comes back to his father asking forgiveness, which he obtains. The elder son is not able to see the reason why the younger son should be thus treated.

The Analysis

(i) Exegesis

Consultation of a standard biblical commentary revealed that:

- In Chapter 15 of Luke we have the grouping of a number of parables dealing with mercy or compassion. There is the parable of the Lost Sheep, and the Lost Coin. The Prodigal Son could be called the Lost Son, as indeed he is in some translations. The impact of the Prodigal Son is thus strengthened when taken in the context of Chapter 15 as a whole.
- there is a refrain of "what was lost is found" which binds the whole of Chapter 15 together (cf. vv. 7, 10, 24, 32);
- the younger son claimed "my share". It was an accepted practice that a father could abdicate before death and divide his wealth;
- the sins of the younger son are identified most clearly as unrestrained sensuality and spendthrift extravagance (v. 30);
- the pigs ate the fruit of the carob tree (pods), but the younger son was too disgusted to eat with the pigs and no one gave him anything else;
- the expression "I will return" is reminiscent of Ho 2: 9: "I will return to my first husband';
- it is the memory of the father's goodness that revives hope and compunction in the younger son;
- the elder son omits the polite address "Father" (unlike the younger son) and refers contemptuously to his brother as "this one".

(ii) Literary Criticism

Repetition often serves as reinforcement of the key ideas. One key phrase is "Father, I have sinned against heaven (God) and against you. I no longer deserve to be called your son", which is first mentioned in vv. 18, 19 and then repeated in v. 21.

Another key idea is that of joy at the younger son's repentance. The word "celebrate" or "celebration" appears in v. 24 (twice), v. 30 and v. 32. With it go the related words "feast" (v. 23), "back to life" (vv. 24, 32), "found" (vv. 24, 32), "music and dancing" (v. 25), "safe and sound" (v. 27), "killed the calf" (vv. 23, 27, 30) and "rejoice" (v. 32).

Contrast is evident throughout the story and some examples have already been alluded to. Perhaps the most striking ones are dead/back to life and lost/found, which occur three times, if we include the "safe and sound" of v. 27. Another contrast is that of hunger/abundance. The younger son being hungry among the pigs contrasts sharply with both the well-fed servants and the feast and fatted calf. The squandering of money and the life of debauchery (v. 13) of the younger son contrasts with the hardworking, obedient, abstemious elder son who never so much as had a party with his friends. The obvious son/servants contrast (vv. 16, 17) helps to emphasize the depth of the younger son's adversity and also to highlight his reinstatement as a son by his father.

Lastly the contrast between all the joyous celebration of the majority and the angry and sulking demeanor of the elder son helps to create in the reader feelings of annoyance at his inability to join in the celebrations.

Folkloric Threesome. There are three main characters: the father and his two sons. The servants as a group do not figure in the story except by reference and the single servant who informs the elder son (v. 27) plays quite a minor role.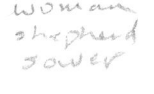

End Stress. If the story ended with v. 24 the conclusion would indeed have the necessary end stress: "this son of mine was dead and has come back to life; he was lost and is found. And they began to celebrate". However the ending of the second part of the story is the father's "all I have is yours" (v. 31) and then a repetition of v. 24. This makes vv. 31, 32 unsatisfactory as the end stress to the whole story because the episode itself is unfinished. We would want to know if the elder son remained angry, went off to a distant country in disgust or whether he was able to "enter into the celebrations".

Structure and Plot. The Prodigal Son as a story is divided into two parts. The first (v. 11–24) forms a discrete part and deals only with the father-younger son relationship although the elder son is mentioned in v. 11. The second part (vv. 25–32) deals with the angry elder son. Both parts end with a parallel statement of celebration and joy at the fact of the younger son having come back.

The two parts of the story have much in common:

(i) both are "in the field(s)";
(ii) the younger son worked hard without much reward on the pig farm; the elder son "slaved" for his father;
(iii) the father went out to meet the younger son "while he was still a long way off"; he also "came out" to plead with the elder son.

Looking at the story as a whole, one notices further how the modes of discourse help to stress the important parts of the story. The introduction, the division of property, the squandering of goods, and famine (vv. 11–16) are all in narrated discourse, whereas the moment of reflection for the younger son among the pigs and the subsequent encounters of both sons with their father are in direct speech.

The main plot of the story is that of a younger son who takes his portion of the family inheritance and makes off to a distant country in search of the good life and maybe fortune. Things go badly for him and he soon finds himself absolutely destitute and hungry. This is the crisis or turning point of the story. He extricates himself from his adversity by deciding to go back to his father's house, where the generous, forgiving welcome his father offers him provides the denouement to the story. The whole episode might have ended there, but for the mention of the two sons in v. 11. Since that reference nothing further is said about the elder son up to v. 24. What we have now is a secondary or sub-plot, which has an unresolved crisis.

The gist of the sub-plot is as follows: the elder son returns from the field, is puzzled by the music and dancing and when he finds out what is happening, he becomes angry at what he sees as his father's unfair treatment of him. The father tries to console him but the story ends with the tension between the father and elder son unresolved.

The question of who the protagonist is raises some problems. One could see the younger son as the protagonist in search of fortune and through his actions being led into relationship problems with his father and brother.

The Return of the Prodigal Son by Murillo.

If one accepts this, and given the fact that he was recklessly wasteful of his inheritance, the title "Prodigal Son" is apt. If however the father is the protagonist, the one who reacts with great generosity and forgiveness to a situation created by his younger son, then a most appropriate title might be "the Prodigal Father" (i.e. "prodigal" in his forgiveness), or simply "the Forgiving Father".

(iii) *Other disciplines*

If we turn to history first of all, we learn that the theme of a younger son leaving home in search of a fortune is well known in Jewish and other folklore. In these tales the elder brother/younger brother relationship is invariably prominent. In the Old Testament the stories of Esau and Jacob as well as Joseph and his brothers are well known. Jacob, we read, had to labor long and hard for his father-in-law and Joseph endured slavery and imprisonment. In both cases, only after this testing do they achieve some kind of prosperity. This prosperity is then revealed to older brothers and the father. It is evident from this that the audience in the time of Jesus would have been familiar with this theme.

Another piece of information which we learn from the history of the Jews is that the division of property was normal practice. Once the younger son had taken his inheritance he had no further claim on the property. The father would have remained in control of the farm and would have consulted the elder son before selling. One notes too that the younger son by becoming a swineherd (an occupation from which Jews were excluded) cuts himself off from membership in the Jewish community—something which further highlights the father's generosity in forgiving him and bringing him "back to life".

Next let us turn to some psychological insights. This story is so rich in its theme of family love and tensions that it readily lends itself to psychological interpretations, as Perkins has shown (1981: 58). In the language of the psychologist Jung, the story could be seen as representing the necessary integration of the shadow side of the personality. Both sons can be seen as negative elements: the younger son represents all tendencies to reckless living—Gentiles, pigs and sexual immorality are symbolic in the Jewish psyche of behavior totally opposed to God; the elder son represents anger and resentment, born of righteousness and dutifulness. All these negative elements must be brought to consciousness in the individual and integrated into the personality. For the younger son, repentance brought about the successful integration of the negative elements in his personality but the elder son's rigid obedience and dutifulness did not allow him to turn his anger and resentment into joy. The elder son's moralism and self-righteousness made him draw back at the sound of the music and dancing and rendered it difficult for him to accept that such a profligate sinner could be put on a par with him—and hence the impossibility for him to join in the celebrations.

In terms of Freudian psychology, the three characters in the story represent three elements of the psyche. The id is the unrestrained, instinctual drives, represented by the younger son; the elder son on the other hand, represents the unrestrained demands of tradition and morality, internalized as superego. The story thus becomes an illustration of the balance required in any healthy adult personality. The ego has to balance instinct and pleasure on the one hand, against duty and societal obligations on the other. In the story the father takes on this balancing role.

Further questions could be raised in terms of psychology about the characters in this family feud. Was the father, for example, in his generosity, overcompensating for his real feelings of anger and hostility towards his younger son? Was the elder son projecting his hostility towards his brother onto the father when accusing him of never having provided a feast? Had his rigid moralism in fact inhibited him from ever asking for one?

The Interpretation

Having worked through all the above steps and having taken the parable apart, as it were, by exegetical and literary analysis, it is necessary to put it together again and consider its overall message in terms of the Kingdom. In the case of the Prodigal Son this is not difficult: God shows an overwhelming generosity and forgiveness to repentant sinners without regard to the degree of depravity to which they might have sunk or to the extent to which they might have cut themselves off from the believing community.

EXERCISE 61:   Using the method for interpreting parables as outlined above, analyze the parables of the Wicked Husbandmen (Mk 12: 1–12), the Unscrupulous Judge and the Importunate Woman (Lk 18: 1–8), the Lost Sheep (Lk 15: 3–7), and the Banquet (Lk 14: 15–24).

THE FATHER

The abba-experience of Jesus is seen by scholars as an important source of the message and lifestyle of Jesus. The term "father" was rarely used of God in the Old Testament—only fourteen times in fact—and not at all in the liturgy of the Synagogue. Among stricter Jews, out of reverence, the very name of God was not to be written down. Even today some Jews write "G-d" to maintain this respect. The Aramaic word *abba* (father) as used for God by Jesus, actually only occurs once in the Gospels at Mk 14:

36. However, it seems the image of God as father most likely originated with Jesus' use of *abba*, and in so doing Jesus would have been breaking with the Jewish tradition. The new reference to God as father became very popular with the disciples and early Christians in the first century. This is reflected in the number of times God is referred to as father in the Gospels: Mk: 4, Lk: 15, Mt: 49, Jn: 109 (Johnson, 1993: 81).

That the image of God as father became very popular does not prescind from the fact that there are many and varied images of God in the Gospels. The parables suggest a plurality of images of God. To name but a few: a woman searching for lost money, a shepherd looking for lost sheep, an employer offending his workers by his generosity, a bakerwoman kneading dough, a king giving a wedding feast for his son, the true vine, and the wind. Nevertheless, it does appear that Jesus' use of the image of God as father did make a lasting impression on the disciples.

What exactly does the word *abba* mean? It was a familiar but reverent term for father among Jews. As Jeremias has pointed out, the word conjures up for Orientals the same range of meanings as we attach to the word "mother". Thus "abba" suggests intimacy, nearness, tenderness, compassion in suffering, love. Pope John Paul I, during his brief pontificate, scandalized some by saying God is our mother, whereas he was recapturing the richness of the Aramaic, *abba*. The term does not therefore in any way suggest a father in the oppressive patriarchal sense, but rather a God of the oppressed.

The term "father" for God helped to highlight the new relationship between us and God as central to the Good News. God is our father, not a distant, impersonal deity. When the followers of Jesus asked for a prayer formula to distinguish them from other groups such as the Baptists, Pharisees and Essenes who all had their own prayers, Jesus gave them the "Our Father" as a distinguishing prayer which reflected a very special relationship with God.

Jesus also said something about his own relationship with the Father. He indicated it was a unique relationship. Jesus always speaks of "my Father" (Mk 14: 36; 11: 25) or "your" Father (Lk 6: 36; 12: 30, 32), or "your heavenly Father" (Mk 11: 25; Mt 23: 9), but never of "our Father". In the prayer, the "Our Father" (Lk 11: 2; Mt 6: 9) he emphatically said: "when you pray, say 'our Father' ". This is supported in the Johannine formula where the distinction is kept: "my Father and your Father" (Jn 20: 17).

This exclusive expression, "my Father" implies therefore a very special, non-transferable, unique relationship between Jesus and God. The Gospel of John, which already shows a deeper reflection by the early Christians on this relationship, dwells more at length on this. Jesus spoke about the Father being in him, and he in the Father; about the Father and he being one; about the Father working in him. "If you know me, you know my Father too" (Jn 14: 7) and "Do you not believe that I am in the Father and the Father is in me?" (Jn 14: 10).

It would take the Christian Church centuries to work out exact formulas about how to express the relationship between Jesus and the Father but already from the Gospels it is evident there is a very special relationship.

EXERCISE 62:  What properties or characteristics do you associate with "father" and "mother"? When you say, God is a "Father", what image of God do you have? Is this image consistent with the image of God Jesus gave us in describing his Father? Is the concept of "father" the same in all cultures? Some people object to calling God "father" today on the grounds that it reinforces a patriarchal concept of God. What is your response to this objection?

What Did Others Say About Jesus? (His Titles)

When we come to consider what others say about Jesus, we find a variety of responses. Some accepted him as an exceptional person with many unanswered questions about his identity. Others rejected him outright. Some Pharisees suggested he was casting out devils through Beelzebul, a pagan divinity (Mt 12: 24); the soldiers in the Praetorium saw him as a would-be king of the Jews (Mt 27: 29); the Sadducees as a breaker of the Law and a charlatan. To his home-town folk he was an enigma. They could not reconcile the carpenter's son with the convincing preacher and miracle worker. To John the Baptist, Jesus was the Great Preacher, for whom he was merely preparing the way. To the poor, sick and oppressed he was a ray of hope, a source of total healing: "At sunset all those who had friends suffering from diseases of one kind or another brought them to him and laying his hands on each he cured them" (Lk 4: 40).

EXERCISE 63:  Look up the following references and put into your own words what the people concerned said about Jesus.
Lk 4: 41; 5: 30; 8: 25; 8: 39; 9: 9; 11: 27; Jn 20: 16;
Mk 1: 28; 2: 16; 3: 6; 7: 37; 8: 29; 10: 47; 14: 63, 64.

In the Gospels we also find a certain small number of recurrent titles used of Jesus by others and sometimes by himself. Many of these titles reflect a post-Resurrection faith and insight as much as they do historical traditions dating from the lifetime of Jesus. The most common of these titles are:

MESSIAH/CHRIST

This title is frequently used of Jesus. It means "the anointed one" from the Greek *Christos* which in turn translates the Hebrew word *messiah*. It stands in the tradition of those who were anointed to office, such as King David, whose task it was to bring God's peace and justice to Israel. The word "messiah" had acquired many shades of meaning among the Jews as we saw in Chapter 3 and hence it was a term to be used with qualifications.

This is particularly the case in Mk 8: 27–30, which refers to Peter's profession of faith "You are the Christ". The qualifications came in the next two paragraphs. The "Christ" or "messiah" is destined to suffer and be put to death (31–33) and his disciples are called to take up his cross and follow him (34–38). Jesus the Messiah is therefore not going to be a political or nationalistic leader. It almost appears that to avoid misunderstanding Jesus did not publicize his Messianic role during his ministry (Mk 8: 30; Lk 4: 41; Jn 10: 24). When he was finally crucified however he was put to death as a would-be Messiah-King.

Paul frequently refers to Jesus as the Christ, giving expression to the belief that Jesus was indeed the one foretold by the Messianic prophecies. This title, Christ, has become the one most frequently used in the history of Christianity and has virtually become a surname of Jesus. Christians refer to him as Jesus Christ.

SON OF GOD

This title is important both because of its frequent use in the New Testament and because of its later different use in theology.

The best place to start when considering this title as used in the New Testament is its use in paganism. Many pagan mythologies have references to sons of gods in a biological or genealogical sense, i.e. men born to divine parents or to a divine father and human mother. In addition, important or very talented people in pagan society were often given the title "son of God". The Jews with their strict monotheistic background were suspicious about such titles. The Old Testament use of "sons of God" must be completely free of any biological connection with God. Sonship for them meant election, mission, obedience and service. Israel in a sense is thus a "son" whom God called out of Egypt. The Messiah (2 S 7: 14) can also be described as the son of God. Later on all pious sons of Israel were said to be sons of God (Ps 73: 15; Ws 5: 5). This concept rests on the idea of adoption.

Jesus never refers to himself as the "Son of God". It was a term used by believers to describe initially his outstanding role in terms of election, mission, obedience and service. Even the term "Son" by itself is a term which Jesus probably did not claim for himself. In Mt 11: 27 Jesus says: "No one knows the Son except the Father, and no one knows the Father except the Son and anyone to whom the Son chooses to reveal him". The question which arises here is: is "Son" in this text a title? Jeremias thinks not. He refers to the Semitic character of the saying. To say the father and the son know each other was a common idiom in the Semitic languages and hence "the Son" here is not a title at all but merely a generally valid proposition.

John has a special interest in using this title of Jesus. The title appears twenty-five times in John's Gospel and twenty-two times in 1 John. By being the Son of God in a uniquely divine sense, Jesus can give to believers "power to become God's children" (Jn 1: 12). John's reflections on Jesus' sonship develops with the reflecting Christian communities. It is really an extension of Mark's use of Son of God (1: 1) where it links up with the concept of the royal Messiah, the inheritor of the promises made to David (2 S 7: 14).

As the Christian communities grew and reflected further, the title "Son of God", as applied to Jesus, would take on more philosophical and metaphysical meaning. In the New Testament the title is dynamic and functional, linking Jesus to the messianic prophesies.

LORD

The word "Lord" translates the Greek *Kyrios* which was the title used by the early believers for the Risen Christ. It has a technical meaning in the sense that before his resurrection he was called by other names such as Son of God, Jesus of Nazareth, Messiah, etc., whereas his resurrection from the dead has enabled the Christians to proclaim him "Lord", i.e. invested with divine power and authority.

In the Septuagint the Hebrew word for Yahweh was rendered by *Kyrios*. Hence in Mt 8: 25, "Lord, save us", the use of "Lord" would have suggested something about the identity of Jesus since only God can command the elements (cf. Ps 107: 29; 65: 7–13). Thomas likewise in confessing "my Lord and my God" (Jn 20: 28) is proclaiming Jesus "Lord". The title was the earliest expression to designate the divinity of Jesus.

SON OF MAN

This title is used eighty-six times in the entire New Testament but most of these references occur in the Gospels. It is the only title that Jesus applies to himself. It seems to be his preferred way of referring to himself from a number of other possible titles.

On the first level the term "Son of Man" is a typical Semitic universal term meaning "human being". It appears in this sense ninety-three times in Ezekiel, and fourteen times in the book of Psalms and Job. However on a second level, it is used as a title in the book of Daniel. In this apocalyptic literature, the figure of the "Son of Man" appears as a vague and mysterious person who participates in the final victory of God's Kingdom. He is pictured as "coming on the clouds of heaven" and in human form. God confers "dominion, glory and kingship" on him (Dn 7: 13–14). The author points out that the figure is symbolic of the Saints of the Most High, i.e. the redeemed community of Israel.

In later Jewish apocalyptic literature (Enoch 37: 71, 2 Esdras), the Son of Man is thought of as an individual. It is debatable if these books influenced the New Testament writers. In any case, the title is virtually absent from all writers other than the four evangelists. This is understandable insofar as "Son of Man" meant most to a Jew who knew the Old Testament allusions (writing to a Jewish audience, Matthew uses the title thirty times). Among Gentile converts other titles would have been more significant.

One reason Jesus might have preferred this title himself is that it allowed him to link it with his suffering and passion predictions, being free of the political overtones that the title "messiah" inevitably carried. In a way, he could see in his public ministry that he was arousing formidable opposition and that his life was heading for human tragedy. He believed that through all his suffering God would have the last word, the final victory. In this sense what we have is an individualization of the Danielic theme. He was "one like the Son of Man".

EXERCISE 64: The Gospel texts that refer to the Son of Man can be placed in four groups. Look up the texts given below and then say:
(a) what is common to the texts in each group;
(b) what the role of the Son of Man is in each.
Group 1: Mt 8: 20; 11: 19
Group 2: Mk 2:10; 2: 28
Group 3: Mk 8: 31; 9: 31; 10: 33, 34
          Lk 22: 22
          Jn 3: 14; 8: 28; 12: 23, 24
Group 4: Mk 8: 38; 13: 26; 14: 62
          Mt 24: 27, 37
          Lk 17: 22, 26; 18: 8

What Did He Do?

Having asked ourselves what Jesus said and what others said about him, we ask the third question: what did he do? We know the importance of actions. We often rely most heavily on what people do rather than on what they say. Jesus stated that those who do the will of his Father will be regarded as his kin (Mt 12: 50). The same applied to the son who initially refused to go and work in the vineyard but afterwards thought better of it and did the work (Mt 21: 28–32).

If we look at the Gospels, the main things that Jesus did during his public ministry were preaching, teaching and curing the sick.

JESUS, PREACHER AND TEACHER

The preaching of Jesus is tied up with what he said about the Kingdom and his parables. When he appeared in public life, people saw him as a kind of John the Baptist preacher. His itinerant lifestyle suggested the prophet-preacher. His sermons, sayings and parables showed he was a consummate teacher. Steeped in the Law and Scriptures he was able to preach and teach with authority, not like Scribes and Pharisees (Mk 1: 22). His language was easily understood by all. He delighted in using sharp contrasts and expressing truths by way of paradoxes. He often turned a question back on his questioner to urge him/her to think further on the issue. He taught by example—he prayed frequently; he worked a cure on the Sabbath to show that the human person is more important than a rule; he spoke out on the injustices the Pharisees imposed on devout Jews; he had compassion on the poor and sick; he forgave his executioners. As a teacher he taught most strongly by the witness of his life.

If one considers the imagery that Jesus used, it is interesting to note, as O'Collins has done (1977: 66–74), certain aspects of his imagination as reflected in his teaching and preaching. Jesus manifested an awareness of a very wide range of human activity, suffering and happiness. One needs only to reflect on his parables and sayings. He noticed the suffering of beggars left starving in the street outside the houses of rich people, but he also observed the joy at wedding feasts and the birth of babies. He had noted the role of stewards in large households, the payment of taxes, shoddy building practices, the investment of money, and the application of the law. Overall it is clear that Jesus had a sensitive perception of a great deal of normal human living.

If Jesus had preferences for certain images one would identify those taken from farming. There is frequent reference to farming methods, the tending of cattle and sheep and agriculture in general. However, he seems also to leave certain gaps in his imagery. Very little appears, for example, on the mother/child, or husband/wife relationships although there is a rich tradition of this in Isaiah and the Psalms. There is very little too of Israel's history or the larger political world of the Mediterranean.

As regards Jesus' method of teaching, it is obvious he preferred to use

Cure of the Blind Man by Duccio Di Buoninsegna (c. 1250–1312).

the inductive method, i.e. he liked to quote concrete cases and allow his hearers to draw their own generalizations. When he is asked "who is my neighbor", for example, he does not attempt a pithy definition but relates the story of the Good Samaritan and invites his listeners to generalize for themselves.

MIRACLES

The miracles of Jesus constitute an important part of what he did. In terms of sheer quantity, accounts of miracles make up about one-third of Mark's Gospel. Miracles, of course, always arouse great curiosity and interest. They did this no less in Jesus' time than in our own. Any reports of miracles at Lourdes, Fatima, Medjugorje or by a local faith-healer never fail to arouse a lively interest. Miracles, in the popular sense, are by nature sensational and demand front-page coverage. However, before taking a closer look at Jesus' miracles, we need to be a bit more critical of the meaning of the word "miracle".

Popular, scientific meaning

In the popular use of the word, a miracle is some event that disregards the laws of nature. If a missing piece of bone is suddenly restored, if the cancer in a body disappears overnight, one has a miracle in the sense that these things do not follow the normal laws of growth and recuperation. They cannot be explained by the laws of nature and hence they are miracles.

This definition is really a scientific description of a miracle and needs qualification. One should speak about the "known" laws of nature. Hence a miracle, in the popular, scientific definition is an event contrary to the known laws of nature. Should more be subsequently learnt about the laws of nature some events might lose their "miraculous" status. For example: the appearance of a rainbow might have been seen as miraculous to a primitive society, but once it was learnt that raindrops were acting as prisms on the sunlight and breaking up the white light into the colors of the spectrum, the rainbow was no longer a miracle. Thus the weakness of the scientific definition of a miracle is that what is a miracle today might not be one tomorrow as a result of increased scientific knowledge.

Biblical meaning

The biblical understanding of the miracle is vastly different to the above. The starting point of the biblical view is creation. God is seen as working in creation. The seeds that fall to the ground and suddenly germinate reveal God's active presence; so does the ripening wheat in the fields, the flowers in the garden, a beautiful sunset or sunrise. The dew precipitated overnight on desert plants providing something to drink is a wonderful sign of God's presence in creation. Creation is wonderful, full of miraculous things. Jesus himself was thinking of this when he said "Think of the flowers. . . not even Solomon in all his regalia was robed like one of these" (Lk 12: 27).

God is Lord of Nature. He is Lord of the storm (Ps 29), he calms the sea (Ps 65: 7), he rules over nature (Ps 89: 9–12). He is God of all creation, yet at times his direction of this creation is more extraordinary than at other times.

God, in the biblical view, was not only seen in creation but in history as well. He was seen to intervene in history from time to time. This is of course a religious understanding of history. In the account of Exodus, the great escape from the Egyptians, the narration frequently mentions Yahweh's influencing of events. "I myself will make Pharaoh's heart stubborn, and perform many a sign and wonder in the land of Egypt" (Ex 7: 3). (The "signs and wonders' were the plagues of Egypt. The plagues however pointed beyond themselves to the supreme miracle of the Exodus.)

Elsewhere in the same book there are other cases of Yahweh's interventions, with the most extraordinary being the parting of the Sea of Reeds and the drowning of the Egyptians—a miracle in the sense of being God's extraordinary intervention. That both the plagues and the passage through the Sea of Reeds might be explained naturally is irrelevant; the important point is that the event was interpreted and believed to be God's intervention and hence "miraculous".

The importance of interpretation of events in the understanding of miracles is superbly echoed by an incident from the musical *Fiddler on the Roof,* as Link has pointed out (1978: 72). In the musical, Motel, the Tailor, wins as his wife Tevye's daughter, who had already been "matched" with another. In an outburst of joy and interpreting the events as miraculous, Motel sings:

> *But of all God's miracles, large and small,*
> *The most miraculous one of all,*
> *Is the one I thought could never be—*
> *God has given you to me!*

In short the concept of a miracle as it is used in the Bible in contrast to the popular, scientific understanding thereof can be expressed thus:

> *The biblical concept of miracle is that of a sign of the intervening action of God, rather than the scientific concept of something that happens contrary to nature.*

New Testament miracles

The above is the biblical background one must have to appreciate Jesus' miracles. The Gospel miracles are thus God's extraordinary intervention in nature and events through Jesus. They are a manifestation of God's power working in and through Jesus. The word *dunamis* is sometimes used meaning "mighty work", the miracle being a mighty work of God. (Other words used in the Gospels are *semeion* meaning "sign" or *ergon*, "work", a favorite Johannine word.) Jesus' miracles are not proofs of his divinity as has been sometimes taught. Neither are they proofs for faith—if they were it would be hard to explain why all the Jews did not believe in Jesus. The miracles of Jesus are rather challenges to faith and signs of God's action in the lives of people who met Jesus.

One can classify the miracles in the Gospels as follows:

(a) *Healings and Exorcisms:* These are miracle stories where Jesus either heals someone of an illness, e.g. the Ten Lepers, or casts out the devil, e.g. the Cure of the Demoniac. These stories often follow a very stylized presentation which would have helped memorization during the period of oral tradition. The pattern invariably followed in these accounts of healing and exorcism is:

(i) Setting: a description of the person and the illness.

(ii) Cure: the method used to cure; the cure performed.

(iii) Acclamation: the people attest the cure and express praise of God etc.

EXERCISE 65: Look up the following healings and exorcisms and see if they conform to the stylized presentation mentioned above.

The Capernaum demoniac (Mk 1: 21–28);
The bent woman (Lk 13: 10–17);
The Gerasene demoniac (Mk 5: 1–20);
The Daughter of the Syrophoenician Woman (Mk 7: 24–30);
The centurion's servant (Mt 8: 5–13);
The Cure of the Woman with a Hemorrhage (Lk 8: 40–56).

(b) *Nature Miracles:* These relate to nature in general and show Jesus' power over the forces of creation, e.g. Jesus walking on the water, multiplying loaves and fishes etc.

EXERCISE 66: Look up the following nature miracles and say briefly over which aspects of creation Jesus is exercising power.

Mk 6: 45–52	Mk 4: 35–41	Lk 7: 11–17
Mt 21: 18–22	Lk 5: 1–11	Jn 11: 1–44

EXERCISE 67: One hears of miracles at Medjugorje where rosary beads are turned to gold.
What is your reaction to such reports?
What place did miracles play in the preaching of Jesus?

(c) *Meaning of the miracles:* In attempting to define miracles we have already mentioned that they are challenges to faith and manifestations or signs of God's actions through Jesus. It is the "sign" aspect we want to pursue a bit further here.

Notice that the miracles have two levels:

(i) the sense level—what people see, hear, touch, etc. In the account of the Ten Lepers, all ten saw Jesus, heard him say "Go show yourselves to the priests' and all observed they were cleansed on the way.

(ii) the sign level—what faith discerns. One leper discerns the power of God acting through Jesus, which brought about his cure, and therefore he comes back praising God and thanking Jesus.

If we take all the miracles on the sign level, i.e. discerning them through the eyes of faith, we can see them as signs of the Kingdom. Mention was made above of the prominence of the Kingdom in what Jesus said and preached (the parables and sayings); a similar prominence is given to the Kingdom by the miracles if we see them as signs of the Kingdom.

Let us backtrack for a moment. In the book of Genesis the author makes much of the entry of sin into the world (the Fall, Gn 3) and then the steady rise of sinfulness signaled by such events as the murder of Abel, the carryings-on between the sons of God and the daughters of men, and the Flood. This reign of evil or of Satan was characterized by sin, sickness and death.

Jesus came into the world to announce the Kingdom and mark the beginning of the end of Satan's reign. Jesus has power over the devils, over sin, sickness and death. The miracles bear testimony to this: he forgives sin, he heals the sick, casts out devils and raises the dead. His miracles are thus signs of the Kingdom, signs of the power of God over evil and signs of God's salvific action: i.e. the miracles are not just displays of power but indicate God's intention to make human beings "whole" again, that is, save them. On the faith level, the miracles are a sign of God's action through Jesus to save us, make us complete, whole, so that we will be free of Satan's reign, and enter into the Kingdom of God, a journey begun here and fully realized at death.

Once it is established that the miracles are a sign of the Kingdom, we can tease out aspects of this Kingdom. Many miracles appear as strong signs of compassion (Lk 17: 11–17; Mk 1: 23; 2: 12) or signs of God's power (Mk 4: 35–45).

The miracles of Jesus in general required some faith in the people who surrounded him. In his home town of Nazareth, Jesus was not able to work many miracles, Matthew observes "because of their lack of faith" (Mt 13: 58). Mark, in a parallel text says Jesus "was amazed at their lack of faith" (Mk 6: 6). Conversely, Jesus praised the woman with a hemorrhage, saying her faith has restored her to health (Mk 5: 34). He makes a similar comment to the woman who was a sinner (Lk 7: 50).

There remains the question of the historical accuracy of the miracle account. We have already pointed out that the meaning of the miracles is to be sought on the sign level of faith according to which miracles are signs of the Kingdom. In spite of this, the question "are the Gospel accounts of miracles accurate descriptions of what happened?" is inevitably raised. To answer this query, a number of points relevant to the Gospels and miracles must be made, as Fallon has pointed out (1980: 146–149).

The first point to be made is that the witnesses of these miracles reported them according to their own mental horizons and perceptions of events. The witnesses gave subjective interpretations of incidents. Thus what one described as an "unclean spirit" 2000 years ago might today be called an epileptic or someone who is mentally unstable. In reading the miracle stories, we must thus allow for this difference of perception between then and now.

Secondly, the way in which the miracles were written allowed for elaboration and embellishment of the story. This is not as strange as one might at first think. We all tend to embellish and exaggerate when recounting an unusual event to impress our audience all the more. Thus the dramatic and exaggerated style of recording these miracles must be allowed for by the reader.

Thirdly, the aim of the evangelist must be kept in mind. The authors of the Gospels wanted to put readers in touch with Jesus of Nazareth now resurrected and living. Their aim was to facilitate contact with Jesus in a prayerful atmosphere—hence the frequent use of Old Testament imagery. The evangelists were not concerned so much with accurately recording a past event as with putting believers in touch with the living Lord.

Given these considerations, it is not difficult to realize that in general, it is not possible to get to the original, actual, unadorned event in the life of Jesus. However, this should not worry us if we can remember that as regards miracles, it is not what happened that is the important thing, but the meaning of the miracle, as mentioned above.

EXERCISE 68: (i) Read the following references and note what they say about Yahweh's relationship to nature:
Ps 29; 65: 7; 89: 9–12; 107: 29.
(ii) Read Ps 44, noting vv. 23 and 24 especially.
(iii) Now read Mk 4: 35–41, the calming of the storm, and write down answers to these questions:
— What do you think was the original unadorned event?
— What is the meaning of the story as told in Mark?
— What response would the Jew who prayed the psalms conscientiously, give to the question, "Who can this be? Even the wind and the sea obey him?"

TABLE OF PARABLES AND MIRACLES IN THE GOSPELS

Name of Parable	Mark	Matthew	Luke	John
The sick and the doctor	2: 17	9: 12	5: 31	
The bridegroom and fasting	2: 19	9: 15	5: 34	
Patch	2: 21	9: 16	5: 36	
Wineskins	2: 22	9: 17	5: 37–39	
Divided Kingdom	3: 24–26	12: 25–28	11: 17–23	
Strongman	3: 27	12: 29	11: 21–23	
Sower	4: 3–9	13: 4–9	8: 5–8	
The lamp	4: 21	5: 15	11: 33	
The seed growing by itself	4: 26–29			
The mustard seed	4: 30–32	13: 31–32	13: 18–19	
Insipid salt	9: 50	5: 13	14: 34	
The wicked husbandmen	12: 1–9	21: 33–43	20: 9–19	
The fig tree	13: 28	24: 32–36	21: 29–33	
Be on the alert	13: 34–37			
A city on a hilltop		5: 14		
Defendant		5: 25	12: 57–59	
The eye, the lamp of the body		6: 22	11: 34–36	
Splinter and plank		7: 3–5	6: 41	
Asking son		7: 9–11	11: 11–13	
False prophets		7: 16–20	6: 43–45	
Two builders		7: 24–27	6: 47–49	
Harvest and laborers		9: 37	10: 2	
Playing children		11: 16	7: 31	
Return of unclean spirit		12: 43–45	11: 24–26	
The darnel		13: 24–30		
Parable of the yeast		13: 33	13: 20–21	
Hidden treasure		13: 44		
Fine pearls		13: 45–46		
Dragnet		13: 47–50		
Household		13: 52		
Blind leading blind		15: 14	6: 39	
The lost sheep		18: 12–14	15: 3–7	
The unforgiving debtor		18: 23–35		
Vineyard laborers		20: 1–16		
The two sons		21: 28–31		
The wedding feast and wedding garment		22: 1–14	14: 15–24	
Burglar		24: 43–44	12: 39	

Name of Parable	Mark	Matthew	Luke	John
The conscientious steward		24: 45–51	12: 42–46	
Ten bridesmaids		25: 1–13		
Talents		25: 14–30		
Sheep and goats		25: 31–46		
Physician, heal yourself			4: 23	
Two debtors			7: 41–43	
Good Samaritan			10: 30–37	
The importunate friend			11: 5–8	
Rich fool			12: 16–21	
Waiting servants			12: 35–38	
The signs of the times			12: 54–56	
Barren fig tree			13: 6–9	
Places at table			14: 7–11	
Tower-builder			14: 28–30	
Warring kings			14: 31–33	
The lost drachma			15: 8–10	
The lost son (Prodigal Son)			15: 11–32	
The crafty steward			16: 1–8	
The rich man and Lazarus			16: 19–31	
Humble service			17: 7–10	
The unscrupulous judge and importunate widow			18: 1–8	
The Pharisee and the publican			18: 10–14	
The pounds			19: 12–27	
The wind				3: 8
Bridegroom's friend				3: 29–30
The imminent harvest				4: 35
The grain of wheat				12: 24
The good shepherd and the robber★				10: 1–10
The shepherd and the hireling★				10: 11–17
The true vine★				15: 1–17

★ allegories rather than parables

Name of Miracle				
Cure of demoniac	1: 21–28		4: 31–37	
Cure of Simon's mother-in-law	1: 29–31	8: 14		
A number of cures	1: 32–34	8: 16	4: 40–41	
Cure of a leper	1: 40–45	8: 2–4	5: 12–16	
Cure of a paralytic	2: 1–12	9: 1–8	5: 17–26	
Cure of a man with a withered hand	3: 1–6	12: 9–14	6: 6–11	
The calming of the storm	4: 35–41	8: 18, 23–27	8: 22–25	
The Gerasene demoniac	5: 1–20	8: 28–34	8: 26–39	

Name of Miracle	Mark	Matthew	Luke	John
Cure of the woman with a hemorrhage (the daughter of Jairus raised to life)	5: 21–43	9: 18–26	8: 40–56	
First miracle of the loaves	6: 30–44	14: 13–21	9: 10–17	6: 1–13
Jesus walks on the water	6: 45–52	14: 22–33		6: 16–21
Cures at Gennesaret	6: 53–56	14: 34–36		
The daughter of the Syrophoenician woman healed	7: 24–30	15: 21–28		
Healing of the deaf man	7: 31–37			
Second miracle of the loaves	8: 1–10	15: 32–39		
Cure of a blind man at Bethsaida	8: 22–26			
The epileptic demoniac	9: 14–29	17: 14–21	9: 37–42	
The blind man of Jericho	10: 46–52	20: 29–34	18: 35–43	
The fig tree withered	11: 20–25	21: 20–22		
Cure of the centurion's servant		8: 5–13	7: 1–10	
Jesus heals the sick	1: 39 3: 7–12	4: 23	4: 14–15	
Cure of two blind men		9: 27–31		
Cure of a dumb demoniac		9: 32–34	11: 14–15	
Cures in Galilean towns		9: 35		
Cure of the blind and dumb demoniac		12: 22		
Healings in a lonely place		14: 14		
Cures near the lake		15: 29–31		
Healings in Transjordan		19: 2		
Cures in the temple		21: 14		
The miraculous draft of fishes			5: 1–11	
The son of the widow of Nain			7: 11–17	
Healings in answer to the Baptist			7: 21	
Healings at Bethsaida			9: 11	
Healing of the crippled woman			13: 10–17	
Healing of a dropsical man			14: 1–6	
The high priest's servant's ear			22: 51	
The wedding at Cana				2: 1–11
Signs in Jerusalem during the Passover				2: 23–25
The cure of the nobleman's son				4: 46–54
The cure of a sick man at the Pool of Bethzatha				5: 1–18
The cure of the man born blind				9: 1–34
The resurrection of Lazarus				11: 1–44

CHAPTER 5

THE PASSION AND RESURRECTION NARRATIVES

INTRODUCTION

The most familiar symbol of Christianity is the cross. You may have noticed the variety of representations that adorn our churches, our meeting places, and perhaps our persons. It is a symbol which touches something that, one way or another, we all know at the level of our own experience: the mystery of suffering, abandonment and death. Each night when we turn on the television news, we are challenged by this mystery in the pain, brokenness and death of people and other aspects of our Planet Earth. So when we take up the Gospel Passion Narratives we are reading a not-unfamiliar story.

But there is another story that we also know at the level of our own experience: the story of the movement towards emergence and transformation. Perhaps it is this dynamic which has led you to your present study of the Gospels. Thomas Berry (1988: 132) talks of the story of the universe as "the story of the emergence of a galactic system through the urgency of self-transcendence". Hydrogen in the presence of extreme heat becomes helium. Stars go through a series of transformations until some explode into the stardust out of which the solar system and the earth take form. Earth goes through a series of transformations "until humans appear at the moment in which the unfolding universe becomes conscious of itself". We are part of the "emergent process" of the universe, knowing in our experience "the urgency of self-transcendence".

The Passion and Resurrection Narratives encompass the experience of both death and transformation. The two stories belong together, and are the culmination of the "emergent process" of Jesus' life.

THE DEATH OF JESUS IN THE GOSPELS

As we have already noted in Chapter 2, the Passion Narratives are very old, self-contained units in the New Testament tradition. Unlike the Resurrection Narratives, they have much in common, perhaps partly because they are older and therefore closer to the events. But they are also contradictory in some details, leaving unanswered questions—for example: did the trial of Jesus take place before Passover (as in John's account) or on Passover Day (as in the Synoptics)? The point is that these narratives are not intended as mere historical reports of events. Above all else, "they are profound theological documents which interpret Jesus' suffering and death upon the cross" (Matera, 1986: 5) from the perspective of post-Easter faith.

It is easy to imagine that the message of a crucified Messiah would not have been readily accepted in the early Christian communities. Jesus' death confounded patriarchal notions of a conquering Messiah with power over others. He became Messiah through standing with the poor and oppressed and seeing his work for the reign of God apparently brought to nothing. The Passion Narratives were an attempt to help Christian believers come to terms with the cross. The gospel writers, from the perspective of the Resurrection, attempted to show why the Messiah died by crucifixion—the "religious-political" punishment which, according to Matera (1986: 2), was usually reserved for rebellious foreigners, slaves and criminals.

The Gospels present the death of Jesus, not as a tragic accident or as appeasement of a demanding God, but as the consequence of the radicalism of what he said and what he did. Each of the gospel writers throws light on Jesus' death from his particular theological perspective—the same perspective that shaped the rest of his Gospel. For Mark, Jesus is a suffering

Persecution, by Weaver Hawkins (1893–1977).

Messiah who stands alone, betrayed and abandoned by his male disciples and trained leaders, and experiencing the absence of God in his darkest hour. It is through his death that his identity as the Christ is finally revealed. Only by accepting the cross can one be a disciple of this suffering Messiah. John, on the other hand, emphasizes the majesty of the only Son of the Father who "lays down his life of his own accord" (Jn 10: 18). He goes to his cross as a king to his throne of glory. For Luke it is the Righteous One, the innocent Prophet-King who is crucified. In Matthew's account of the Passion, the Chosen People of Israel, through their leaders, reject Jesus the Son of God, so now the promise is given over to a new people, the Church.

EXERCISE 69: (a) Read the Passion Narrative in at least Mark and Luke.
(b) Research the Passover festival. What is the significance, as seen by Luke, of the last Passover meal of Jesus with his disciples? (Lk 22: 14–20)
(c) What is the significance of the references to Ps 22 and 31 in the Passion Narrative (cf. Mk 15: 21–41; Mt 27: 43; Jn 19: 24; Lk 23: 46)?
(d) Why did Jesus die?

EXERCISE 70:  Crossan (1991: 411–416) observes that Mark framed the passion of Jesus with the story of the unnamed woman in 14: 3–9 and the unnamed centurion in 15: 39. Read the two stories and note how each of the unnamed acknowledges Jesus. Compare the actions of the unnamed with those of the named in Mark's Passion Narrative. What do you find?

EXERCISE 71: (a) Choose a particular Gospel. Imagine you are a member of Mark's (Luke's, Matthew's or John's) community.
Then read the Passion Narrative carefully, noting the different scenes that make up the Narrative.
What impression do you get of Jesus? of the people involved?
(b) What image of Jesus comes through most strongly for you in the Passion Narrative?
What in the Narrative contributes to this image (themes, actions, names, repeated words/phrases)?
Is this image consistent with the presentation of Jesus throughout the Gospel? (Give examples.)

In the earliest of the post-Easter traditions, Jesus' death was already interpreted as a saving and expiatory death "for us" and "for many". "Jesus was handed over to death for our sins and raised up for our justification" (Rm 4: 25). This interpretation was elucidated in terms of the 4th Servant Song, used in the very early creed in 1 Co 15: 3–5 and early tradition of the Last Supper to interpret the death of Jesus as a representative expiatory death for the salvation of people. This interpretation became fundamental to the Christian understanding of the Redemption.

Did Jesus himself know the saving (soteriological) power of his death? We do not know. All we can say is that the concept of the sufferings of the just man and the expiatory power of these sufferings were common in his day (2 M 7: 6, 9), and Jesus may well have recognized this in his self-understanding.

EXERCISE 72: Many people die without any particular meaning being attached to their death. What importance does Scripture attach to the death of Jesus?
How can you express that in today's language?

Jesus' death climaxed and actualized the pattern of his life:

> *His redemptive work is not restricted to his death, but his death gives it final clarity and definitiveness. The story of Jesus, and its end, remain a question to which only God can give the answer. Unless Jesus' work failed, this answer can only say that a new age dawned in his death. That is what is meant by the belief that Jesus was raised from the dead. (Kasper, 1976: 121).*

THE RESURRECTION

When you hear the word "Easter", what comes to mind? For many of us, it may well be images that go back to our earliest years and are associated with joy and new life: the sun dancing, a butterfly emerging from its chrysalis, the Easter bunny, the Easter egg or beautiful Ukranian Pysânky eggs. Some of us may have in mind one of the many pictures by famous artists depicting Jesus in the process of emerging from the tomb—though none of the Scriptures ever recorded anyone seeing Jesus rising "from the dead". Perhaps we recall one of a number of stories of Jesus' post-Resurrection appearances to his disciples.

Even the name "Easter" has the ring of new life and transformation about it. According to the Oxford Dictionary, Easter or "Eostre" was the ancient Anglo-Saxon goddess of spring, whose festival was celebrated at the spring equinox. In European languages (French *Pâques*, Spanish *Pascuas*, Italian *Pasqua*), the name given to Easter recalls its origin in the Hebrew *Pesach*, which is the word for the Jewish celebration of Passover, the feast of deliverance from slavery and oppression.

Each of these images, stories and names is an attempt to throw light on what is the central event in the Gospels—a life-after-death event for which we have no image or story adequate in itself. Indeed, controversial writing on the Resurrection in our own time, nearly 2000 years after the event, testifies to the continuing effort to gain greater insight into this central mystery.

The resurrection of Jesus is the central affirmation of the Christian faith. To confess that "Jesus is Lord" is to believe that "God raised him from the dead" (Rm 10: 9), and "if Christ has not been raised then our preaching is useless and your believing it is useless" (1 Co 15: 14).

'The Christ': you may remember that we looked at this title in Chapter 4. After the Easter event, "Jesus is Lord" (Christ, Messiah, the Anointed One of God) became the central act of faith of those living in recognition of what God had done in raising Christ from death (e.g. Ac 2: 36; 3: 20). In the Easter event, the disciples had seen the saving activity of God visible in Jesus; for in spite of appearances, even Jesus' death, God had not abandoned him. As before, through their long history, God still remained the Faithful One.

But more; for they remembered that Jesus had, out of the depths of his own self-understanding and the immediacy of his unique relationship with God, called God Father (cf. Chapter 4). The Easter event was from beginning to end the work of the Father, according to John. In that God had raised Jesus from the dead God had, to the bewildered astonishment of the disciples, established Jesus' messianic title. Further, God had established him as Savior and Liberator.

The early Christians recognized the saving activity of God, they remembered "all that Jesus had done and taught", and seeing this anew in the light of the Easter event, recognized its true meaning. The Resurrection was at the heart of their recognition of and faith in Jesus as Lord.

This Resurrection faith is expressed in the New Testament in three ways:

a) The disciples proclaim their faith: the kerygma (e.g. in the speeches in Acts, where they announce it to non-believers).
b) The disciples celebrate their faith: creeds and hymns. There are many instances in the writings of Paul of both credal statements and hymns—fragments of the liturgy of the early Christians. (We will return to the topic of Creeds in Chapter 6.)
c) The disciples tell of their faith: narratives. It is this form that we find in the later New Testament texts, the Gospels. They say in yet another way—in the form of story—what is expressed in the kerygma, the creeds and the hymns (cf. Charpentier 1981: 33–39).

It is with this narrative form in the Gospels that we are concerned in this chapter.

The Holy Women at the Sepulchre, Armenia 1038.

THE RESURRECTION NARRATIVES

The Resurrection Narratives present a bewildering array of material:

1) Mk 16: 1–8 is the conclusion of the Gospel of Mark in the best Greek manuscripts, and reports the empty tomb and the Easter message "He has risen, he is not here". It does not describe the Resurrection itself nor any appearance of Jesus.

2) Mt 28: 1–20 also reports the empty tomb and the Easter message: "He is not here, for he has risen, as he said he would." It goes on to report appearances of the risen Christ in Jerusalem and Galilee (with the focus on Galilee), and the sending forth of the Apostles.

3) Lk 24: 1–53 tells of the finding of the empty tomb and of the message, "He is not here; he is risen". Luke goes on to talk of appearances of the risen Jesus at Emmaus and in Jerusalem (but not in Galilee), of his commission to witness, and the ascension.

4) Jn 20: 1–29 tells of the empty tomb, and Jesus' appearance to Mary Magdalene and two appearances to the disciples in Jerusalem.

5) The epilogue to John's Gospel (21: 1–23) tells of Jesus' appearance to seven disciples in Galilee.

6) The appendix to Mark's Gospel (16: 9–20)—added much later and

found only in some Greek manuscripts—reports three appearances on Easter Sunday and his being "taken up" on that same day. It reads rather like a summary of Matthew and Luke.

THE APPEARANCES AND THE EMPTY TOMB TRADITIONS

Except for the accounts of the empty tomb, the Gospel writers seem to go their own way and thus there is a variety of appearances stories, with some obvious discrepancies. Scholars have concluded from this that the reports of Jesus' appearances are not reflections of the earliest preaching about the risen Christ, but rather are later attempts to fill out the reports of appearances of the risen Christ in the earlier proclamations, such as 1 Co 15: 3–7.

Perrin (1977) suggests that because each evangelist is writing from a particular theological perspective (as we have already seen in Chapters 2 and 3), the real question is not "Did Jesus do this or that?" (Did he appear as risen from the dead to his disciples or not [Mark], in Galilee [Matthew], or only in Jerusalem [Luke]?". Instead, we ask ourselves: "What is Mark trying to say to us by deliberately omitting appearance stories, or Matthew by locating the major appearance in Galilee, or Luke by limiting appearances to the Jerusalem area?" These are the real questions, because they are questions about the convictions and perceptions of the Gospel writers themselves; what is it that the particular writer is challenging us to accept or deny by means of this particular narrative? (cf. Perrin, 1977: 7–9).

EXERCISE 73:  **(a)** Read the Empty Tomb narrative in each of the Gospels (Mk 16: 1–8; Mt 28: 1–8; Lk 24: 1–12; Jn 20: 1–18). Compare the different emphases in the telling of the story.
(i) Focus on the characters: who went to the tomb? what were they expecting to find? what did they find? what were their reactions?
(ii) What is each of the gospel writers trying to say in telling the story? What does the story mean?
(b) Read Mk 16: 1–8 again. This time note references to time, place and characters. Show how the writer uses these to indicate transformation (e.g. the early morning—transition into a new day).

The Empty Tomb story appears in all four Gospels, although it is not mentioned by Paul in 1 Co 15: 3–8 where he uses a confession of faith that may go back in the tradition to 35 A.D.—some thirty years before the first Gospel was written:

> *Well then, in the first place, I taught you*
> *what I had been taught myself,*
> *namely that Christ died for our sins,*
> *in accordance with the scriptures,*
> *that he was buried;*
> *and that he was raised to life on the third day,*
> *in accordance with the scriptures;*
> *that he appeared first to Cephas*
> *and secondly to the Twelve.*
> *Next he appeared to more than five hundred*
> *of the brothers at the same time,*
> *most of whom are still alive,*
> *though some have died;*
> *then he appeared to James, and then to all the*
> *apostles.*
> *and last of all he appeared to me. . .*

The fact that the Empty Tomb story does not appear in this early statement of belief possibly indicates that this story circulated later than the report of appearances, was incorporated by Mark into his Gospel, and was subsequently used by Matthew and Luke as they worked from the Marcan source. Some scholars say that the Empty Tomb narrative may have been closely connected with a tradition of pilgrimage by early Christians to the empty tomb of Jesus, and the liturgical celebration there of the mystery of the Resurrection. Others believe that the narrative does have a basis in history, given the similarities of the accounts in all four Gospels (in contrast to the variations in the appearance stories), and also given that the story focuses on the witness of women—an unlikely invention since, according to Jewish law, women could not legally bear witness.

Whatever the origins of the story, the Empty Tomb tradition reflects the deliberation of faith about what happened to Jesus' body, for it seems that the early disciples were convinced of Jesus' Resurrection, not by the tomb, but by the appearances. Their belief made sense of the empty tomb.

The Empty Tomb tradition may have had greater importance in early times than it has today, since it would have counteracted the gnostic denial of the bodiliness of Jesus and his Resurrection.

How did the early Christians themselves interpret the emergence of their faith in the living Crucified One?

EXERCISE 74: 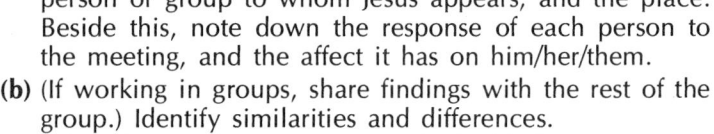 **(a)** Read the Gospel stories of the appearances. (If preparing for a group discussion, choose one of the Gospels. Your group leader will ensure that all four Gospels are covered by the group.) As you read, write down the name of the person or group to whom Jesus appears, and the place. Beside this, note down the response of each person to the meeting, and the affect it has on him/her/them.

(b) (If working in groups, share findings with the rest of the group.) Identify similarities and differences.
What does each writer seem to be highlighting in particular?

(c) Which person/group in the story do you identify with most, in terms of response to Jesus?

In your exploration of the Empty Tomb Narratives and the appearances, you will have noticed the active role played by the women, who are mentioned by name (thus indicating their importance in the early Christian communities). Mary Magdalene in particular plays a crucial role in these events, and is the primary witness to the Resurrection.

You will remember that in your study of Mk 8 (Appendix A), you discovered that the writer spoke of discipleship in terms of seeing and not-seeing. Fallon (1980: 442–443) draws our attention to the richness of the word "see" in English and the variety of ways in which we use the word, not only for seeing with our physical eyes but also for understanding/comprehension/enlightenment. The most common word for "see" in the Resurrection Narratives is the Greek word *horao*, which is the source of our English word "aware" (cf. Lk 21: 27; 24: 34, 39; Jn 16: 16; 20: 18, 20, 25, 27). The disciples "become aware of" who Jesus is in their encounters with the risen Jesus.

Fallon, speaking of the appearance stories, underlines their importance:

> *They are profound texts born of prayer and of real experience, and they express in powerful symbolic language the most meaningful experiences that formed the early Church, and founded their faith in the presence of the risen Jesus in their midst. They must be read from within the same prayer, and while reflecting on our own experiences of the risen Jesus (Fallon, 1980: 443).*

An attentive reading of the appearances narratives shows a close link between these stories of the experience of Jesus' presence among them and the Eucharist:

> *It was especially when Jesus' disciples came together to remember him at the "Breaking of Bread" that they experienced his living presence among*

them . . . The experience of the Eucharist is central to the "Resurrection appearances" (Fallon, 1980: 442).

EXERCISE 75: Read again the Emmaus story (Lk 24: 13–35) and trace the pattern of Eucharistic celebration in the structure and imagery of the story.

NEW LIFE

Was the Resurrection something that happened to Jesus? Or was it, as some have argued, something that happened only to his disciples—a particularly vivid religious experience, for example? Fuller describes the Resurrection itself as "an eschatological event between God and Jesus ('God raised Jesus from the dead'), not merely something that happened to the disciples" (R. Fuller, quoted in O'Collins, 1978: 11). Moreover, in their emphasis on the bodily aspect (e.g. Jn 20: 27; Lk 24: 41–43; Jn 21: 15–22), the Gospel writers appear to be stressing the continuity between the historical Jesus and the risen Lord. (The fact that it is Luke and John who are making the point so emphatically suggests that they may have been resisting Greek and gnostic tendencies to undermine the physical.)

Yet there was something different about him; the disciples sometimes failed to recognize him (Lk 24: 16; Jn 20: 14; 21: 4; Mt 28: 17; Lk 24: 41). Mark states that he "appeared in another form" (16: 12). Some transformation has certainly taken place in Jesus and perhaps, in their consistent underlining of this, the Gospel writers are trying to shift our attention and our questions from the purely physical aspect to the (new) total reality of Jesus. Charpentier points out that there were two main kinds of imagery at work in the early Christians' efforts to express their understanding of the Easter mystery, Resurrection imagery and exaltation imagery:

> *The disciples felt that they had to use both kinds of imagery: Jesus was risen, so the one who was now alive was the same being whom they had known earlier: his friends recognized him. But he was also exalted, glorified, he had ascended into heaven; so this was not just a matter of rediscovering life as it was before: Jesus was introduced to a new life, the life of God. (Charpentier, 1981: 35)*

Was the Resurrection an historical event? Not in the sense of our being able to go out with notebook and pen and make a full report as the details unwind before our eyes. But the fact that it can hardly be called an historical event in our ordinary sense of the word does not mean, as McBrien points out, that the Resurrection was not a real event for Jesus with historical implications for others. McBrien suggests the word *transhistorical*, rather than historical or unhistorical. The reality of the risen Lord transcends history as we know it (cf. McBrien, 1980: 412).

SOME COMMON MISUNDERSTANDINGS

Fitzmyer (1979) claims that one of the major modern problems with the Resurrection of Jesus is the way in which we tend to picture to ourselves what the New Testament says about the risen Jesus. It is worth noting that:

(1) Nowhere is it stated that anyone witnessed the Resurrection of Jesus (Ac 1: 22 = "a witness to the risen Christ").

(2) The New Testament never presents the Resurrection of Jesus as a resuscitation, i.e. a return to his former mode of existence (like, for example, Lazarus).

(3) Jesus is never depicted as walking the earth for forty days, or appearing as a spook; Lk 24: 37ff. specifically rejects the latter idea.

(4) Though the New Testament does not state it explicitly, it implies again and again that when the risen Christ appeared, he appeared from glory, in the presence of the Father: "Christ was raised from the dead by the glory of the Father" (Rm 6: 4). Furthermore, the only difference between the appearance of the risen Christ to Paul on the Damascus road and the other appearances is a temporal one (after or before Pentecost).

(5) Whereas the risen Jesus who appeared insisted on his identity, he is also said to have appeared "in another form" (Mk 16: 12). Again (as we have already seen above), he was not immediately recognized by the disciples on the way to Emmaus, nor by Mary Magdalene. We recall Paul's statement that there is a difference between a "physical body" sown in death and a "spiritual body" raised from death.

(6) The question of whether the Resurrection appearances were physical or spiritual has long puzzled people. The Gospels seem to be saying "both physical and spiritual", as we have already seen. The proclamation of the death, burial, rising and appearances of Jesus originated in a culture which did not have a dichotomized concept of body/soul. Whatever the explanation, the emphasis in each Gospel is that the one

who appeared was the same Jesus who had been crucified, "translated at his Resurrection into an entirely new mode of existence".

EXERCISE 76: **(a)** With regard to "some common misunderstandings': which ones did you grow up with? when did you correct your understanding?

(b) Go back to Berry's concept of the universe as "emergent process" driven by the "urgency of self-transcendence". How do you see the Resurrection in this context?

(c) What would you like to explore further about the Resurrection?

CHAPTER 6

▼

EXPRESSING BELIEFS: THE CREEDS

Today people are concerned about many things. On the global scene the most serious and urgent problems seem to be what one could refer to as human rights issues, the North-South conflict and the ecological crisis. These concerns are not felt equally by all, but one has only to consider the rapid growth of the Peace Movement or the various environmentalist groups, to realize that people (including politicians) are taking these issues more seriously. And as people become more convinced and feel more strongly about these burning issues, they begin to articulate their beliefs in concrete terms. The environmentalists say, for example, that unless we cut down drastically on our use of chlorofluorocarbons, we will, by the end of the century, have irreparably destroyed the ozone layer. In other words when people feel strongly about something they tend to come out with belief statements which clarify for themselves and others where they stand.

In a way this also happened to the early Christians. They felt strongly about Jesus and attempted to express their beliefs in words. For a moment let us contrast these early Christians with ourselves. To believers today, two thousand years after the event, Jesus is of course, the Promised One, the Son of God, the Second Person of the Blessed Trinity. For the first group of believing Christians, the articulation of the identity of Jesus was not all that simple. They did not, like us, have the benefit of numerous Church Councils and two thousand years of tradition. As a preaching and reflecting community they were faced with the problem of expressing in words what they believed in their hearts. In proclaiming the kerygma, they were obliged to search for the appropriate words which would attempt to explain the mystery of Jesus' life and death. In this way they would clarify for themselves and others where they stood.

WHAT ARE CREEDS?

As has been already mentioned, the first attempt to express the mystery of Jesus after the Resurrection, was the simple phrase "Jesus is Lord". Other similar phrases were of course also used. With time attempts to speak of

Boat and lighthouse as symbols of belief in life's journey ending in eternal life; third century, Rome.

belief in Jesus became fixed into set patterns which were eventually called "creeds". What we want to do now is trace the initial steps of the early Church in its growing realization and articulation of who Jesus really is, as expressed in creeds.

The word "creed", as we use it today, needs to be defined before we proceed any further. The following definition could be a useful starting point:

> *A creed is a concise statement of essential articles of faith expressed in a fixed formula approved by Church authorities.*

It is worth noting that although a creed contains essential articles of faith it does not claim to contain all articles. Lengthier and more comprehensive statements of faith are called theological treatises. Creeds however are relatively concise statements of faith which have the advantage of being easy to learn by rote. A glance at their origin and history will prove informative.

Early Creeds

The exact origin of creeds is not easy to trace. There was a legend at one time that the twelve Apostles got together in solemn conclave before setting out on their mission to the four corners of the earth and actually composed the Apostles' Creed as we know it today. Modern scholars however reject this theory as belonging to pious legend.

In seeking the origins of early creeds, one has really to look at the New Testament. Certainly there are no creeds or formulas of faith as we know them today, but there are short phrases, initially centered on Jesus' identity, which served as a starting point for lengthier statements later to be called creeds. These initial phrases were really simple one-clause Christologies,

164

almost catchwords, such as "Jesus is Lord" (1 Co 12: 3; Rm 10: 9; Ph 2: 11; Col 2: 6) or "Jesus is the Son of God" (Ac 9: 21; 1 Jn 4: 15; 5: 5).

The next step beyond these one-clause phrases was a movement to fuller expressions of faith, often a kind of summary drawn up for catechetical purposes. A good example of such a formula is 1 Co 15: 3–5:

> *Well then, in the first place, I taught you what I had been taught myself, namely that Christ died for our sins in accordance with the scriptures, that he was buried; and that he was raised to life on the third day in accordance with the scriptures, that he appeared first to Cephas and secondly to the twelve . . .*

EXERCISE 77: Look up the following references to other fuller expressions of faith or primitive catechetical formulas: Rm 1: 3f; Rm 8: 34; 2 Tm 2: 8; Ga 1: 4; 1 Th 4: 14; 5: 9f.

The plan of those early formulas seems basically to be that of the name of JESUS plus selected incidents in the story of redemption. From these formulas it was a quick step to binitarian or two-clause statements with reference to the Father and the Son. 1 Co 8: 6 speaks of us having "one God and Father" and "one Lord Jesus Christ" (cf. also 1 Tm 2: 5f.; 6: 13f.; 2 Tm 4: 1; Rm 4: 24). The catchword "God, who has raised the Lord Jesus from the dead" was another such binitarian formula which soon became a cliché in the community of believers.

Following on this development we have the next step—the trinitarian statements; these though were not as common as the single-clause or binitarian formula. A well-known example is of course 2 Co 13: 13: "The grace of the Lord Jesus Christ, the love of God and the fellowship of the Holy Spirit be with you all". Another common one is the baptismal formula of Mt 28: 19, "baptise them in the name of the Father, and of the Son and of the Holy Spirit" (cf. also 1 Co 6: 11; 12: 4ff.; 1 Th 5: 18f.; Ga 1: 3 with 3: 11–14; 4: 4–7; 1 P 1: 2; Heb 10: 29).

A safe conclusion we can draw from all this is that single-clause, binitarian and trinitarian expressions flourished side by side in the Apostolic Church as parallel formulations of the one kerygma. We can also point out that the trinitarian pattern which dominated later creeds was already present in New Testament times.

It is important to note that these formulas of faith, later to be known as creeds, were local to begin with. Christianity was spread over the Mediterranean countries and local churches would have their own particular wording for the profession of faith and with time no doubt borrowed from

other churches or from itinerant preachers such as Paul and later mission-
aries.

Although the connection between baptismal liturgy and the creeds will
be discussed below, we need to remind ourselves of the origin of these
fixed formulas called creeds. In the first instance they were statements of
belief about Jesus. Secondly, they were used or they developed to instruct
adult pagans and Jews into the Christian faith, i.e. they were used
catechetically. Thirdly, they were also used in a slightly different way in
the actual baptismal ceremony which we will explain shortly. Fourthly,
they developed under pressure from attacks by heretics. The Church found
it necessary to state and clarify its beliefs about important matters such as
the divinity of Christ and the relationship of the Son and Holy Spirit to
the Father. The Nicene Creed is a good example of this fourth factor in
the origin of creeds.

MAIN CREEDS

The Apostles' Creed

This creed is thought to come from an older second century creed called
the Old Roman Creed which was really composed of a short trinitarian
formula followed by an originally independent Christological summary.
Little is known about the Apostles' Creed except that it was first used in
Western baptismal liturgies, whereas the Greeks used the Nicene. Today
the Apostles' Creed is rarely used in liturgical services.

The text of this creed is as given below. Note how there are three
main statements (in bold type) which constitute a trinitarian statement and
how most of the creed is really a Christological summary.

> **I believe in God, the Father almighty,**
> **creator of heaven and earth.**
> **I believe in Jesus Christ, his only Son, our Lord.**
> *He was conceived by the power of the Holy Spirit*
> *and born of the Virgin Mary.*
> *He suffered under Pontius Pilate,*
> *was crucified, died and was buried.*
> *He descended to the dead.*
> *On the third day he rose again.*
> *He ascended into heaven,*
> *and is seated at the right hand of the Father.*
> *He will come again to judge the living and the dead.*

I believe in the Holy Spirit,
the holy Catholic Church,
the communion of saints,
the forgiveness of sins,
the Resurrection of the body,
and the life everlasting.

The Athanasian Creed

This creed is also seldom used today. It is sometimes called by its Latin title *Quicunque Vult* ('whosoever will be saved. . .") taken from its opening words. Thought to have originated in South Gaul in the middle of the fifth century, it is called Athanasian, not because St Athanasius wrote it, but because the anonymous author, like St Athanasius, had obviously made a close study of St Augustine's writings, particularly his theology and his doctrine on the Trinity. It is quite a long, wordy creed, the first part dealing with the Trinity, the second with the person of Christ. The text is as follows:

> ★Whosoever will be saved: before all things it is
> necessary that he hold the Catholic Faith.
> Which Faith except everyone do keep whole and
> undefiled: without doubt he shall perish everlastingly.

I. And the Catholic Faith is this: That we worship one God in Trinity, and Trinity in Unity;
    Neither confounding the Persons: nor dividing the Substance.
    For there is one Person of the Father, another of the Son; and another of the Holy Ghost.
    But the God-head of the Father, of the Son and of the Holy Ghost, is all one: the Glory equal, the Majesty co-eternal.
    Such as the Father is, such is the Son: and such is the Holy Ghost.
    The Father un-create, the Son un-create: and the Holy Ghost un-create.
    The Father incomprehensible, the Son incomprehensible: and the Holy Ghost incomprehensible.
    The Father eternal, the Son eternal: and the Holy Ghost eternal.
    And yet they are not three eternals: but one eternal.
    As also there are not three incomprehensibles, nor three un-created: but
    one un-created, and one incomprehensible.
    So likewise the Father is Almighty, the Son Almighty: and the Holy Ghost Almighty.
    And yet they are not three Almighties: but one Almighty.
    So the Father is God, and Son is God: and the Holy Ghost is God.

And yet they are not three Gods: but one God.

So likewise the Father is Lord, the Son is Lord: and the Holy Ghost is Lord.

And yet not three Lords: but one Lord.

For like as we are compelled by the Christian verity: to acknowledge every

Person by Himself to be God and Lord;

So we are forbidden by the Catholic Religion: to say, there be three Gods,

or three Lords.

The Father is made of none: neither created, nor begotten.

The Son is of the Father alone: not made, nor created, but begotten.

The Holy Ghost is of the Father and of the Son: neither made, nor created, nor begotten, but proceeding.

So there is one Father, not three Fathers; one Son, not three Sons: one Holy Ghost, not three Holy Ghosts,

And in this Trinity none is afore, nor after other: none is greater, or less than another;

But the whole three Persons are co-eternal together: and co-equal.

So that in all things, as is aforesaid: the Unity in Trinity and the Trinity in Unity, is to be worshipped.

> ★He therefore that will be saved:
> must thus think of the Trinity.

II. Furthermore, it is necessary to everlasting salvation: that he also believe rightly the Incarnation of our Lord Jesus Christ.

For the right Faith is, that we believe and confess: that our Lord Jesus Christ, the Son of God, is God and Man;

God, of the Substance of the Father, begotten before the worlds: and Man, of the Substance of His Mother, born in the world;

Perfect God, and perfect Man: of a reasonable soul and human flesh subsisting;

Equal to the Father, as touching His God-head and inferior to the Father, as touching His Manhood.

Who although He be God and Man: yet He is not two, but one Christ;

One, not by conversion of the God-head into flesh: but by taking of the Manhood into God;

One altogether; not by confusion of Substance; but by unity of Person.

For as the reasonable soul and flesh is one man: so God and Man is one Christ;

Who suffered for our Salvation: descended into hell, rose again the third day from the dead.

He ascended into heaven, He sitteth on the right hand of the Father,

---

NICAEA

Πιστεύομεν εἰς ἕνα θεόν, πατέρα, παντο-κράτορα, πάντων ὁρατῶν τε καὶ ἀοράτων ποιητήν. Καὶ εἰς ἕνα κύριον Ἰησοῦν Χριστόν, τὸν υἱὸν τοῦ θεοῦ, γεννηθέντα ἐκ τοῦ πατρὸς μονογενῆ, τουτέστιν ἐκ τῆς οὐσίας τοῦ πατρός, θεὸν ἐκ θεοῦ, φῶς ἐκ φωτός, θεὸν ἀληθινὸν ἐκ θεοῦ ἀληθινοῦ, γεννη-θέντα οὐ ποιηθέντα, ὁμοούσιον τῷ πατρί, δι' οὗ τὰ πάντα ἐγένετο, τά τε ἐν τῷ	We believe in one God, the Father, almighty, maker of all things visible and invisible; And in one Lord Jesus Christ, the Son of God, begotten from the Father, only-begotten, that is, from the sub-stance of the Father, God from God, light from light, true God from true God, begotten not made, of one substance with the Father, through

Part of the Nicene Creed in Greek and English.

God Almighty: from whence he shall come to judge the quick and the dead.

At whose coming all men shall rise again with their bodies: and shall give account for their own works.

And they that have done good shall go into life everlasting: and they that have done evil into everlasting fire.

> ★This is the Catholic Faith: which except a man
> believe faithfully, he cannot be saved.

The Nicene Creed

This creed is the one used in the Sunday liturgy of many Christian Churches. It was the formula agreed on by the Council of Constantinople in 381, so really it is incorrect to speak of it as the Nicene Creed. However, some scholars have maintained that the creed agreed upon in 381 was really a touching up of the previous formula established in 325 by the Council of Nicea.

The context of these two Councils, Nicea and Constantinople, was one of polemics and heresy. Both were concerned with rebuffing Arianism and establishing correct formulae of faith. The environment in which those conciliar creeds arose was very different indeed from the catechetical one of the first two centuries. It has been said that the old creeds were for catechumens and the new ones for bishops. Certainly the "new ones" (conciliar creeds) were devised as touchstones of orthodoxy for teachers and preachers.

Before exploring the background to the Nicene Creed, the actual text will be cited:

> *We believe in one God,*
> *the Father, the Almighty,*
> *maker of heaven and earth,*
> *of all that is, seen and unseen.*

We believe in one Lord, Jesus Christ,
the only Son of God,
eternally begotten of the Father,
God from God, Light from Light,
true God from true God,
begotten, not made,
of one Being with the Father.
Through him all things were made.

For us and for our salvation
he came down from heaven;
by the power of the Holy Spirit
he became incarnate from the Virgin Mary
and was made man.

For our sake he was crucified under Pontius Pilate;
he suffered death, and was buried.
On the third day he rose again in accordance with the Scriptures;
he ascended into heaven and is seated at the right
hand of the Father.
He will come again in glory to judge the living and
the dead, and his kingdom will have no end.

We believe in the Holy Spirit, the Lord, the giver of life,
who proceeds from the Father and the Son,
With the Father and the Son he is worshipped and glorified.
He has spoken through the Prophets.
We believe in one holy catholic and apostolic Church.
We acknowledge one baptism for the forgiveness of sins.
We look for the Resurrection of the dead,
and the life of the world to come. Amen.

THE POLEMIC CONTEXT

Heresies

Although the main heresy associated with the origin of the Nicene Creed was Arianism, there was certainly no shortage of heresies in the first few centuries of the Christian era as Christological and Trinitarian problems were ironed out. Many of the heretics were sincere and sometimes saintly people who were striving to come to terms with the mystery of the Incarnation.

The Ebionites, for example, in the second century were Judaisers who feared worshipping Christ lest by so doing they offended the unity of Godhead. The Docetists held to the divinity of Christ but maintained he only appeared to be human—in reality they said his physical appearance was an optical illusion and mere "semblance" (*dokesis*—hence "Docetism"). They rejected any genuine incarnation. The Sabellians denied Jesus had the same substance as the Father; Arius that Christ was divine. Nestorius thought Christians should call Mary Christotokos (mother of Christ) but not Theototokos (mother of God) because she was mother of his humanity not his divinity. Eutyches and the monophysites asserted Christ only had one nature not two. And so the list goes on. With each new heresy the Church was either forced to refine its previous statements or make new ones.

Linguistic and Conceptual Problems

When reading the history of the early Councils and the theological debates, one is struck by the substantial difficulties associated with language usage and differing theologies. As regards language it must be remembered that the Eastern part of the Roman empire was Greek-speaking and influenced by a Greek or Eastern outlook. The West was Latin-speaking and had its own pagan worldview. The early Church was Jewish in origin but soon became very much "Gentile", or a church of converted pagans. Distances were great and transport slow, with the result that centers of Christianity and secular learning developed strong identities in relative isolation. "Schools" of philosophy and theology existed with strong traditions.

Having said the above by way of background, we can return to the Creeds. The original Nicene Creed arose in response to the heresy of Arius, a presbyter of Alexandria in North Africa. He held that Christ was not really divine and hence not equal to the Father. The Arians, in general, held a pagan view of God as unknowable, unchangeable and unreachable. This kind of God would certainly not become a man nor become involved in human affairs. This God was One and Supreme. Christ therefore, they argued, must be a subordinate, created deity, a mediator between the Godhead and the world. The Arian Christ was neither properly God nor properly man, but something in between. He was a creature of God's rather than an incarnation of God. They quoted texts from St Paul which seem to support the notion of Christ being subordinate to the Father, e.g. 1 Co 11: 3; 15: 28; Col 1: 15.

In response the "orthodox" believers quoted passages which seem to place Christ in the same category as the Father, e.g. Jn 10: 30; 14: 9; Rm 9: 5. To counter Arius, the proposal before the Council of Nicea (325) was that the Son is "of one substance with the Father", in Greek *Homoousion*. Bear in mind that the Council was attended by about 318 bishops, mainly Greek-speaking.

There was much debate about the introduction of the new word *homoousion* (one, same substance). It was not scriptural and had been associated with previous heresies. Arians were quick to see that if the word was accepted, their position might be able to be harmonized with it. The clause "of one substance (*homoousios*) with the Father" declared the Father and the Son are "the same". However to some this meant a personal or specific identity in the sense of the Son being identical with, or the same as the Father. To others it simply meant a much broader, generic identity in the sense of the Son being similar to the Father. Partly because of this ambiguity, all except two bishops voted in favor of the term, which has come down to us. The circumstances surrounding the origins of the Nicene Creed thus explain the emphasis on the relationship between the Son and the Father:

> *"We believe in one Lord, Jesus Christ,*
> *the only Son of God,*
> *eternally begotten of the Father,*
> *God from God, Light from Light*
> *true God from true God,*
> *begotten, not made,*
> *of one Being* (homoousios) *with the Father. . ."*

The Council of Constantinople (381) reaffirmed the Nicene faith. It approved and reaffirmed the key word *homoousios*, but the creed that was promulgated was worded differently from that of Nicea and contained a clause on the Holy Spirit. The difference between the Son and the Spirit, it was pointed out, is that the Son is begotten of the Father, but the Holy Spirit "proceeds" from the Father. This formulation reflected Eastern thinking and that of Basil of Caesarea in particular. (Stating that the Holy Spirit proceeds from the Father only is known as the single procession. Later on the double procession was introduced into the Nicene Creed, i.e. the Holy Spirit proceeds from the Father and the Son.)

We have been discussing the linguistic and doctrinal problems arising from the word "substance". There was a similar debate over the word "person" with respect to the Trinity and the Athanasian Creed. The Trinity was spoken of as three persons in one God but the understanding of the word "person" varied. It is worth examining this in greater detail.

The Latin word *persona* originally meant a part played in social life, the function of an individual in society and later on the actual occupier of such a role or function. In drama it was used of both the role and the individual in that role. Thus today we still speak of the dramatis personae in a play, i.e. the actors in the play in their roles. (This Latin use of *persona* is thus different from the contemporary use of "person" in the sense of "personality" stressing individuality and identity.) Tertullian in the West popularized the Trinitarian formula "one Substance, three Persons", in the Latin sense of *persona*.

The Greek word *prosopon* corresponded to the Latin *persona*. However, because of its links with Sabellianism it never came to be used for the Persons of the Trinity. Sabellius had argued that the three Persons of the Trinity were merely temporary manifestations (*proposa*) of the divine Essence. As this view was rejected the Eastern theologians settled on another word, namely *hypostasis*—the equivalent of the Latin *substantia*, "substance"—to indicate Persons in the Trinity. So when the Latins used *persona* for a person in the Trinity, the Greeks used *hypostasis*.

These two terms, *persona* and *hypotasis* avoid the two extreme meanings of an abstract substance and a concrete individual being. There is no English equivalent. Our word "person" stresses too much the idea of a separate individual being and suggests Tritheism when applied to the Trinity, while the word "mode" is vague and leans towards Sabellianism.

Thus any translation of the Latin or Greek runs the risk of losing some aspects of its meaning. Augustine was a Latin and when he wrote about the Trinity he deliberately chose to put forward different thinking. He did not like the Eastern use of three "hypostases" thinking it stressed pluralism of the divine Persons too much. The Greeks also spoke of the Son as begotten of the Father and the Spirit proceeding from the Father. Augustine thought this smacked of Arianism (Son "begotten") and sub-ordinationism (Son subordinate to Father). He thought the unity of the Trinity was best safeguarded by speaking of the Holy Spirit as proceeding from the Father and the Son (double procession).

Augustine made use of an analogy to illustrate his point. He spoke of the triad of memory (center of personality including subconscious mind), intelligence and will within the one person. The intelligence is a reflection, he thought, of the divine Reason who is the Son; the will mirrors that love which is the Holy Spirit, while the center of the personality is analogous to the Father. If anything this analogy bends towards "modes" of existence but it should be borne in mind that Augustine was struggling with a great mystery of faith. It was when the mystery was put into words in the form of a profession of faith that difficulties of understanding and language appeared.

Augustine's formulation of the double procession appears in the

"Athanasian" Creed. The double procession surfaced again in Spain in the seventh century in the Nicene Creed. Gradually this *Filioque* clause (so named because *Filioque*—"and from the Son" was added to "who proceeds from the Father") was accepted in the West with the encouragement of Charlemagne, although the Popes held out until the eleventh century.

The Eastern Christians were, however, most offended that the Latin Church should act unilaterally against the decision of the Council of Constantinople in 381, and alter the Nicene Creed by adding "and from the Son". This difference between East and West was just one of a number which led to the East/West Schism of 1054.

Given the above history of debates surrounding the Athanasian Creed one can appreciate the emphasis placed on the Trinity and on Christ.

CREEDS AND THE LITURGY

We have already indicated that baptism, catechetical instruction and anti-heretical polemics all provided occasions for the rise and use of fixed formulas of the main articles of Christian belief. Now we want to focus on the liturgy and those creeds. It is accepted today that the primary use of creeds, their true and original use, was to serve as solemn affirmations of faith in the context of baptismal initiation.

A distinction must be made at this point between declaratory and interrogatory creeds. When the adult catechumens presented themselves for instruction they were taught over a number of weeks with the bishop "handing out" or "giving" the creed in the later weeks of Lent and commenting on it phrase by phrase. Then at baptism the catechumens were expected to "give it back", i.e. to recite it by rote as a demonstration that they knew their new faith. In a way the declaratory creeds became a by-product of the teaching of catechumens.

The interrogatory creeds were really the baptismal questions. At baptism, the candidate was asked a series of questions about the faith and had to respond to each. A good example of this liturgy is mentioned in the Apostolic Tradition written about 215 by St Hippolytus, which probably reflects known liturgical practice of the third century. It reads:

> *And when he who is to be baptized goes down to the water, let him who baptizes lay hands on him saying thus, "Dost thou believe in God the Father almighty?" And he who is being baptized shall say, "I believe". Let him forthwith baptize him once, having his hand laid upon his head. And after this let him say, "Dost thou believe in Christ Jesus, the Son of*

*Eleventh century Romanesque
Church of Saints Gervasius and
Protasius, and octagonal baptistry,
Baveno, Northern Italy.*

*God, Who was born by the Holy Spirit from the Virgin Mary, Who was
crucified under Pontius Pilate and died, and rose again on the third day
living from the dead, and ascended into the heaven, and sat down on the
right hand of the Father, and will come to judge the living and the
dead?" And when he says, "I believe", let him baptize him the second
time. And again let him say, "Dost thou believe in the Holy Spirit, in the
holy Church, and the Resurrection of the flesh?" And he who is being
baptized shall say, "I believe". And so let him baptize him the third time.*
(Kelly, 1972: 46)

It was this interrogatory creed which properly belonged to the baptism as
such. The declaratory creed later began to be recited at the baptismal
ceremony but after the actual questions and answers and the plunging into
the water. The candidate was able to recite the creed which had been
learned during the weeks of instruction. Thus although the declaratory
creed found a place within the baptismal liturgy, its function was secondary.

Here we might note the rise of an odd name for the creeds, namely
"symbolum". It was used in the third century to denote the baptismal
questions and answers. The basic meaning of the word was that of a "sign"
or "token". Thus to speak of the baptismal interrogatory creed as a "sign"
meant it was taken as a sign of one's faith, a symbol of faith. Although

interrogatory creeds were not extensive interrogations of faith, nevertheless they stood for acceptance of the total faith of Christianity. Again with time "symbolum" was used to refer to the declaratory creeds. Thus the Nicene Creed today would be called a "symbol", "sign" or "token" of faith.

Given that the creed really belongs to baptism, its appearance in the Eucharistic liturgy makes for interesting reading. The fifth-century Monophysites (believed in one nature in Christ) inserted the Nicene Creed into their Eucharistic liturgy in a dramatic protest against what they saw as "innovations" of the Council of Chalcedon. The Chalcedonians however refuted the idea that they were not orthodox, by also inserting the Creed into their Eucharistic liturgy. This custom became general in West and East where it came to be recited after the Gospel.

Under Charlemagne in the West, as we saw above, the Filioque clause was added and popularized. The pope in Rome was not immediately affected by this innovation as his rite of the Mass did not have a place for a creed at all! But by the eleventh century even the pope was reciting the Nicene Creed with the Filioque clause. As with the Easter Vigil, the recitation of the creed during the Eucharistic Liturgy after hearing the Word of God serves as a renewal of commitment.

EXERCISE 78:   (a) Which of the above creeds do you personally prefer? Say why. Comment on the language used in each.
(b) Read the following examples of a creed:

(i) *An African Creed*
We believe in the one High God, who out of love created the beautiful world and everything good in it. He created man and wanted man to be happy in the world. God loves the world and every nation and tribe on the earth. We have known this High God in the darkness, and now we know him in the light. God promised in the book of his word, the Bible, that he would save the world and all the nations and tribes.

We believe that God made good his promise by sending his son, Jesus Christ, a man in the flesh, a Jew by tribe, born poor in a little village, who left his home and was always on safari doing good, curing people by the power of God, teaching about God and man, showing that the meaning of religion is love. He was rejected by his people, tortured and nailed hands and feet to a cross and died. He lay buried in the grave, but the hyenas did not touch him, and on the third day he rose from the grave. He ascended to the skies. He is the Lord.

We believe that all our sins are forgiven through him. All who have faith in him must be sorry for their sins, be baptized in the Holy Spirit of God, live the rules of love and share the bread together in love to announce the good news to others until Jesus comes again. We are waiting for him. He is alive. He lives. This we believe. Amen. (Donovan, 1973: 200)

(ii) *A Contemporary Creed*

We believe in a loving God, creator of all humankind, who forms and sustains the universe in power and love. We believe in a God who has not divided people into the poor and the rich, specialists and the ignorant, owners and slaves.

We believe in Jesus Christ, God incarnate, who showed us by his words and work, suffering with others and conquest of death, what human life ought to be and what God is like.

We believe in Jesus Christ who rose, and continues to rise for our life, so that we may be liberated from prejudice and arrogance, from fear and hate, so that we may transform the world into the city of God.

We believe in the Spirit who came with Jesus into the world, who is present with us now and always, and can be experienced in prayer, in action, in forgiveness, in the Word, and in the community of the Church.

We believe in the community of all peoples and in our responsibilities for making our world either into a place of misery, hunger and tyranny, or into the City of God.

We believe that it is possible to build a just peace.

We believe that a life of meaning is possible for all, and we believe in the future of this world of God. Amen.

(Adapted from a poem by German theologian Dorothy Solee, and the Latin credo.)

(iii) *A Creed About Justice*

I believe in a color-blind God.
Maker of technicolor people,
Who created the universe
And provided abundant resources
For equitable distribution
among all God's people.[1]

(iv) *An Australian Creed*

We believe in God,
We believe in ourselves as the image of God,

We believe in Australians,
  in their black Aboriginal beauty,
  in their migrant struggles,
  in their search for identity.

We believe in the Australian place,

with its Asian context,
its northern culture,
with all its nearness and all its distance,
with its possibilities for growth,
in dream time, southern time, our time.

We believe in our responsibility for creation;
the trust of every mountain range,
of every forest and harbor,
of every city, of plans for the future.

We believe in our hopes for the human family as Christ
wishes it,
in ourselves in the mobility that God has given us, to
experience the beauty of our vast land,

We believe that we are a community of saints,
called to build God's kingdom of peace,
and the kingdom of justice and mercy for all,
among all peoples, in this country of Australia.

Amen.[2]

(c) Now compose your own short creed, stressing those
aspects of your faith which you think need emphasizing today.

[1] Canaan Banana, The Gospel According to the Ghetto, Geneva: World Council of
Churches, 1974, p. 8. (quoted in C. S. Song's *The Reign of God*, p. 45).
[2] Bulletin, Holy Name Parish, Wahroonga, Sydney, Australia, 4/7/93.

GLOSSARY

Allegory	A literary composition in which each detail is given a meaning.
Canon	Greek "rule" or "measure". List of writing accepted as Sacred Scripture by the Church. Only at the Council of Trent (1546) did the Roman Catholic Church define the list of books of the Old Testament (46) and the New Testament (27). The Roman Catholic, Protestant and Jewish Bibles vary in the number of books they recognize as canonical.
Chiasm	Greek *chiasma* = "crossing". Inverted parallelism. The arrangement of words in a sentence or the elements in a pericope in such a way that they form corresponding pairs, often around a center, thus: a b—c—b a.
Chiliasm	From Greek *chilioi* = 1000. The theory that the earthly Kingdom of Christ would be initiated by the Second Coming in the year 1000.
Christology	A theological interpretation of the person and work of Christ.
Creed	A concise statement of essential beliefs enjoying the sanction of ecclesiastical authority.
Eschatology	From Greek *eschaton* = the last things. Doctrines concerning the last things, i.e. the end of the world, death, heaven and hell.
Essenes	A religious group within Judaism whose members followed a strict rule of life and believed themselves to be the true remnant of God's people.
Exegesis	Practical application of the theoretical rules of interpretation supplied by hermeneutics (see "hermeneutics" below).
Exorcism	The casting out of evil spirits.
Fundamentalism	Indicates a literal understanding of the Bible and in theology in general, extreme conservatism.
Form criticism	Analysis of Gospels based on the assumption that early

	Christian communities, during the period of oral tradition, adapted material to their own circumstances.
Genealogy	An account or listing of the family tree.
Gentile	Not of the Jewish race.
Hermeneutics	The science of interpretation of Scripture.
Homoousios	Of the same substance.
Homoiousios	Like in substance.
Inclusion	The repetition at the end of a piece of writing (pericope/chapter/book) of the same words/idea/theme that occurred at the beginning, thus drawing the reader's attention back to the beginning and providing a frame for the whole.
Inspiration	The doctrine that God has chosen to speak through people who in turn have recorded this communication in written form (Scripture).
Kerygma	From Greek *kerygma* = proclamation. Refers to the initial preaching or public proclamation of the Gospel.
Messiah	From the Hebrew for "anointed'; refers to the Jewish expectation of a savior.
Messianism	A group of ideas including the hope of a Messiah, the expectation that the Israel of the future would be identical with the universal Kingdom of Yahweh.
Midrash	(pl. = midrashim) Ancient Jewish commentary on part of the Hebrew Scriptures (Old Testament). A reflection on some text of Scripture in the light of the current situation.
Parable	Similitudes, comparisons or short stories drawn by Jesus from daily life to make his message plain and vivid.
Parousia	Greek for "presence". Technical term for the second coming of Christ at the end of time.
Pericope	A short passage or unit of Scripture.
Pharisee	A lay religious movement or party in Judaism characterized by their attention to the Torah (Law).
Redaction criticism	Analysis of the Gospels based on the assumption that authors have edited material, giving it theological bias.
Redactor	The final editor of a particular Gospel.
Sanhedrin	Highest Jewish tribunal during Greek and Roman periods.
Sadducee	Jewish aristocratic religious sect in the time of Jesus with a rigid understanding of the Torah (Law).
Sitz im Leben	The technical term referring to the actual life-setting of a text in Scripture.
Soteriology	From Greek *soteria* = salvation. The study of the theology of salvation and redemption.
Source criticism	Analysis of the Gospels or other Scriptures which examines the origins of various texts and their dependence on common or particular sources.

Synagogue   Jewish institution for the reading and exposition of the Old Testament.

Synoptic   From Greek *synoptikos* = seeing the whole together. It is used in reference to the first three Gospels of the New Testament because they take a common view (to some extent) of the events in the life of Jesus.

Torah   (a) Law, or "Teaching"; (b) The name given to the first part of the Hebrew canon of the Old Testament, comprising the five books Genesis, Exodus, Leviticus, Numbers, Deuteronomy.

Zealots   A militant group of nationalists in Judaism determined to overthrow the Romans by armed revolution.

BIBLIOGRAPHY

General

Abbott, W. (ed.) (1966), *The Documents of Vatican II*, London: Chapman.

Black, M. (ed.) (1977), *Peake's Commentary on the Bible*, Middlesex: Nelson.

Brown, R., Fitzmyer, J., & Murphy, R., (eds.) (1990), *The New Jerome Biblical Commentary*, London: Geoffrey Chapman.

Butterick, G. et al. (ed.) (1962), *The Interpreter's Dictionary of the Bible*, New York: Abingdon.

McBrien, R. (1980), *Catholicism*, Melbourne: Collins Dove.

Newsom, C. & Ringe, S. (ed.) (1992), *The Women's Bible Commentary*, London: SPCK.

Rahner, K. (ed.) (1975), *Encyclopedia of Theology*, London: Burns & Oates.

Chapter 1: The Setting for the Story

Anderson, B. (1975), *Understanding the Old Testament*, Englewood Cliffs: Prentice Hall.

Bornkamm, G. (1981), *Jesus of Nazareth*, London: Hodder & Stoughton.

Charpentier, E. (1981), *How to Read the New Testament*, London: SCM.

Crown, A. (1981), "The Dead Sea Scrolls", *Current Affairs Bulletin*, July, 1981.

Ellis, P. (1976), *The Men and the Message of the Old Testament*, Collegeville: Liturgical Press.

Fallon, M. (1981), *The Four Gospels*, Sydney: Catholic Adult Education Centre.

Goergen, D. (1986), "Jesus' Roots in Palestinian Judaism", Ch. 2, *The Mission and Ministry of Jesus*, Wilmington: Michael Glazier.

Gottwald, N. (1979), *The Tribes of Yahweh*, London: SCM.

Grosvenor, M.B. & Vosburgh, F.G. (1968), *Everyday Life in Bible Times*, Washington: National Geographic Society.

Hammond, C.S. (1959), *Atlas of the Bible Lands*, Maplewood: W.J. Hammond Inc.

Kee, H.C. & Young, F. (1974), *The Living World of the New Testament*, London: Darton, Longman & Todd.

LaSor, W. (1972), *The Dead Sea Scrolls and the New Testament*, Michigan: Eerdman.

May, H. (ed.) (1974), *Oxford Bible Atlas*, London: O.U.P.

Murphy, F. (1991), *The Religious World of Jesus: An Introduction to Second Temple Palestinian Judaism*, Nashville: Abingdon Press.

Nolan, A. (1977), *Jesus Before Christianity*, London: Darton, Longman & Todd.

Perkins, P. (1978), *Reading the New Testament*, New York: Paulist Press.

Perrin, N. (1974), *The New Testament*, New York: Harcourt Brace.

Rops, D. (1962), *Daily Life in Palestine in the Time of Christ*, London: Weidenfeld & Nicolson.

Rowley, H. (1965), *Student's Bible Atlas*, Thetford: Lutterworth.

Senior, D. (1975), *Jesus*, Dayton: Pflaum.

Spivey, R. & Smith, D. (1982), *Anatomy of the New Testament*, New York: Macmillan.

de Vaux, R. (1961), *Ancient Israel*, New York: McGraw Hill.

Wijngaards, J. (1979), *The Homeland of Jesus*, Great Wakering: Mayhew-McCrimmon.

Winton, Thomas D. (1961), *Documents from Old Testament Times*, New York: Harper & Row.

Wouk, H. (1960), *This is My God*, New York: Cape.

Chapter 2: The Growth and Development of New Testament Studies

Abbott, W. (ed.) (1966), "Dogmatic Constitution on Divine Revelation", *The Documents of Vatican II*, London: Chapman.

Baker, T. (1969), *What is the New Testament?*, London: SCM.

Beare, F. (1968), "Concerning Jesus of Nazareth", *Journal of Biblical Literature*, Vol. 87, 125–135.

Belo, F. (1981), *A Materialist Reading of the Gospel of Mark*, New York: Maryknoll.

Bonino, J. Miguez (1975), *Doing Theology in a Revolutionary Situation*, Philadelphia: Fortress Press.

Bornkamm, G. (1960), *Jesus of Nazareth*, London: Hodder & Stoughton.

Childs, B. (1979), *Introduction to the Old Testament as Scripture*, London: SCM.

Collins, R. (1983), *Introduction to the New Testament*, London: SCM.

Crossan, D. (1991), *The Historical Jesus*, Edinburgh: T & T Clark.

Culpepper, R. (1983), *Anatomy of the Fourth Gospel*, Philadelphia: Fortress Press.

Esler, P. (1987), *Community and Gospel in Luke-Acts: The Social and Political Motivations of Lucan Theology*, Cambridge: SNTS Monograph Series 57.

Flanagan, N. (1978), *Mark, Matthew, and Luke: A Guide to the Gospel Parallels*, Collegeville: Liturgical Press.

Fiorenza, E. Schüssler (1983), *In Memory of Her: A Feminist Theological Reconstruction of Christian Origins*, London: SCM Press.

—— (1984), *Bread Not Stone: The Challenge of Feminist Biblical Interpretation*, Boston: Beacon.

—— (1985), "The Will to Choose or Reject: Continuing Our Critical Work", L. Russell (ed.) *Feminist Interpretation of the Bible*, Oxford: Blackwell.

—— (1992), *But She Said: Feminist Practices of Biblical Interpretation*, Boston: Beacon.

Fitzmyer, J. (1981), "The Dead Sea Scrolls and the New Testament after Thirty Years", *Theology Digest*, Vol. 29, No.4.

Gager, J. (1975), *Kingdom and Country: The Social World of Early Christianity*, Englewood Cliffs, New Jersey: Prentice-Hall.

Gamble, H. (1985), *The New Testament Canon*, Philadelphia: Fortress Press.

Gutiérrez, G. (1973), *A Theology of Liberation*, London: SCM.

Hampson, D. (1990), *Theology and Feminism*, Oxford: Basil Blackwell.

Holmberg, B. (1980), *Paul and Power: The Structures of Authority in the Primitive Church as Reflected in the Pauline Epistles*, Philadelphia: Fortress Press.

Jewett, R. (1988), *The Social World of Formative Christianity and Judaism*, Philadelphia Press.

Judge, E.A. (1960), *The Social Pattern of the Christian Group in the First Century*, London: Tyndale.

Keegan, T. (1985), *Interpreting the Bible*, New York: Paulist Press.

Kingsbury, J. (1986), *Matthew as Story*, Philadelphia: Fortress Press.

Krentz, E. (1985), *The Historical-Critical Method*, Philadelphia: Fortress Press.

Leon-Dufour, X. (1980), *Dictionary of the New Testament*, London: Geoffrey Chapman.

Loades, A. (ed.) (1990), *Feminist Theology: A Reader*, London: SPCK.

Mack, B. (1993), *The Lost Gospel: the Book of Q and Christian Origins*, San Francisco: Harper Collins.

Malherbe, A. (1983), *Social Aspects of Early Christianity*, Philadelphia: Fortress Press.

Maisch, I. & Vogtle, A. (1975), "Jesus Christ", *Encyclopedia of Theology*, London: Burns & Oates.

McKnight, E. (1969), *What is Form Criticism?*, Philadelphia: Fortress Press.

Meeks, W. (1983), *The First Urban Christians: the Social World of the Apostle Paul*, New Haven: Yale University Press.

Osiek, C. (1984), *What Are They Saying About the Social Setting of the New Testament?*, New York: Paulist Press.

Perkins, P. (1978), *Reading the New Testament*, New York: Paulist Press.

Perrin, N. (1974), *The New Testament*, New York: Harcourt Brace.

—— (1969), *What is Redaction Criticism?*, Philadelphia: Fortress Press.

Pesch, R. (1975), "Jesus Christ", K. Rahner (ed.), *Encyclopedia of Theology*, London: Burns & Oates.

Peterson, N. (1978), *Literary Criticism for New Testament Critics*, Philadelphia: Fortress Press.

Pius XII (1943), *Divino Afflante Spiritu*, London: Catholic Truth Society.

Pontifical Biblical Commission (1964), "Instruction on the Historical Truth of the Gospels", *Catholic Biblical Quarterly*, 26, 1964, 305–312.

Powell, M. (1990), *What is Narrative Criticism?* Minneapolis: Fortress Press.

Redlich, E. (1939), *Form Criticism*, London: Duckworth.

Rhoads, D. & Michie, D. (1982), *Mark as Story*, Philadelphia: Fortress Press.

Russell, L. (ed.) (1985), *Feminist Interpretation of the Bible?*, Oxford: Blackwell.

Schneiders, S. (1986), *Women and the Word: the Gender of God in the New Testament*, New York: Paulist.

—— (1991A), *Beyond Patching*, New York: Paulist.

—— (1991B), *The Revelatory Text*, San Francisco: Harper Collins.

Segundo, J. (1976), *The Liberation of Theology*, New York: Orbis Books.

Spivey, R. & Smith, D. (1982), *Anatomy of the New Testament*, New York: Macmillan.

Stambaugh, J. and Balch, D. (1986), *The Social World of the First Christians*, London: SPCK.

Theissen, G. (1978), *Sociology of Early Palestinian Christianity*, Philadelphia: Fortress Press.

—— (1992), *The Gospels in Context: Social and Political History in the Synoptic Tradition*, Edinburgh: T & T Clark.

Thiselton, A. (1992), *New Horizons in Hermeneutics: The Theory and Practice of Transforming Biblical Reading*, London: Harper Collins Publishers.

Trible, P. (1978), *God and the Rhetoric of Sexuality*, Philadelphia: Fortress Press.

—— (1984), *Texts of Terror*, Philadelphia: Fortress Press.

—— (1990), "Feminist Hermeneutics and Biblical Studies", Loades, A. (ed.), (1990), *Feminist Theology: A Reader*, London: SPCK.

Wainwright, E. (1992), "If I But Touch His Garment", *Women-Church* 11, Spring, 1992: 13–20.

Chapter 3: The Gospel Stories

Brown, R. (1977), *The Birth of the Messiah*, London: Geoffrey Chapman.

—— (1966), *The Gospel According to John* (2 Vols), Anchor Bible, London: Geoffrey Chapman.

—— (1979), *The Community of the Beloved Disciple*, New York: Paulist Press.

Brown, R. & Meier, J. (1983), *Antioch and Rome*, New York: Paulist.

Charpentier, E. (1981), *How to Read the New Testament*, London: SCM.

Dodd, C.H. (1953), *The Interpretation of the Fourth Gospel*, C.U.P.

Doohan, L. (1985), *Matthew: Spirituality for the 80s and 90s*, Santa Fe: Bear & Co.

—— (1985), *Luke: The Perennial Spirituality*, Santa Fe: Bear & Co.

—— (1986), *Mark: Visionary of Early Christianity*, Santa Fe: Bear & Co.

—— (1988), *John: Gospel for a New Age*, Santa Fe: Bear & Co.

Edwards, O. (1981), *Luke's Story of Jesus*, Philadelphia: Fortress Press.

Ellis, P.F. (1984), *The Genius of John: a Composition Critical Commentary on the Fourth Gospel*, Collegeville: Liturgical Press.

Fallon, M. (1981), *The Four Gospels*, Sydney: Catholic Adult Education Centre.

Fiorenza, E. Schüssler (1983), *In Memory of Her*, London: SCM.

Fitzmyer, J. (1981), *The Gospel According to Luke I–IX*, New York: Doubleday.

Hendricks, H. (1984), *The Infancy Narratives*, London: Chapman.

Kelber, W. (1979), *Mark's Story of Jesus*, Philadelphia: Fortress Press.

Kingsbury, J.D. (1986), *Matthew as Story*, Philadelphia: Fortress Press.

Kysar, R. (1984), *John's Story of Jesus*, Philadelphia: Fortress Press.

—— (1976), *John: the Maverick Gospel*, Atlanta: John Knox Press.

Mack, B. (1988), *A Myth of Innocence: Mark and Christian Origins*, Philadelphia: Fortress Press.

McKenzie, J. (1968), "The Gospel According to Matthew", *Jerome Biblical Commentary*, New Jersey: Prentice-Hall.

Moloney, F. (1984), *Woman, First Among the Faithful*, Blackburn: Collins Dove.

—— (1986), *The Living Voice of the Gospel*, Blackburn: Collins Dove.

Perkins, P. (1978), *Reading the New Testament: An Introduction*, New York: Paulist Press.

Perrin, N. (1974), *The New Testament*, New York: Harcourt Brace.

Rhoads, D. & Michie, D. (1982), *Mark as Story*, Philadelphia: Fortress Press.

Spivey, R. & Smith, D. (1982), *Anatomy of the New Testament*, New York: Macmillan.

Stuhlmeuller, C. (1968), "The Gospel According to Luke", *Jerome Biblical Commentary*, New Jersey: Prentice-Hall.

Taylor, M. (1983), *John: The Different Gospel—A Reflective Commentary*, New York: Alba House.

Chapter 4: A Portrait of Jesus

Alter, R. (1981), *The Art of Biblical Narrative*, London: Allen & Unwin.

Barr, J. (1988), "Abba Isn't 'Daddy' ", *Journal of Theological Studies*, 39: 1, 28–47.

Crossan, J.D. (1973), *In Parables*, New York: Harper & Row.

—— (1975), *The Dark Interval*, Niles: Angus.

Elsen, A. (1962), *Purposes of Art*, New York: Hold, Rinehart, Winston.

Fallon, M. (1981), *The Four Gospels*, Sydney: Catholic Education Centre.

Fuller, R. (1963), *Interpreting the Miracles*, London: SCM.

Hahn, F. (1973), *The Worship of the Early Church*, Philadelphia: Fortress Press.

Hunter, R. (1960), *Interpreting the Parables*, London: SCM.

Jeremias, J. (1972), *The Parables of Jesus*, London: SCM.

Johnson, E. (1993), *She Who Is: the Mystery of God in Feminist Theological Discourse*, New York: Crossroad.

Josephus (1960), *Josephus: Complete Works*, Grand Rapids: Kregel.

Kasper, W. (1976), *Jesus the Christ*, Malvern: Dove.

Kealy, J. (1977), *Who is Jesus of Nazareth?*, Denville: Dimension Books.

Kee, H. (1983), *Miracle in the Early Christian World*, New Haven: Yale University Press.

Kennedy, G. (1960), *The Parables*, New York: Harper & Row.

Link, M. (1978), *The Seventh Trumpet*, Niles: Argus.

Loades, A. (ed.), (1990), *Feminist Theology: A Reader*, London: SPCK.

Loisy, A. (1902), *Evangile et l'Eglise*, Paris.

McFague, S. (1975), *Speaking in Parables: A Study in Metaphor and Theology*, Philadelphia: Fortress Press.

Moloney, F. (1986), *The Living Voice of the Gospel*, Blackburn: Collins Dove.

O'Collins, G. (1977), *What Are They Saying About Jesus?*, New York: Paulist Press.

O'Hagan, A. & Crowe, J. (1973), *In Various Ways, God Spoke*, Melbourne: Polding Press.

Perkins, P. (1981), *Hearing the Parables of Jesus*, New York: Paulist Press.

Perrin, N. (1974), *The New Testament*, New York: Harcourt Brace.

Senior, D. (1975), *Jesus*, Dayton: Pflaum.

Shea, J. (1980), *Stories of God*, Chicago: Thomas More Press.

Thomas, D. (1979), *The Face of Christ*, London: Hamlyn.

Tolbert, M. (1979), *Perspectives on the Parables*, Philadelphia: Fortress Press.

Via, D. (1967), *The Parable: Their Literary and Existential Dimension*, Philadelphia: Fortress Press.

Chapter 5: The Passion and Resurrection Narratives

Berry, T. (1988), *The Dream of the Earth*, San Francisco: Sierra Club.

Boff, L. (1987), *Passion of Christ, Passion of the World*, Maryknoll: Orbis.

Brown, R. (1977), *The Virgin Birth and the Resurrection*, London: Geoffrey Chapman.

—— (1991), A *Risen Christ at Eastertime*, Collegeville: Liturgical Press.

Charpentier, E. (1981), *How to Read the New Testament*, London: SCM.

Crossan, D. (1991), *The Historical Jesus*, Edinburgh: T & T Clark.

Fallon, M. (1981), *The Four Gospels*, Sydney: Catholic Adult Education Centre.

Fitzmyer, J. (1987), "The Resurrection of Jesus Christ according to the New Testament", *The Month*, Nov. 1987, 20: 11; 402–410.

Grassi, J. (1987), *Rediscovering the Impact of Jesus' Death*, Kansas City: Sheed & Ward.

Hendrickx, H. (1984), *The Resurrection Narratives of the Synoptic Gospels*, London: Geoffrey Chapman.

Kasper, W. (1976), *Jesus the Christ*, London: Burns & Oates.

Matera, F. (1986), *Passion Narratives and Gospel Theologies: Interpreting the Synoptics through their Passion Stories*, New York: Paulist Press.

Marxsen, W. (1970), *The Resurrection of Jesus of Nazareth*, London: SCM.

McBrien, R. (1980), *Catholicism*, Malvern: Dove.

O'Collins, G. (1973), *The Easter Jesus*, London: Darton, Longman & Todd.

—— (1978), *What Are They Saying About the Resurrection?*, New York: Paulist Press.

—— (1977), *The Calvary Christ*, London: SCM.

—— (1987), *Jesus Risen*, London: Darton, Longman & Todd.

—— (1988), *Interpreting the Resurrection*, New York: Paulist.

O'Collins, G. & Kendall, D. (1987), "Mary Magdalene as Major Witness to Jesus' Resurrection", *Theological Studies*, 48: 4, 631–646.

Perkins, P. (1984), *Resurrection: New Testament Witness Contemporary Reflection*, London: Geoffrey Chapman.

Perrin, N. (1977), *The Resurrection Narratives*, London: SCM.

Rahner, K. (ed.) (1975), *Encyclopedia of Theology*, London: Burns & Oates.

Senior, D. (1984), *The Passion of Jesus in the Gospel of Mark*, Wilmington: Michael Glazier.

—— (1985), *The Passion of Jesus in the Gospel of Matthew*, Wilmington: Michael Glazier.

—— (1991) *The Passion of Jesus in the Gospel of John*, Collegeville: Liturgical Press.

Chapter 6: Expressing Beliefs: The Creeds

Chadwick, H. (1967), *The Early Church (The Pelican History of the Church Vol. 1)*, Penguin Books.

Danielou, & Henri-Marrou (1964), *The Christian Centuries*, London: DLT, Vol. I, Part Two: A, "The Countries of the East", Chapters 27–31.

Donovan, V.J. (1973), *Christianity Rediscovered*, Notre Dame; Fides–Claretian.

Hellwig, M. (1973), *The Christian Creeds*, Dayton: Pflaum.

Kelly, J.N. (1972), *Early Christian Doctrines*, London: Longman Group Limited.

Kelly, M. (1972), *Early Christian Creeds*, London: Longman.

Marthaler, B. (1987), *The Creed*, Mystic: Twenty-Third Publications.

O'Collins, G. (1977), *What Are They Saying About Jesus?*, New York: Paulist Press.

Richardson, A. (1935), *Creeds in the Making*, London: SCM.

Rogier, L. et al. (1964), *The Christian Centuries*, Vol. I London: Darton, Longman & Todd.

Stevenson, J. (ed.) (1960 revised), *A New Eusebius*, London: SPCK.

Stevenson, J. (1966), *Creeds, Councils and Controversies*, London: SPCK.

World Council of Churches (1992), *Confessing One Faith: An Ecumenical Explication of the Apostolic Faith as it is Confessed in the Nicene-Constantinopolitan Creed* (381), Geneva: World Council of Churches.

Young, F. (1991), *The Making of the Creeds*, London: SCM.

APPENDIX A

THE GOSPEL OF MARK—READING WORKSHEET

Read the Gospel of Mark as a whole first, then answer the questions below.

Introduction 1: 1 – 13

1. List the names of those whom Mark has used to introduce Jesus, in rather dramatic fashion, to his readers.
2. As you read, identify places mentioned on your map. Notice how the author makes use: of place names, e.g. provinces, towns; of specific spots—sea, boat, synagogue, house.

Galilee 1: 14 – 3: 6

3. As you read, identify places on your map.
4. In this section dealing with Jesus' ministry in Galilee, a number of healing miracles are recorded. List details of each, according to the sample in the diagram below:

Chapter	Where	Who and What	How Jesus responded	Response of person and/or crowd
1: 23	Synagogue, Capernaum	Man with evil spirit	"Come out of him"	Crowd amazed at his authority

5. Chapters 1 – 3:
    (a) Name the disciples who are called individually.
    (b) Where were they when they were called?
    (c) The appointment of the Twelve: what were they called to do?
6. What is the common factor in Mark's account of the picking of the corn and the cure of the man with the withered hand?
7. What does Mark say about the attitude of (a) the Pharisees, (b) the Scribes in 2: 23 – 3: 30?
8. Chapter 4 contains three parables about the sowing and growth of seed. In simple diagrammatic form, illustrate each.
9. In the story of the Calming of the Storm, Jesus reproaches his disciples. For what?
10. Chapter 5:
    (a) Identify "the country of the Gerasenes" on your map.
    (b) Three miracles are described in detail in this chapter. Record:

Chapter	Where	Who and What	How Jesus responded	Response of person and/or crowd

11. Chapter 6:
    (a) Why did Jesus not cure many people in his home town?
    (b) Sum up in one sentence instructions to his apostles before they set out.
    (c) There is an interlude in which John the Baptist suddenly reappears in Mark's story. Why was John arrested, and what happened to him?
    (d) Apostles' return: what did Jesus plan to do? what happened?
    (e) After the meal, where did Jesus go? where did his disciples go?
    (f) Mark gives a reason for the disciples being "utterly and completely dumbfounded" (6: 52). What is this reason?
    (g) Identify on your map the place where they finished the trip.
12. Chapter 7: The Pharisees and Scribes return to the story.
    (a) What do they complain about?
    (b) In one sentence, sum up Jesus' response to them.

Journeys Outside Galilee
7: 24 – 10: 52

In this section particularly we see Mark as a master craftsman of storytelling. He is a writer with a purpose, a message, and he shapes his story accordingly.

13. 7: 24 – 8: 38:
    (a) Identify places on map.
    (b) Healing miracles at Tyre and in the Decapolis region: record who, what etc.
    (c) After the second miracle of the loaves, what do the Pharisees ask for? What is the significance of placing their request straight after the loaves story?
    (d) Why has Mark placed the story of the cure of the blind man (8: 22 – 26) immediately after Jesus' comment in 8: 21?
    (e) Suggest a reason for this master storyteller's placing of Peter's profession of faith immediately after the story of the cure of the blind man.
    (f) 8:27 – 38 has been called the climax of the first half of Mark's Gospel and of Jesus' training of his disciples. What does Jesus tell his disciples about himself and about those who follow him?
14. Chapter 9:
    (a) Locate on your map the places mentioned.
    (b) Name all the people in the Transfiguration story.
    (c) Cure of the epileptic: record where, who and what, etc.
15. 9: 33 – 10: 52: In this section there are several incidents of the disciples wanting to be greatest, or first, or rewarded. Identify these incidents, and Jesus' response in each case.

Jerusalem 11: 1 – 16: 20

16. Identify Jerusalem and Bethany on your map.
17. 11 – 12: 12 contains a story of triumph contrasted with stories of desolation. Identify these briefly.
18. 12: 13 – 44: Write one sentence each on the attitude of:
    (a) Pharisees   (b) Sadducees   (c) Scribes in general   (d) Widow
19. Chapter 13: Using clues within this chapter, can you suggest anything about the situation of the community which Mark is addressing?

Passion and Resurrection
14: 1 – 16: 20

20. Read the story straight through, as a whole. Then write a sentence on the part played by each of the following in the story:
    (a) The women   (c) The Twelve
    (b) Judas   (d) The Three

(e) Peter
(f) The disciples
(g) Scribes and Priests
(h) The High Priest
(i) Pilate
(j) The young man
(k) Barabbas

(l) The soldiers
(m) Simon of Cyrene
(n) The Centurion
(o) Joseph of Arimathea
(p) The robbers
(q) The crowd
(r) Jesus

21. Where are the disciples told to go and find Jesus after the Resurrection?
22. Having read the whole Gospel, what is your impression of the Jesus whom Mark presents?

THE GOSPEL OF MATTHEW—READING WORKSHEET

Read the Gospel of Matthew as a whole first, then answer the questions below.

The Birth and Infancy of Jesus 1: 1 – 2: 23

1. What is Matthew trying to show by the genealogy in 1: 1 – 1: 17?
2. Why is the child to be called "Jesus"? (1: 21)
3. Locate Jerusalem, Bethlehem, Judaea, Egypt, Nazareth and Galilee on your map. (2: 1 – 2: 23)
4. How many magi are mentioned? (2: 1 – 2: 12)

The Kingdom of Heaven Proclaimed 3: 1 – 7: 29

5. What is the difference between John's and Jesus' baptism? (3: 1 – 3: 12)
6. Name the three places of the temptations. (4: 1 – 4: 11)
7. What did Simon and Andrew and then James and John do when they were called by Jesus? (4: 18 – 4: 22)
8. Locate on your map new names mentioned in 4: 23 – 25.
9. What do 5: 1; 17: 1; and 28: 16 have in common as regards the *place*? Do you think this is significant? Why/why not?
10. What is the difference between Matthew's first beatitude and Luke's (Lk 6: 20)?
11. What was Jesus' role regarding the Law?
12. What things should be done in secret and why?
13. How is one to know false prophets?

The Kingdom of Heaven is Preached 8: 1 – 10: 42

14. In this section a number of healing miracles occur. They may be analyzed as follows:

Chapter	Where	Who and What	Jesus' Response	Response of person and/or crowd
8: 14 – 15	Peter's house	Peter's mother-in-law. Fever.	Touched her	She got up and waited on him.

Fill in your own table, as appropriate, for the following miracles:
  (a) Cure of the centurian's servant
  (b) The demoniacs of Gadara
  (c) Cure of a paralytic
  (d) Cure of the official's daughter
  (e) Cure of two blind men
15. Regarding the mission of the disciples (10: 1 – 42), why were they *not* to go to pagan territory?
16. On your map add the places mentioned in 8: 5; 8: 28; 10: 15; 11: 21.

The Mystery of the Kingdom of Heaven 11: 1 – 13: 52.

17. List the names of the parables in this section.

The Church, First-Fruits of the Kingdom of Heaven (13: 53 – 18: 35)

18. How did Jesus react to the news of his cousin's death?
19. Name incidents in this section where Peter plays a prominent part.

The Approaching Advent of the Kingdom of Heaven 19: 1 – 25: 46

20. What exception to the rule of no divorce is mentioned?
21. What was Jesus' reply to the request of the mother of Zebedee's sons?

22. How do the priests and scribes react to this story of the parable of the Wicked Husbandmen according to Matthew?
23. What two major events are mentioned in the discourse of 24: 1 – 25: 46?
24. The Last Judgment: what will the virtuous say to the King? and what will his reply be?

Passion and Resurrection 26: 1 – 28: 20

25. State briefly the role of each of the following in the Passion Narrative:
    (a) Judas
    (b) Peter
    (c) Servant-girls
    (d) Pilate
    (e) Caiaphas
    (f) Barabbas
    (g) Soldiers
    (h) Simon of Cyrene
    (i) Joseph of Arimathea
26. After the Resurrection, why did the chief priests bribe the soldiers?
27. What is the mission of the disciples as mentioned in 28: 19?
28. Looking at the Gospel as a whole, describe Matthew's portrait of Jesus.
29. What picture of the Pharisees emerges from Matthew's Gospel? Refer to texts to support your opinion.

THE GOSPEL OF LUKE—READING WORKSHEET

Read the Gospel of Luke as a whole first, then answer the questions below.

The Prologue 1: 1 – 4

1. To whom is this Gospel addressed?
2. To whom is the Acts of the Apostles addressed? (Ac 1: 1)

The Infancy Narrative 1: 5 – 2: 52

3. Fill in the missing parts:

1: 5 – 25	Birth of John announced
1: 26 – 38	Birth of
1: 11	Angel appears to Zechariah
1: 26	
1: 13	Elizabeth is to have a son
1: 31	
1: 18	Zechariah is puzzled
1: 34	
1: 20	
1: 35	Angel assures Mary
1: 68 – 79	
1: 46 – 55	Mary's Hymn of Thanksgiving
1: 80	John grows and matures
2: 52	

4. Having answered Q. 3, what do you notice?
5. Fill in all the place names (towns, provinces, districts) mentioned in 2: 1 – 28, on your map.
6. What was Jesus' parents' reaction at finding him (2: 41 – 50)?

The Preparation for the Public Ministry of Jesus 3: 1 – 4: 13

7. What was the essence of John's proclamation?
8. List the three temptations of Jesus:
(i)
(ii)
(iii)

The Galilean Ministry of Jesus 4: 14 – 9: 50

9. In this section a number of healing miracles occur. They may be analyzed as follows:

Chapter	Where	Who and What	Jesus' Response	Response of person and/or crowd
4: 31 – 37	Synagogue, Capernaum	Demoniac	"Be quiet. Come out of him." Authority	Amazed at power and told everyone.

Fill in your own table, as appropriate, for these miracles:
  (a) Simon's mother-in-law
  (b) the Paralytic
  (c) the Centurian's servant
  (d) the son of the widow of Nain
  (e) the woman with a hemorrhage
10. Jesus prays the whole night through (6: 12): why do you think Luke emphasizes this at this particular point?
11. What was the mission of the Twelve? (9: 1 – 6)

The Journey to Jerusalem 9: 51 – 19: 27

12. Fill in, on your own map, the places mentioned in 10: 13 – 15.
13. Why do you think Luke places the Lord's Prayer (11: 1 – 4), the Importunate Friend (11: 5 – 8) and Effective Prayer (11: 9 – 13) together?
14. Simply list the titles of the parables in this section.
15. Name the titles of the three parables in 15: 4 – 7; 8 – 10 and 11 – 32. Why do you think Luke has placed them together? What aspect of God's nature do they highlight?

The Jerusalem Ministry 19: 28 – 21: 38

16. What effect did the parable of the Wicked Husbandmen have on the Scribes and chief priests and why?
17. Of what is the blossoming fig tree a sign?

The Passion 22: 1 – 23: 56

18. State briefly the role of each of the following in the Passion Narrative:
  (a) Judas
  (b) Peter
  (c) Herod
  (d) Pilate
  (e) Servant-girl

(f) Guards
(g) Sanhedrin
(i) Simon of Cyrene
(i) The Good Thief
(j) Centurion
(k) Joseph of Arimathea

After the Resurrection
24: 1 – 53

19. What was the reaction of the eleven to the women's story?
20. At what stage were the disciples' eyes opened in the Emmaus story and what is the significance thereof?
21. What mission did Jesus give the Apostles?
22. What do verses 1: 8 – 10 have in common with 24: 52 – 53? What is the significance thereof?
23. Looking at the Gospel as a whole, describe Luke's portrait of Jesus.

APPENDIX B

List of Some Literary Forms Found in the Gospels

FORM	PAGE REFERENCE IN TEXT
Announcement Stories	90–91
Call Stories	119, 120
Infancy Narratives	88–93
Judgment Sayings	55
Miracle Stories	55, 137–142
Parables	55, 121–130
Passion Narratives	55, 149–152
Pronouncement Stories	54
Proverbs	55
Short Sayings	55

APPENDIX C

Instruction on the Historical Truth of the Gospels

Our Holy Mother the Church, which is "the pillar and ground of the truth,"[1] has invariably made use of Sacred Scripture in her work of ministering eternal salvation to souls, safeguarding it always from every sort of false interpretation. Problems there will always be, and the Catholic exegete, engaged in expounding the word of God and answering the difficulties brought forward against it, should not lose heart. He must keep on vigorously at his work of bringing out ever more clearly the genuine sense of the Scriptures, not relying merely on his own capabilities, but putting his trust chiefly and unshakably in the help of God and the light shed by the Church.

It is highly gratifying that the Church today can number so many faithful sons, possessed of that proficiency in matters biblical which is required at the present time, who have responded to the call of the Supreme Pontiffs and are devoting themselves wholeheartedly and with unflagging energy to their weighty and exacting task. "And all other children of the Church should bear in mind that the efforts of these valiant laborers in the vineyard of the Lord are to be judged not only with fairness and justice, but also with the greatest charity,"[2] for even interpreters of the highest reputation, such as Jerome himself, in their endeavors to clear up certain more difficult points, have on occasion arrived at results which were far from happy. [3] All should be on their guard "lest in the heat of debate the limits laid down by mutual charity be transgressed; and lest, in debate, the impression be given that it is the revealed truths and the divine traditions themselves that are being controverted. For unless the various studies of many different scholars are pursued by them together in a spirit of harmony and with the principles themselves placed beyond dispute, we cannot well expect them to accomplish any great progress in this branch of learning."[4]

Today the labors of exegetes are all the more called for by reason of the fact that in many publications, circulated far and wide, the truth of the events and sayings recorded in the Gospels is being challenged. In view of this the Pontifical Biblical Commission, in the discharge of the duty entrusted to it by the Supreme Pontiffs, has thought it opportune to set forth and to insist on the following points:

1. The Catholic exegete, under the guidance of the Church, must turn to account

all the resources for the understanding of the sacred text which have been put at his disposal by previous interpreters, especially the holy Fathers and Doctors of the Church, whose labors it is for him to take up and to carry on. In order to bring out with fullest clarity the enduring truth and authority of the Gospels he must, whilst carefully observing the rules of rational and of Catholic hermeneutics, make skillful use of the new aids to exegesis, especially those which the historical method, taken in its widest sense, has provided; that method, namely, which minutely investigates sources, determining their nature and bearing, and availing itself of the findings of textual criticism, literary criticism, and linguistic studies. The interpreter must be alert to the reminder given him by Pope Pius XII of happy memory when he charged him "to make judicious inquiry as to how far the form of expression or the type of literature adopted by the sacred writer may help towards the true and genuine interpretation, and to remain convinced that this part of his task cannot be neglected without great detriment to Catholic exegesis."[5] In this reminder Pius XII of happy memory is laying down a general rule of hermeneutics, one by whose help the books both of the Old Testament and of the New are to be explained, since the sacred writers when composing them followed the way of thinking and of writing current amongst their contemporaries. In a word, the exegete must make use of every means which will help him to reach a deeper understanding of the character of the Gospel testimony, of the religious life of the first churches, and of the significance and force of the apostolic tradition.

In appropriate cases the interpreter is free to seek out what sound elements there are in "the Method of Form-history," and these he can duly make of to gain a fuller understanding of the Gospels. He must be circumspect in doing so, however, because the method in question is often found alloyed with principles of a philosophical or theological nature which are quite inadmissible, and which not infrequently vitiate both the method itself and the conclusions arrived at regarding literary questions. For certain exponents of this method, led astray by rationalistic prejudices, refuse to admit that there exists a supernatural order, or that a personal God intervenes in the world by revelation properly so called, or that miracles and prophecies are possible and have actually occurred. There are others who have as their starting-point a wrong notion of faith, taking it that faith is indifferent to historical truth, and is indeed incompatible with it. Others practically deny a priori the historical value and character of the documents of revelation. Others finally there are who on the one hand underestimate the authority which the Apostles had as witnesses of Christ, and the office and influence which they wielded in the primitive community, whilst on the other hand they overestimate the creative capacity of the community itself. All these aberrations are not only opposed to Catholic doctrine, but are also devoid of any scientific foundation, and are foreign to the genuine principles of the historical method.

2. In order to determine correctly the trustworthiness of what is transmitted in the Gospels, the interpreter must take careful note of the three stages of tradition by which the teaching and the life of Jesus have come down to us.

Christ our Lord attached to Himself certain chosen disciples[6] who had followed Him from the beginning,[7] who had seen His works and had heard His words, and thus were qualified to become witnesses of His life and teaching.[8] Our Lord, when expounding His teaching by word of mouth, observed the methods of reasoning and of exposition which were in common use at the time; in this way He accommodated Himself to the mentality of His hearers, and ensured that His teachings would be deeply impressed on their minds and would be easily retained in memory by His disciples. These latter grasped correctly the idea that the miracles and other events of the life of Jesus were things purposely performed or arranged by Him in such a way that men would thereby be led to believe in Christ and to accept by faith the doctrine of salvation.

The Apostles, bearing testimony to Jesus,[9] proclaimed first and foremost the death and Resurrection of the Lord, faithfully recounting His life and words[10] and, as regards the manner of their preaching, taking into account the circumstances of their hearers. [11] After Jesus had risen from the dead, and when His divinity was clearly perceived,[12] the faith of the disciples, far from blotting out the remembrance of the events that had happened, rather consolidated it since their faith was based on what Jesus had done and taught.[13] Nor was Jesus transformed into a "mythical" personage, and His teaching distorted, by reason of the worship which the disciples now paid Him, revering Him as Lord and Son of God. Yet it need not be denied that the Apostles, when handing on to their bearers the things which in actual fact the Lord had said and done, did so in the light of that fuller understanding which they enjoyed as a result of being schooled by the glorious things accomplished in Christ,[14] and of being illumined by the Spirit of Truth.[15] Thus it came about that, just as Jesus Himself after His Resurrection had "interpreted to them"[16] both the words of the Old Testament and the words which He Himself had spoken,[17] so now they in their turn interpreted His words and deeds according to the needs of their hearers. "Devoting (themselves) to the ministry of the word,"[18] they made use, as they preached, of such various forms of speech as were adapted to their own purposes and to the mentality of their hearers; for it was "to Greek and barbarian, to learned and simple,"[19] that they had a duty to discharge.[20] These varied ways of speaking which the heralds of Christ made use of in proclaiming Him must be distinguished one from the other and carefully appraised: catecheses, narratives, testimonies, hymns, doxologies, prayers and any other such literary forms as were customarily employed in Sacred Scripture and by people of that time.

The sacred authors, for the benefit of the churches, took this earliest body of instruction, which had been handed on orally at first and then in writing—for many soon set their hands to "drawing up a narrative"[21] of matters concerning the Lord Jesus—and set it down in the four Gospels. In doing this each of them followed a method suitable to the special purpose which he had in view. They selected certain things out of the many which had been handed on; some they synthesized, some they explained with an eye to the situation of the churches, painstakingly using every means of bringing home to their readers the solid truth of the things in which they had been instructed.[22] For, out of the material which they had received, the sacred authors selected especially those items which were adapted to the varied circumstances of the faithful as well as to the end which they themselves wished to attain; these they recounted in a manner consonant with those circumstances and with that end. And since the meaning of a statement depends, amongst other things, on the place which it has in a given sequence, the Evangelists, in handing on the words or the deeds of our Savior, explained them for the advantage of their readers by respectively setting them, one Evangelist in one context, another in another. For this reason the exegete must ask himself what the Evangelist intended by recounting a saying or a fact in a certain way, or by placing it in a certain context. For the truth of the narrative is not affected in the slightest by the fact that the Evangelists report the sayings or the doings of our Lord in a different order,[23] and that they use different words to express what He said, not keeping to the very letter, but nevertheless preserving the sense.[24] For, as St Augustine says: "Where it is a question only of those matters whose order in the narrative may be indifferently this or that without in any way taking from the truth and authority of the Gospel, it is probable enough that each Evangelist believed he should narrate them in that same order in which God was pleased to suggest them to his recollection. The Holy Spirit distributes His gifts to each one according as He wills;[25] therefore, too, for the sake of those Books which were to be set so high at the very summit of authority, He undoubtedly guided and controlled the minds of the holy writers in their recollection of what they were to write; but as to why, in doing so, He should have permitted them, one to follow this order in his narrative, another to follow that—that is a question whose answer may possibly be found with God's help, if one seeks it out with reverent care."[26]

Unless the exegete, then, pays attention to all those factors which have a bearing on the origin and the composition of the Gospels, and makes due use of the acceptable findings of modern research, he will fail in his duty of ascertaining what the intentions of the sacred writers were, and what it is that they have actually said. The results of recent study have made it clear that the teachings and the life of Jesus were not simply recounted for the mere purpose of being kept in remembrance, but were "preached" in such a way as to furnish the Church with the foundation on which to build up faith and morals. It follows that the interpreter who subjects the testimony of the Evangelists to persevering scrutiny will be in a position to shed further light on the enduring theological value of the Gospels, and to throw into clearest relief the vital importance of the Church's interpretation.

There remain many questions, and these of the gravest moment, in the discussion and elucidation of which the Catholic exegete can and should freely exercise his intelligence and skill. In this way each can contribute individually to the advantage of all, to the constant advancement of sacred learning, to preparing the ground and providing further support for the decisions of the Church's teaching authority, and to the defence and honor of the Church herself.[27] But at all times the interpreter must cherish a spirit of ready obedience to the Church's teaching authority, and must also bear in mind that when the Apostles proclaimed the Good Tidings they were filled with the Holy Spirit, that the Gospels were written under the inspiration of the Holy Spirit, and that it was He Who preserved their authors immune from all error. "For we received our knowledge of the economy of our salvation by means of no others than those same by whose means the Gospel came to us: that Gospel which they first proclaimed as heralds and afterwards, by the will of God, passed on to us in the Scriptures to be the ground and pillar of our faith. Thus no one has any right to say that they preached before they had the perfect Knowledge, as some venture to assert, boasting that they are correctors of the Apostles. For after our Lord had risen from the dead and they were invested with power from on high by the descent of the Holy Spirit upon them, they were filled with all the gifts, and had the perfect Knowledge; they went forth to the ends of the earth spreading the good tidings of the blessings we have from God and announcing heavenly peace to man, all of them and each of them equally possessing the Gospel of God."[28]

3. Those charged with the duty of teaching in Seminaries and similar establishments "must make it their first care to see . . . that the teaching of Holy Writ is carried out in a manner thoroughly in keeping with the importance of the subject itself, and with the requirements of the present day."[29] Professors should make theological doctrine the main subject-matter of their exposition, so that the Sacred Scriptures "may become for the future priests of the Church a pure and never-failing source of spiritual life for themselves, and of nourishment and vigor for the office of sacred preaching which they are to undertake."[30] Professors, when they make use of critical methods, especially of what is called literary criticism, should not do so for the mere sake of criticism, but with a view to gaining by means of it a deeper insight into the sense intended by God speaking through the sacred writer. They should not stop halfway, therefore, resting on the discoveries they have made from the literary point of view, but should go on to show how such findings make a real contribution towards the better understanding of revealed doctrine or, if occasion arises, towards the refutation of misleading views. By following these guiding principles teachers will ensure that their pupils find in Sacred Scripture themes of a nature "to raise their minds to God, nourish their souls, and foster their interior life."[31]

4. But it is those who instruct the Christian people by sacred preaching who need the greatest prudence. It is doctrine above all that they must impart, mindful of the admonition of St Paul: "Pay attention to yourself and to the doctrine which you teach; be persistent in these things. For by doing so you will bring salvation to yourself and to your hearers."[32] They must altogether shun what is merely new-fangled or what is insufficiently proved. New views for which there is solid support they may when necessary put forward, using discretion and taking into account the qualifications of their audience. When they narrate biblical events they are not to introduce imaginary additions at variance with the truth.

This same virtue of prudence should be especially practiced by those who write for the Christian public at popular level. They should make it their study to bring out the treasures of the word of God "in order that the faithful may be moved and spurred on to shape their lives in conformity with it."[33] Let them regard themselves as in duty bound never to depart in the slightest from the common doctrine and tradition of the Church. And whilst undoubtedly they should lay under contribution whatever real advances in biblical knowledge the labors of modern scholars have brought about, they should keep altogether clear of the precarious fancies of innovators.[34] They are strictly charged not to yield to a mischievous itch for novelty by recklessly giving wide publicity, indiscriminately and without any previous shifting, to each and every tentative solution of difficulties that happens to be proposed; this way of acting disquiets the faith of many people.

Already on a previous occasion this Pontifical Biblical Commission thought it opportune to recall to mind that books, and also magazine and newspaper articles, dealing with biblical matters, are subject to the authority and jurisdiction of Ordinaries, since they are concerned with religious topics and with the religious instruction of the faithful.[35] Ordinaries are requested, therefore, to be particularly vigilant where such popular publications are concerned.

5. Those in charge of biblical associations must observe inviolably the laws already laid down by the Pontifical Biblical Commission.[36]

If all these instructions are kept, the study of the Sacred Scriptures will redound to the advantage of the faithful. All without exception will experience even today the truth of what St Paul wrote: that the Sacred Scriptures "can make wise unto salvation, which is had by faith in Christ Jesus. All scripture inspired by God is profitable for teaching, for reproving, for correcting, for training in right conduct: so that the man of God may be complete, equipped for every good."[37]

Our Most Holy Lord, Pope Paul VI, in an audience graciously granted to the undersigned Right Reverend Consultor-Secretary on April 21, 1964, approved this Instruction and ordered its publication.

Rome, April 21, 1964

Benjamin N. Wambacq, O. Praem.,
Consultor-Secretary

1   Tm 3, 15.
2   Divino afflante Spiritu; Enchiridion Biblicum (EB), 564.
3   Cf. Spiritus Paraclitus; EB, 451.
4   Litt. Apost. Vigilantiae; EB, 143.
5   Divino afflante Spiritu; EB, 560.
6   Cf. Mk 3: 14; Lk 6: 13.
7   Cf. Lk 1: 2; Ac 1: 21–22.
8   Cf. Lk 24: 48; Jn 15: 27; Ac 1: 8; 10: 39; 13: 31.
9   Cf. Lk 24: 44–48; Ac 2: 32; 3: 15; 5: 30–32.
10   Cf. Ac 10: 36–41.
11   Cf. Ac 13: 16–41 with Ac 17: 22–31.
12   Ac 2: 36; Jn 20: 28.
13   Ac 2: 22; 10: 37–39.

14 Jn 2: 22; 12: 16; 11: 51–52; cf. 14: 26; 16: 12–13; 7: 39.
15 Cf. Jn 14: 26; 16: 13.
16 Lk 24: 27.
17 Cf. Lk 24: 44–45; Ac 1: 3.
18 Ac 6: 4.
19 Rm 1: 14.
20 1 Co 9: 19–23.
21 Cf. Lk 1: 1.
22 Cf. Lk 1: 4.
23 Cf. St John Chrys., In Mat. Hom. I, 3; PG 57, 16–17.
24 Cf. St August, De consensu Evang. 2, 12, 28; PL 34, 1090–1091.
25 1 Co 12: 11.
26 De consensu Evang., 2, 21, 51 s.; PL 34, 1102.
27 Cf. Divino afflante Spiritu; EB, 565.
28 St Iren., Adv. Haer., III 1, 1; Harvey, II, 2; PG 7, 844.
29 Litt. Apost. Quoniam in re biblica; EB, 162.
30 Divino afflante Spiritu; EB, 567.
31 Divino afflante Spiritu; EB, 552.
32 1 Tm. 4: 16.
33 Divino afflante Spiritu; EB, 566.
34 Cf. Litt. Apost. Quoniam in re biblica; EB. 175.
35 Instructio ad Exc. mos locorum Ordinarios. . . 15 Dec. 1955; EB, 626.
36 EB, 622–633.
37 2 Tm. 3: 15–17.

APPENDIX D

The Canon of the New Testament

The New Testament is a collection of books which were written at different times in different places around the Mediterranean Sea. The first such writing was Paul's letter to the Thessalonians, about 52. Thereafter other letters and the Gospels followed (cf. Appendix E).

It is difficult to determine when exactly these writings came to be put together as a composite book and how it was decided which books were worthy of inclusion and which had to be rejected. These issues will be pursued below. For the present it can be noted that the final collection of books to be considered the New Testament is known as the New Testament "Canon". Similarly the list of books considered as comprising the Old Testament is the Old Testament Canon. A useful definition of "Canon" is as follows:

> The "Canon" is the list of books accepted by the Church as inspired. These books constitute the Bible.

HISTORY OF THE NEW TESTAMENT CANON

In 2 P 3: 15f. (written after 100) reference is made to a collection of Pauline letters. Polycarp (c. 69–c. 156, Bishop of Smyrna) seems also to know of nine of the canonical letters of Paul. The Gospels, written in the second half of the first century A.D., were already in a single collection by 130. Justin (Apol.1.67) recommends they be read in the Liturgy alongside the Old Testament prophets. The third group of writings, the Catholic letters, the Acts of the Apostles, Revelation and Hebrews, became accepted in the second half of the second century (i.e. 150–200). Even then the degree of authority attached to each book varied (cf. The *New Jerome Biblical Commentary* on New Testament Canon).

The Church was prompted into action regarding the New Testament writings because of the position of Marcion.

208

Marcion, the son of a bishop and shipowner of Sinope on the Black Sea, was founder of the Marcionites, an ascetic Gnostic (= secret knowledge) sect. He came to Rome somewhere between 120–130. Marcion rejected the entire Old Testament on the ground that it portrayed a vengeful God. He admitted only ten Pauline letters as well as a version of Luke's Gospel which had been purged of its Old Testament citations and the infancy narrative. He was excommunicated in 144.

In response to Marcion's list of books (his "canon") the Church affirmed the four Gospels, the ten Pauline letters Marcion had named as well as the pastoral letters, Acts of the Apostles and Revelation. This collection finds some official expression towards the end of the second century in the Muratorian fragment, which lists twenty-two New Testament writings: the four Gospels, Acts, thirteen Pauline letters, three Catholic letters, the Apocalypse of John and the Apocalypse of Peter. Thus a "canon" was formed towards the end of the second century, without Hebrews and with uncertainty about the number of Catholic epistles.

What *criteria* were used in accepting some books and not others? According to Gamble (1985: 68–72), the early Church was guided by the following criteria:

(1) Apostolicity — was the document written by an Apostle or thought to be associated with one?

(2) Catholicity — was the document relevant to the Church as a whole? Some of Paul's letters were not catholic in this sense, as they were written to specific local communities.

(3) Orthodoxy — was the document's contents in agreement with the faith of the Church?

(4) Traditional Usage — had the document been customarily used in the worship and teaching of the various Churches?

In the *Greek Church* Hebrews was recognized but not Revelation (until the sixth century). The number of Catholic Epistles was also a problem. In 367, Athanasius identified twenty-seven books of the New Testament. Subsequent synods of East and West confirmed this number.

Although no new decrees on the canon are found after the fifth century, discussion on the authorship and validity of individual books continued.

It was left to the *Council of Trent* in 1546 to define the canon of the Old and New Testaments once and for all. Regarding the New Testament (cf. Appendix E) the Council said:

> "It has thought it proper, moreover, to insert in this decree a list of the sacred books, so that no doubt may remain which books are recognized by this Council . . . New Testament: the four Gospels, according to Matthew, Mark, Luke and John; the Acts of the Apostles written by Luke the Evangelist; fourteen epistles of the Apostle Paul—to the Romans, two to the Corinthians, to the Galatians, Ephesians, Philippians, Colossians, two to Timothy, to Titus, Philemon, and the Hebrews; two epistles of the Apostle Peter, three of the Apostle John, one of the Apostle James, one of the Apostle Jude, and the Apocalypse of the Apostle John. Council of Trent, 1546."

In the *Reformation* era doubts were expressed by Erasmus about the apostolic origins of Hebrews, James, 2 Peter, 2 and 3 John and Apocalypse. Luther felt the New Testament books needed to be graded in importance.

Vatican II: Dei Verbum Chapter 5 refers to the New Testament and gives prominence to the Gospels:

> *"It is common knowledge that among all the Scriptures, even those of the New Testament, the Gospels have a special pre-eminence, and rightly so, for they are the principal witness of the life and teaching of the Incarnate Word, our Savior."* *(18; cf. also 17–20).*

LIST OF THE TWENTY-SEVEN NEW TESTAMENT BOOKS

1. *Pauline Corpus*   *No. of Books*

   1 Thessalonians★   )   Early Letters
   2 Thessalonians#   )

   Galatians★   )
   1 Corinthians★   )
   2 Corinthians★   )   Great Letters
   Romans★   )
   Philippians★   )

   Philemon★   )
   Colossians#   )   Captivity Letters
   Ephesians#   )

   1 Timothy+   )
   Titus+   )   Pastoral Letters
   2 Timothy+   )   13

   ★ Genuine Pauline letters (7)
   # Deutero-Pauline letters (3)
   + Pseudonymous letters (3)

2. *Gospels*
   Mark   )
   Matthew   )   Synoptic Gospels
   Luke   )

   John   4

3. *Catholic Epistles*
   1 Peter
   2 Peter
   James
   Jude
   1 John
   2 John
   3 John   7

4. *Other Writings*
   Acts
   Hebrews
   Revelation   3
                                                                         ———

                                                          Total: 27

APPENDIX E

Timeline of the New Testament and Other Early Christian Books

Approximate Dates

A.D.	New Testament	Other Early Christian Books
50–52	1 Thessalonians	
	2 Thessalonians	
56	Philippians	
57	1 Corinthians	
	Galatians	
	2 Corinthians	
	Romans	
58	James	
61–63	Colossians	
	Ephesians	
	Philemon	
64	1 Peter	
65	1 Timothy	
	Titus	
67	Hebrews	
	2 Timothy	
	Mark's Gospel	
70–80	Acts of the Apostles	
	Jude	
	2 Peter	
81–90	Matthew's Gospel	
	Luke's Gospel	
91–100	Revelation	Letter of St Clement
	John's Gospel	
	1, 2, & 3 John	Didache
100		Gospel of Thomas (?)
110		Seven Letters of Ignatius of Antioch

Approximate Dates

A.D.	*New Testament*	*Other Early Christian Books*
		Polycarp's letter to the Philippians
		Odes of Solomon
130		Letter of Barnabas
135		Gospel of the Hebrews
		Shepherd of Hermas
170		Diatesseron (Tatian)

INDEX